The Making of a History

The Making

Gregory M. Tobin

# of a History

Walter Prescott Webb
and The Great Plains

University of Texas Press Austin & London

Library of Congress Cataloging in Publication Data

Tobin, Gregory M   1936–
   The making of a history.

   Originally presented as the author's thesis, University of Texas at Austin, 1972.
   Bibliography: p.
   Includes index.
   1. Webb, Walter Prescott, 1888–1963.
   2. Webb, Walter Prescott, 1888–1963. The Great Plains.
   3. Great Plains—History. 4. Mississippi Valley—History. I. Title.
E175.5.W4T62 1976   978'.007'2024 [B]   76–3120
ISBN 0–292–75029–3

Set in Times Roman by G & S Typesetters, Inc.

Printed in the United States of America by
Edwards Brothers, Inc.

Frontispiece: Walter Prescott Webb by Alan E. Cober

To K. M. T.—and our four close friends

Contents

Acknowledgments

IT IS A MEASURE of the standing of Walter Prescott Webb among his friends and associates that any request for advice and assistance made during the course of this study invariably met with a generous response. I am indebted to members of the Webb family—Mrs. Walter Prescott Webb, Miss Mildred Webb, and Mrs. Ima Wright—for their willingness to share their recollections with me. Mr. C. B. Smith, Sr., of Austin, Texas, made it possible for me to consult what proved to be a very important collection of Webb papers which had recently come into his possession. Dr. Chester V. Kielman of the University of Texas Archives and Dr. Dorman H. Winfrey of the Texas State Archives gave me every assistance in locating materials, as did the staff of the Barker Texas History Center. Professor William A. Owens of Columbia University kindly gave me access to a taped interview with Walter Prescott Webb recorded in 1953.

Webb's long association with the history department at the University of Texas at Austin meant that I could draw on the comments of a number of those who had worked with him in the later stages of his career, and I am grateful to Professor Barnes A. Lathrop, Professor Robert C. Cotner, and Professor Joe B. Frantz for their advice and assistance. The dissertation which eventually emerged owes a great deal to the careful and kindly attention of my supervisor, Professor John E. Sunder.

Many others contributed to the development of this study, and in ways that are difficult to categorize. The American Studies Program of the American Council of Learned Societies supported my research, and I am grateful to Mr. Richard W. Downar and his staff for making it possible for me to devote an extended period of time exclusively to writing. A travel grant from the Australian-American Educational Foundation helped me get to the United States, and the task of getting a program of graduate studies underway was made much easier than it might have been by the kindness of members of the Austin community—in particular, Professor C. Hartley Grattan and Mrs. Grattan, Professor Phillip L. White, and Gene and Betty White. There are others whose encouragement and friendship made an indirect but no less distinct contribution; for example, Emeritus Professor Norman D. Harper pioneered the study of American history in Australia, and my interest in the West dates from his courses at the University of Melbourne. Professor Howard R. Lamar provided me with detailed and helpful comments, and I am grateful for his interest in the work.

Finally, there are those who made it possible for me to complete the study by taking heavier loads on their own shoulders—my colleagues at Flinders, and in particular Trudi Hislop, Paul Bourke, and Don DeBats. Jenny Elliott and Sue Forrest helped type the final draft, Madeleine Davis and Carolyn Clementi checked sections of the manuscript, and Andrew Little prepared the map. The journey which took me eventually to the edge of the Plains, and the research and writing which were part of that journey, could not have been made without the encouragement and support of my family; this is their book, as much as it is mine.

Introduction

ROUGHLY ONE-FIFTH of the territory of the United States lies in the area generally designated as the Great Plains—a vast tract stretching from the eastern slopes of the Rockies to a nebulous line west of the Mississippi and in the vicinity of the ninety-eighth meridian. It was in this area that the last act in the long drama of American settlement was played out; as much as forty years had elapsed between the time of acquisition and the fact of settlement, and during that period the Plains were crossed and recrossed by itinerant trappers and by settlers moving through to the more attractive lands of the Pacific Coast. The image of the Plains as a great ocean of grassland and limitless horizons that had so appealed to earlier observers still held good at the midpoint of the nineteenth century—save that there were now well-traveled sea lanes as well as empty expanses; an ocean that for centuries had supported its own distinctive life now felt the presence of strange craft and narrow lines upon its surface. Those who crossed took only what they needed for the moment; they showed no inclination to stay, for to them the Plains were simply a wide corridor to the Promised Land, and of no intrinsic importance.

In the thirty years that followed the end of the Civil War, the eastern heartland of the United States entered into the industrial age with a vengeance, and the products of its factories made it possible for the herdsman and the cultivator to mount the first concerted assault on the grasslands that stretched from west of the Mississippi to the Rockies. Urbanized northeasterners, who were only one generation away from their own roots in the soil, forged the rails that brought the iron age to the Plains; the nomads of the Plains and their seminomadic white counterparts made way for the pastoralist and the tiller of the soil, and the same technology that had brought these new inhabitants to the Plains made it possible for them to grow food for those who tended the machines, both at home and abroad. For a brief period two different stages of development stood side by side on the one continent and within the one civiliza-

tion—the city and its processing mechanisms, the Plains with their
meat and grain. Though closely interlocked, heartland and colony
stood for a moment sharp and clear within a single polity; a generation later, and the lines of demarcation were already becoming
blurred.

The elements of contrast should not be overstressed; most of
those who settled the Plains in those decades had been reared in
the framework of a common cultural heritage and took with them
a general commitment to a common set of values and assumptions
that already had the weight of a century of national life behind it—
even allowing for the great trauma of the Civil War. The relatively
few cultural differences that did survive into the second half of the
nineteenth century had little chance of prevailing against the impact
of a catapulting technology that eradicated distance and laid con-
duits for the printed and spoken word across even the most extensive deserts and plains. Colonial appendages though they were, the
settled areas of the new West were not allowed to savor their physical isolation for very long; incorporation proceeded alongside development and exploitation, ensuring the extension to the West of that
larger sense of identity that marked the American off from the
world community. So effective was this process of continuous as-
similation and cross-fertilization that within a generation a distinctively western type—the cowboy—had won acceptance as a symbol
at the national level.

But beneath the network of steel and wire that riveted the nation
together at the very point when its population spilled over into the
prairies and into the new industrial cities, some of the tensions and
the frustrations that are characteristic of the colonial experience
struggled for expression and release in the West. Those who had
moved to the new West in the decades after the Civil War were
more troubled by the harshness of their physical existence than by
any sense of cultural isolation. Their cultural needs were relatively
few and uncomplicated and were adequately met from the store of
tradition brought with them from the older sections of the country
in which they had spent their formative years. Once the initial tasks
of establishing homes and farms had been completed, the sense of
urgency that had driven them in the early years gave way to the assumption that permanency and stability had been achieved. The
farmer still had to struggle for his livelihood, but it was now a struggle against predators of his own kind—the politicians and middle-
men who coveted his meager gains. With all their problems, the settlers knew that the social order they represented had triumphed

over the wilderness and that there would be no turning back; individuals might falter, but the wider community had appropriated the Plains and would hold them permanently for its children. But their offspring had no memories of an older land against which to measure their experience of life. For them, the Plains environment was an unavoidable and ever-present fact that bore down on their existence at every level and demanded recognition and comprehension. Their situation was not unlike that of the children of the immigrants who poured into the eastern cities in the same period. Both groups faced the same problem of establishing an acceptable identity in a world very different from the one their fathers had known. They could not identify with a traditional world, because it lay beyond their direct experience; at the same time, those who grew up on the frontier were formed by communities that in many cases were less than a quarter of a century old and had not as yet developed a life of their own.

There was little that could act as a point of attachment for the rising generation, yet the urge to find some point of contact, some sense of being part of a wider community, was an important part of the process of establishing a sense of personal identity. Very few of those who were born on the frontier were equipped to examine their own relationship with their physical and social environment in any detail; relative isolation and the thin spread of population in the early stages of settlement meant a slowing down in the movement of ideas, and a lack of social intercourse made it difficult for those who lived in the area to achieve a sense of identity, either as individuals or as communities.

It is within this broad framework that the career of Walter Prescott Webb should be examined. The son of a pioneer schoolteacher and farmer, Webb grew up tantalizingly close to the cattle kingdom and witnessed its disappearance. From his vantage point on the edge of the Plains, he saw enough of that vanishing era to feel drawn to it and to need some way of identifying with its style and values. But he was also the son of a dirt farmer, and prolonged exposure to the tedium and apparently pointless labor involved in farm life produced a determination to have done with it. Webb became one of the characteristic western types—the young man who turned his face eastward in search of opportunity and the better life, but could never cure himself of the habit of looking back over his shoulder and wondering about the land he had left. Yet there was one element that marked him off from the backtrailers depicted in Hamlin Garland's midwestern novels: though Webb turned away from the land of his childhood, he never moved far from its edge. As the years went by and he became more aware of the bonds that held him to that land, his focus began to shift and eventually fixed itself on the continuing struggle between man and the hostile environment of the Plains. ("I have never been able to get away from the dry country. I returned to it intellectually after having escaped it physically. I have sought to understand what I hated and feared . . .")[1] He was to cling almost grimly to that land as long as he lived, and he found his greatest satisfaction in trying to plumb its character.

No one knew better than Webb that the edge of the Plains was not the most pleasant or satisfying environment for an intelligent and sensitive youngster, and he respected it at a distance. But it is important that he did respect it; with all its limitations, it was the home of his own people, and it had sheltered the friends and neighbors of his childhood. It had helped to form his personality in ways that he could only partially understand, and he could never separate himself from a mold that had in fact become part of him. In the course of time, he found himself impelled to probe the history of the region in which he had spent the first twenty years of his life and to write of it in a way that demanded recognition—compelled, perhaps, by the realization that without such knowledge and the recognition that went with it, his own personality would in some way remain disjointed and incomplete. The possibility that the humble lives of his own parents and the men and women of their generation might slip unnoticed into the forgotten past disturbed him—and in part because some element of his own existence would inevitably follow them into obscurity. That this should happen while the chronicles of the older parts of the country were being probed and weighed with minute care seemed to Webb to be an arrogant and willful act of injustice, and, until that situation was rectified at least in part, he remained at war with those he felt to be chiefly responsible.

A student by choice and a scholar by accident, Webb represents several strands in the attempt to form what might be called a western mind, in the sense in which author Wilbur J. Cash applied the term to the South. His role in fixing the image of a major segment of the western landscape can hardly be questioned; forty years after its publication, *The Great Plains* still stands as the point of departure for most studies of the region, and Webb's interpretation of the process of settlement has bitten deep into the public mind. But the book also represents one of the most successful attempts by a first generation westerner to produce an integrated view of his immediate historical context, over and against the national perspective that inevitably followed on the heels of political and economic incorporation. Though as ardent a nationalist as any of his generation, Webb also harbored the characteristic resentments of a colonial toward the arrogant assumptions of superiority on the part of the imperial heartland. The urge to demonstrate that there was something unique about the experience of the Plains communities that marked it off from that of the older sections of the country and gave it a special character is never very far below the surface in Webb's work; it is an element that may help to explain his lifelong reluctance to identify himself as a follower of Frederick Jackson Turner, whose vision of the frontier as a distinctive force in American history dominated the thinking of a generation of western historians. By the time Webb came to write *The Great Plains*, the Turner approach was almost a part of the orthodoxy against which he needed to assert the special claims of the Plains region. A midwestern view was, in his eyes, not all that different from a northeastern one: Boston and Chicago seemed like close neighbors when viewed from the perspective of North Central Texas.

The impulse to explore and delineate the social context that had shaped a generation was one thing; translating it into action was a far more difficult problem. Lonely and introspective as a youngster, Webb had to discover in painful and solitary fashion the concepts that would allow him to organize his view of the world around him and the vocabulary to express and link them together into a satisfying whole. In itself, the slow expansion of his intellectual and imaginative framework constitutes something of a case study in the formation of a western mind under the conditions operative in the first decades of the century. Webb's intellectual development reflected some of the limitations inherent in the social conditions prevailing in a remote segment of an outlying state. Some of those limitations had a permanent impact and made it difficult for him to function as an intellectual or a professional historian in the way that most of his colleagues took for granted; others he circumvented or developed into compensatory strengths, giving his intellectual profile something of the curious flatness and imbalance that are characteristic of the landscape of his region.

At the same time, Webb's educational development was something more than a chronicle of deficiencies. Almost by chance, he became the heir to a set of ideas and an intellectual orientation that had its roots deep in nineteenth century European scholarship and came to him as a variant of what was generally known as institutional history—a variant that stands apart from the germ theory that Turner had earlier rejected as irrelevant. When Turner was at the height of his career, Webb was captivated by the lectures of a man whose approach to history ran along lines rather similar to those Turner had adopted but was applied on a global rather than a national level. Webb was to apply the approach he had learned from Lindley Miller Keasbey to explore the development of his own region, but he never lost the inclination to look for the underlying structures that ran beneath the political and social framework and gave meaning to the fabric they supported. Toward the end of his career, he was to give this tendency full rein by reverting to Keasbey's global perspective, while at the same time remaining anchored, in a way that Keasbey never was, to his own hearth and the ways of his people. It is this exposure to the workings of a formidable and exciting intellect that marks Webb off from those of his generation who followed the same path from frontier obscurity to professional standing and that accounts for the curious tension between his tenacious provincialism and his penchant for global generalization.

This study is an attempt to trace the making of an environmentalist by placing his development within the framework of his own intellectual and social setting and, in a sense, subjecting his career to the same type of scrutiny that he advocated as the basis of the study of evolving cultures. The procedure itself is a familiar one; those who tabulate the changing modes in the writing of history take for granted the need to relate the work of a mature scholar to the climate of ideas prevailing during his productive years. Few would regard a major piece of historical writing as an autonomous deposit quite distinct from the personality of the author; questions concerning the nature and scope of his education, the impact of the individuals and the institutions with which he was associated, and shifts within the relevant schools of interpretation—all are recognized as elements that can condition an individual historian's approach to his subject. The assumption is that a faithful adherence to the canons of the discipline ensures that the historian reduces the impact of such influences to an acceptable level or at least controls them by being aware of their existence.

In Webb's case, however, there are unusually strong grounds for probing the relationship between the writer and his milieu. In the case of *The Great Plains*, the final work was not the outcome of an intellectual process in which rationality was simply tempered by the operation of psychological and emotional considerations; if anything, the conventional approach was reversed, and disciplined rationality became the handmaiden of a deeply founded emotional reaction. Webb was right to stress that he would have preferred to have been a creative writer rather than an academic historian, and there is a sense in which he is best cast as a writer who found that history provided him with the only material he knew how to use—material that had some bearing on his inward concerns.

All of this points to the need for a much closer study of the relevant biographical material than is customary and a questioning of the assumption that scholarly habits are an adequate proof against the assertion of the individual psyche. To suggest that Webb wrote *The Great Plains* to justify the Plainsman and his works and that the task drew as heavily on his emotional resources as on his intellect does not reduce the significance of the work itself, but it does add an additional perspective that is not evident at first reading. What one can observe here is a first generation colonial, brought up in a community without a clearly articulated sense of its own identity and then trained to value the ability of older societies to specify their heritage, grappling with the contradictions of his own situation. Like others of his generation, he tried to define that sense of community with the land and those who live close to it that often seems to become all-important to men uncertain of their place within the wider community; in reaching out for that definition, in trying to merge the subjective and objective worlds, Webb slowly built up a picture of the interplay between a rigid geographical framework and the fluid patterns of social life that emerged within its boundaries. What he saw there convinced him that there were present elements of creativity and adaptation that satisfied his sense of the special character of the Plains experience. In making his examination, he was less concerned about method than about the ultimate goal to be achieved; regional sensitivity easily mastered any loyalty to academic disciplines whose methodological principles he only partially accepted.

In the course of the present study, no attempt will be made to assess the value of Webb's later work or to make any more than a passing reference to his studies of the Texas Rangers or of economic sectionalism in the 1930's. The preparation and the writing of *The Great Plains* was critical enough to warrant the narrower focus —critical both in forming Webb's own historical perspective and in defining a regional sense of identity. Whatever the quality or significance of his later work, the importance of that initial base seems undeniable. Nor is any attempt made to determine whether Webb's interpretation of the Plains experience is a valid one, or whether subsequent research in geography, anthropology, or other relevant disciplines has qualified or invalidated sections of the work; the focus remains limited to the relationship between an individual imagination and its formal expression.

If Webb had been an isolated figure, whose writings were known only to specialists and academic colleagues, the assessment of his early career might well take on a different form. But what makes him an especially interesting figure in the development of western historical writing is that he managed to project both his personality and his ideas across a wider section of his immediate community than is usually the case, and that he did this without in any way modifying his basic role as a university teacher. The accidental death of a retired historian does not ordinarily make front page news in a sizable community, and it is significant that Webb is one of the few individuals granted interment in the state cemetery at Austin on the basis of services to the state in other than a military or political capacity. More than ten years after his death, evidence of his impact on an important segment of his generation is more apparent in the general community of which he was a determined member than in the university where he spent most of his working life.

Yet Webb was not active in local politics or in many of the non-academic activities that sometimes earn a university teacher special standing in his community. His influence, both in terms of his students and of those who knew him only on the basis of more casual contacts, stemmed to some degree from a recognition that he took local people and local concerns seriously; even the fact that he invested heavily in the growth of his community was a tangible indication of a personal involvement in the everyday life of his community and his confidence in its future. But more important was the fact that he was willing to talk in simple terms of things that were of interest to his own people, to speak of their common past in a way that gave dignity and meaning to their historical experience. For that, the generation of which he was part remained grateful; another generation, brought to maturity in a very different social environment, would have less need for the kind of reassurance he offered.

Such an identification between a historian and his community suggests something about the character of his work that is worth exploring and which may throw light on the cultural and psychological pressures that operate in societies that are modern and at the same time still in the process of formation. But apart from these interpretive premises, certain other considerations have held this study to what might be regarded as an unduly restricted framework, and some of these are of a personal and perhaps arbitrary character. This examination of Webb's early development is made from the perspective of one who never met or studied under Webb —the perspective of a foreigner whose contact with the United States and the university in which Webb spent most of his career does not go back beyond late 1969. Acquaintance with his work does go back earlier; the writer first came across *The Great Plains* during an undergraduate course at the University of Melbourne in the mid-1950's and found that its treatment of pioneer life showed some similarities to the experience of sections of the local Australian farming community.

To anyone familiar with life in the Australian wheat belt, where drought is a constant preoccupation and both the windmill and the wire fence are so much a normal part of the agricultural landscape that they are rarely noticed, Webb's account of the problems faced by the early settlers of the Plains had an obvious relevance. In neither area have man and nature ever come to a completely acceptable accommodation. That sense of grim and unresolved contest between the two, which Webb conveyed as few other students of the West have done, is also a very pervasive element in the Australian pioneering experience; drought and fire remain as weapons held in reserve and capable of wiping out the accumulated efforts of a generation.

Similarities of background and environment provide part of the basis for an interest in Webb and his interpretation of the Plains experience, but in no sense is this intended as a comparative study. Its framework is limited to Webb's social setting, and its purpose is to probe the relationship between that setting, the cultural matrix it supported, and a book that was at the same time both an attempt to define that setting and a product of it.

alan E. Cober '75

The Making of a History

1. Family and Community

THE GENERATION OF southerners born during the Civil War and brought to maturity in the wake of Reconstruction were something of a forgotten race. Scarred by the consequences of defeat and left to pay the price for the miscalculations of their forebears, many of these young people parted with the traditions of the Old South and rejected the hopes of the New. Nothing very much was said, but their actions were evidence of their sense of discouragement in the face of the social tensions and restricted opportunities that bedeviled the South during their formative years. In the late 1870's and early 1880's increasing numbers began to follow the example set by Confederate veterans and others whose lives had been turned into chaos by the war: they began to resume the great curving movement that had swept so many people out of the exhausted lands of Virginia and the Carolinas fifty years before and deposited them in the rich lands of the Gulf and the Delta.[1]

This time the curve flattened out and drove due west to the broad acres of East Texas and perhaps even beyond to the very edge of the settled areas. Here the migrant could expect to be among friends, for he was still within the boundaries of the old Confederacy; yet he would also be in a land where the ravages of war were not so evident and where there was a possibility of quick access to land and the status that inevitably went with it. To men and women embittered by the chaos in which they had grown up, these attractions canceled out the isolation, the physical dangers, and the rawness characteristic of the new environment. Harshness they could live with; for many, it was all they had ever known.

Casner Webb was of that generation, and, like so many of his contemporaries, he abandoned Mississippi very early in his adult life. At the age of twenty-one, he took his wife and daughter and moved from Monroe County, Mississippi, across Louisiana and into East Texas.[2] Little is known of the particular motives that brought about this move, other than those that are credited to the bulk of his fellow migrants. Perhaps it was not a difficult decision to make;

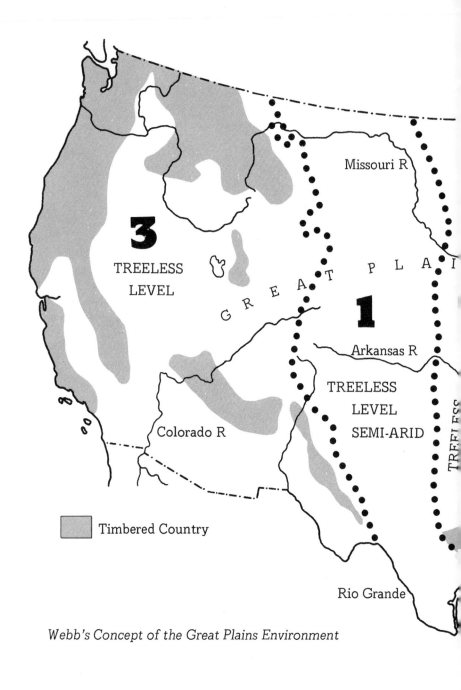

Webb's Concept of the Great Plains Environment

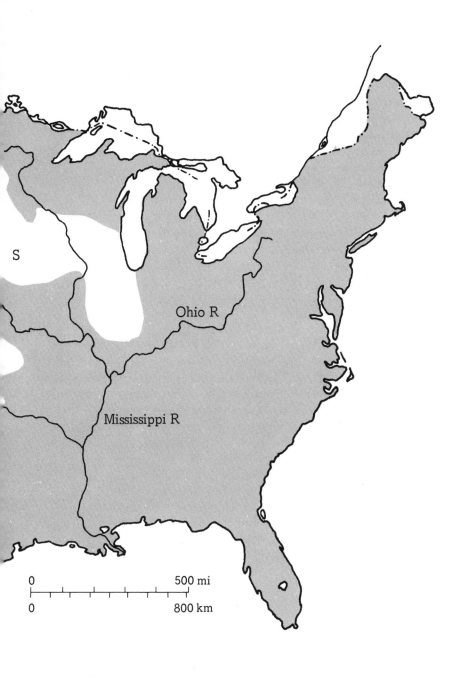

S

Ohio R

Mississippi R

0   500 mi
0   800 km

his own forebears and those of his wife had probably come to the
Deep South as part of that earlier migration from the older parts
of the region, and their example may have predisposed Casner to
move when opportunities were lacking in Mississippi.[3] It seems likely that the decision was Casner's rather than his wife's; nervous and
inclined to be overanxious, Mary Kyle Webb does not appear to
have figured prominently in family decisions. In later years their
son remembered the contrast in temperament between Casner and
Mary—her timidity paired against his fractious and high-spirited
nature.[4] Quickwitted and adaptable, Casner Webb would prosper
if given half a chance—and in the 1880's Mississippi did not seem
to offer even that.

The Webb migration was not as solitary and lonely as some of
that period, for Walter's childhood memories of the four years spent
in East Texas were peopled with uncles and cousins who lived in
the neighborhood, and it may be that his father worked for some of
these relatives when not teaching school.[5] Casner had not launched
himself into an unknown venture; there were friends ahead of him
to ease the way a little. The land itself was familiar enough; Panola
County, where the family remained for about four or five years,
was deep within the Piney Woods region of East Texas, and in
terms of climate and vegetation was in many ways a westward extension of the South. This was one of the older settled portions of
Texas, and its social and economic structure corresponded more
to that of the Old South than to that of Central Texas or even the
Gulf Coast. Here cotton was the dominant crop, and nearly half
the population was black.[6] Though technically within the area
claimed by Spain in earlier centuries, it was too far beyond the effective control of the Spanish authorities for even a vestige of Spanish influence to remain into the nineteenth century. The whole area
was an extension of the cotton belt into Texas and a natural haven
for southern men looking for an economy and a way of life similar
to the one they had known in the older regions of the South.

It was while the Webbs lived in East Texas that Walter, their
third child, was born on April 3, 1888. Alma, the eldest of the family, had been born while the family was still in Mississippi, and a
boy, Houston, died at the age of two. Another boy died not long
after the family moved to West Texas: "It was here that I waked
in the dead of night to discover a commotion in the house. A
screech owl had entered and my father was trying to get it out. I do
not remember whether there was any comment on this ill-omen, but
I know that most ill-omens were known to my mother. I recall

awaking in the night after this and there was again commotion, tears and frantic efforts. Death had entered the humble place and claimed the youngest member."[7] For some reason, Walter Webb rarely made any reference to the fact that he was the only one of four brothers to survive childhood; Houston, Kyle, and Bruce Webb all died young, leaving Walter with one elder and two younger sisters.[8] As a child he found this midway position bothersome, and the absence of a brother no doubt made his position lonelier than it might otherwise have been. By the time he was five, his family had left East Texas, and his memories of life there were only the vague and disconnected flashes so typical of early childhood— the fragrance of the pipesmoke as a boarder sat by the door in the evening and talked of his native London, the excitement when a pair of oxen bolted and charged into the house, the feel of crushed cutworms underfoot as he walked among the rows of cotton, and the rain, ". . . big drops coming down from high, making tracks in the dry sand, a small boy running around the house, full of delightful guilt at being out when he should be in."[9]

There is nothing to suggest that his circumstances were any different from those of hundreds of other children of his age living in rural East Texas at that time. His parents were still young and had yet to find their permanent niche in society; they do not appear to have been any more impoverished than the bulk of their neighbors at a time when farmers as a group were a depressed section of the community.[10] Perhaps the only element that distinguished Casner Webb from his contemporaries was that he was comparatively well educated and could qualify as a rural school teacher. It was probably the desire to capitalize on the asset that persuaded him to move again, leaving East Texas well behind and traveling over a hundred miles to the eastern edge of the lower Plains and the western limits of the agricultural frontier—to Stephens County and the Western Cross Timbers, a belt of blackjack and post oak which reached south from Oklahoma and divided the Grand and Blackland prairies from the Plains of West Texas. It was in this region on the edge of the Plains that the family made their permanent home.[11]

By the time the Webbs made their final move, young Walter was just beginning to observe his larger surroundings with a certain amount of interest and to find himself as a person within that framework. His reminiscences of the period between his sixth and twelfth years, all of which were spent in the area around Stephens County, suggest the rapid expansion of his imagination—but the influences bearing in on the growing boy were anything but conventional. The family had now reached an area where the crust of settlement was far thinner than anything they had previously known, so that the distinctive features of the area stood out all the more clearly. The actual journey to the new location had not left much of an impression, except for one incident that stood out because it awakened a sense of unease in a boy still very dependent on his parents in an unfamiliar situation. His father had gone on alone to make preparations for the family, and Mary Webb followed with the children. They arrived at Waco at the dead of night, and Walter remembered the scene vividly: "The station was lit with pin-points of light, and cab-men with lanterns calling 'This way to this and that hotel.' I have heard my mother speak of how trying this experience was, this deciding where to go, and I think I caught then some of her anxiety . . ."[12] They made their first stop in Eastland County, at the home of Uncle Jasper Webb, a white-bearded eccentric who had left Mississippi at some earlier point and settled near Merriman. Soon after their arrival, Casner moved the family again, this time to the home of another relative living closer to the community where he planned to teach.[13] Walter disliked the company of the elder cousins who seemed to swarm through his home, and he was relieved when his father found a home to rent. This was to be only the first of a series of moves that would take the family over wide areas of Stephens and Eastland counties during the next ten years, for most of Casner's teaching assignments were for one year only and it was essential that he go wherever the chance of a job presented itself. Teaching was still an irregular business, and those who depended on it for a living had to fit in with the fluctuating demands of the frontier communities.[14]

There was nothing genteel about Casner Webb's role in the local community, for it was his physical strength rather than his learning that qualified him for his work; the raw and refractory youths who made up the school population at the time were quite capable of driving a teacher out of the school, and the parents expected that the teacher be a strict disciplinarian. Though small and wiry, Casner had learned how to defend himself in those earlier years in Mississippi, and he made his reputation by his willingness to fight it out with older children. Some he disarmed, and others he half-strangled into submission; he made some enemies, but he managed to keep employed in a three-county area as long as there were schools where the students needed a firm hand.

Many of the children were already hardened by farm work and were reluctant to waste their time in the schoolroom.[15] Casner apparently provided the encouragement they needed.

The constant moving from one small community to another provided the boy with a certain amount of stimulus and variety that would have been lacking if the family had remained tied to a farm right through his boyhood. There were new friendships and new sights and an occasional glimpse of the life of the small towns scattered through the area. For a boy whose exposure to formal education was to be at best irregular, impressions drawn from life became all the more important, and what he saw in those early years left him with a somber respect for rural life that persisted into later life. Though he later rebelled against the hard and apparently useless routine of farm work, he never lost his sympathy for those who made their living from the soil; at the same time, he knew enough of the reality of their life to avoid being sentimental about it.

There were many Wests, and the one that Webb saw as a child was of a kind that has attracted little in the way of romantic legend. It had some of the harshness associated with pioneering and practically none of the local color that would appeal to a later generation. The two counties with which he was most familiar—Stephens and Eastland—had been almost uninhabited at the time of the Civil War, and those who did live there were virtually manning the outposts on the last perimeter of settlement. It was an area where, as late as the 1870's, the Indians still possessed the power to snuff out life when and if they saw fit, and it required a considerable military effort to make the land safe for the settlers who came in during the next decade. By 1876 conditions had improved; Stephens County was reorganized, given a new county seat, and made ready for the arrival of farmers and their families.[16]

What followed was something of a telescoping of the usual process of settlement into one continuous blur of activity.[17] The few ranchers who managed to operate in the area during the period of Indian activity had made little impact, and, at the point when the cattle industry was reaching its peak on a statewide basis, they were being overrun by the flow of settlers coming in from the north and east. In the 1880's, would-be farmers—many of them from Arkansas, together with large contingents from Louisiana and Mississippi—began to arrive in such numbers that they swamped the older population and rapidly shifted the basis of the local economy from ranching to agriculture.[18]

This is not to suggest that the area was heavily populated when the tide of immigration began to ease early in the following decade; but compared to the unsettled years following the end of the Civil War, this part of Texas had changed dramatically during the 1880's. Farms were under cultivation, communications were good, and the first generation of settlers were beginning to fill out the structures of county organization that had been there on paper for twenty years.

The rapidity of settlement reflected in part the pressures forcing population out of the South, and in part the promotional activities of the railroads.[19] In their anxiety to tap the lucrative transcontinental traffic, a number of companies had built lines across Central Texas to link up with the Pacific Coast routes; railroads appeared in the North Central counties either before or alongside the inflow of settlers, accelerating the process of settlement and transforming the economic potential of the area.[20] At the very time when the farming sector of the national economy was experiencing a decline, incoming settlers began to grow cotton and raise stock on the edge of the Texas Plains. Under the circumstances, few could hope to become wealthy, but the land would provide a living for those who were frugal and prepared to wait for better times. It was the possession of land and not the prospect of sudden wealth that held men to the soil, despite the discouragement of low prices, drought, and the labor involved in bringing new lands into production.

Nor was there any significant gap between the taking up of land and the appearance of the small towns with their tiny commercial services. The unusually early arrival of the railroads triggered the growth of small centers like Cisco and Albany, little clusters of homes grouped around a general store, a blacksmith's shop, and—in the case of a county seat—a newly built courthouse.[21] In some cases, the arrival of the railroads caused the relocation of existing hamlets; in fact, the railroads were the major element in determining the distribution of population in the county. The little towns that grew up along the railroads became in turn the natural centers for church and school development, and a surprising number maintained a newspaper quite early in their lives.

The net result was that the small communities on the edge of the Texas Plains emerged from the decade of the 1880's with most of the structural requirements of organized society already in place. The machinery of local government was already functioning, thanks to provisions made by the state legislature long before they were settled to any extent; as soon as the Indian threat disappeared in the late 1870's, small groups of settlers had carried out the procedures laid down for the formation of county government. By the 1880's taxes were being collected, some schools were operating, and the churches were well in evidence. A transportation system was already in place: two rail lines served the needs of Eastland County at a time when the roads were still in a very rudimentary condition and were maintained by a system of corvée.[22] Though late on the scene in terms of nineteenth century development, these little communities had shown some capacity for political organization and a reasonable degree of efficiency in the conduct of their own affairs; by the end of the century they must have appeared as stable and as permanent as any other group of settlements in the nation, and they were to remain quiet backwaters until the oil boom threw them into confusion in the years that followed the First World War.

Yet there was still an element of harshness in the lives of those who worked in the area when the Webbs first reached there in 1892 or 1893. A decade and a half does not provide time for a farming community to bring any more than a fraction of the settled land under cultivation; there were still large tracts of land awaiting the plow, and others remained unoccupied. Much of the cleared land had been given over to cotton, since this was the crop best known to the predominantly southern immigrants. But it took time to learn the special characteristics of the land, and to make the necessary adjustments. As late as 1902, Casner Webb was able to demonstrate that some parts of the district were well adapted to fruit growing, and he managed to tap a regional market at a time when the arrival of the boll weevil had thrown a damper on the prospects of cotton.[23] Later still, the humble peanut would become one of the major crops in the area, a development not suspected in the 1890's.

To an intelligent observer, there was still plenty of evidence of what the country must have been like in its raw state some thirty years before; the migrants had penetrated and subdued the land, but they had not completely changed its face. This fact, together with the physical presence of most of the pioneering generation, made it possible for young Webb to let his imagination run freely over the terrain. The Indians were gone, but the signs of their presence were still evident, and the discussions among the older residents as they sat around the firesides on long winter evenings did not center on legendary events in the distant past but on incidents in their own lives a decade or two earlier.[24] There was little room for a romantic gloss in these reminiscences, for the tales they told were of realistic dangers and the deaths and injuries of people they had known. Occasionally a small boy had to make some imaginative adjustments to put individuals in their proper perspective: Amos Fincher seemed a very old man to childish eyes, but Walter could still see him as the buffalo hunter he had been rather than the farmer he had become.[25]

Very early in his life he sensed the special values attaching to horsemanship, values that went beyond the element of sheer practicality: "All West Texas was on horseback at that time, especially the young men. . . . I can see the saddled and sweaty horses standing tied to trees, while men stood or talked or drew figures in the earth, line boundaries, directions, or just plain sand doodling."[26] This image, with its suggestions of the open range and masculine independence, remained fixed in his memory, but it has to be put alongside the more humdrum scenes of daily life that were too numerous to be memorable—the daily routine of mules or horses drawing open farm wagons or turning the sod for the incoming crops. There was still open range in the counties that Webb knew best as a child, but most farmers cleared land and followed the plow, raised chickens, and put down wells for water. Theirs was a plain existence, with little of the supposed glamour of the cattle kingdom a little farther to the west.

A plain life, but not necessarily an isolated one, thanks to the railroads and the small towns they brought with them. Webb could remember his father hauling a wagonload of freight from the railhead in Cisco to a store at Wayland and the pair of them spending the night at the wagon yard in Cisco—a cheerful outdoor hostelry where travelers could pitch camp and make their own fires for a small fee. There was food for the horses, and in the morning men cooked an early breakfast of coffee and bacon and talked as the wood smoke curled upward and hung lazily over the yard. To a country boy, the late sleeping and dilatory habits of his town cousins seemed to suggest a lack of interest in practical matters that would lead to disaster if practiced on a farm.[27] But for all that, town and farm were not too far apart, and neither one could function without the other.[28]

There were still some suggestions of the open ways of the range era; weapons were still carried, but mostly by the young men, and on social occasions at that—suggesting that the revolver had become something of a status symbol rather than a practical necessity.[29] Older men with land and family responsibilities possibly felt less inclined to condone violence or to become involved in situations that could bring disaster on their dependents—but clashes could still occur. Walter could remember an occasion when his father drew a revolver during an argument with some associates; but it is significant that he had to borrow the weapon from a friend when he realized that a clash might occur. Ironically, the friend who supplied the weapon was the local justice of the peace and a Baptist preacher.[30] The more dangerous incidents were those involving family groups, and there was always the possibility of a resurgence of the old-type family feuds. Once the Webbs met an armed contingent of the Heatley clan on their way into town to confront a rival group that had given offence; nothing happened, but the incident showed how easily such conflicts could erupt and how thin was the line between the violent ways of the old order and the newer urge for improvement: the Heatleys were the patrons of Casner Webb's little rural school.[31]

There were other aspects of local life that a growing boy could sense, even though he could not put them in proper perspective. He realized very early in life that to be poor was to be in some way humiliated and deprived, and he resisted anything that would suggest that his own family were in that condition. In particular, the appearance of "thicken gravy" (a mixture of bacon grease, flour, and water) on the family table or eating corn bread for breakfast were both signs of degradation.[32] Not many families in those farming communities could be classified as poverty-stricken; self-sufficiency was the norm, and a surplus meant mild prosperity unless drought or a tornado threw the local economy into chaos. But lack of opportunity affected many of the growing young men and forced some of them to look hard at the traditional escape route to the west. Once the demands of getting the family farm into production had been met, there was little for the younger sons to do on their own account; their parents had taken most of the better land in the area when they first arrived, and the land that remained was unattractive and difficult to clear. Occasionally, young men would leave home and look for work in the cattle country to the west— but this was often a revolt against parental discipline, and it ended in a forced return.[33] The more orderly approach, and the one favored by young men who wanted land and the chance to establish a family in a farming community, was to head north to the newly opened lands of the Indian territory.

The decision to move was a serious one, and the actual departure was marked by gatherings of relatives and friends to make their farewells. Webb remembered attending one of these farewells for a group of brothers who were leaving for Oklahoma the following morning. ("That night the children played base amid the fireflies while the older ones talked and were no doubt suitably sad. How the women loved sadness.")[34] Later, when the Webbs lived near Eliasville, they could watch the daily procession of wagons traveling to Oklahoma and note the return of the casualties. One of the great internal migrations of the United States was nearing its end, and the growing boy saw something of it and guessed at the pressures that had generated such a movement.[35]

Only one generation could pioneer in the authentic sense, and in North Central Texas that generation was now well established and settling down to enjoy the modest comfort that had been their original objective. Their children, however, were caught in a difficult situation: if not to Oklahoma or to the still more uncertain prospects of the West, where could they go? The local towns were too small to offer any prospects, and to go beyond their orbit required something more than a rudimentary education. So the last decade of the nineteenth century saw the beginnings of a significant shift in emphasis among the rural families of the area; realizing that education was the key to their children's prospects—and their own ability to provide it an indicator of their own success in life— some of the farmers who had settled in the area in the 1880's were now moving into the local towns, if only on a temporary basis, so that their children could have access to the new secondary schools. The flight from the land had already begun, and in a sense these farmers were trying to equip their children to make their own way in a world that was already becoming very different from the one they had known.[36]

It was only in his later years that Webb came to value the experience of that period, and even then his comments suggest a general respect rather than a personal affection. He never yearned for the days of his childhood, or cast them in a romantic light; instead, he stressed the harshness and the capacity of men and women to survive and build, grounding his sense of respect on the hard rock of experience. Nothing about the life of those communities made him nostalgic or sentimental; they were essentially utilitarian structures that provided needed services and took no particular joy in their own existence. Too raw to have developed any sense of identity or common heritage, they were geographic and economic rather than social units. The churches provided one kind of linkage, but neither Casner nor Walter Webb displayed much enthusiasm for Christian fellowship; if evangelical Protestantism ever obtained any foothold in Walter's soul, it slipped away fairly quickly under his father's critical glare.[37] The only institution that provided Walter with any form of social contact and involvement in the affairs of others was the school, and his contact with formal education was irregular until he was seventeen years of age.

The elements that he missed in those years were the intangibles that are often the by-products of community life and are especially important in the development of a balanced and integrated consciousness—companionship, recreation, involvement in the affairs of others, entertainment, a rudimentary sense of the aesthetic, mental stimulus; all of these tended to wither when exposed to the rawness of an unremitting nature. Even the structures that men placed upon the earth seemed temporary and at the mercy of the landscape, like "empty cardboard boxes which the wind would soon blow away."[38] The county courthouse and an occasional church reflected some of the solidity and the tradition characteristic of the institutions that produced them; but more typical was the frame dwelling clinging uneasily to an unfriendly soil and already beginning to crack and wither under the sun. Adobe makes its peace with the terrain and with sun and sky; board and box frame suggest a temporary occupation and an inevitable deterioration and collapse.

Without the deeply rooted social bonds that come from generations of shared community life, individuals were thrown exclusively on their own resources and on the support of the immediate family. In Webb's case this meant his parents only, and in particular his father; temperament and necessity made the bond between father and son a strong one, with the mother somewhat in the background.[39] But parental influence could not solve many of the problems of a boy who knew that his inclinations were taking him away and out of their range of interests; it was because neither the community he lived in nor the parents who sheltered him could provide the direction he needed that he had to depend on what he read of the outside world or what he heard from the few individuals who knew that world at first hand.

2. The Making of
an Imagination

FOR AN INTELLIGENT child who sensed that there was no place for him on the frontier, the avenues of escape were not immediately evident. In the absence of the guidance and example provided by an extended family network or the alternatives that an urban community usually displays for its discontented, young Webb was thrown almost entirely on the resources of the local school. This was his one opportunity to feed and stimulate an eager imagination, and his only chance to enjoy the company of children of his own age outside the family circle. It was also a source of information about the outside world, information that a child would need when he found that there was little incentive for him to stay close to the farm. A great deal depended on the individual teacher, and, under the loose arrangements then prevailing, it was quite possible for a teacher to be no more familiar with the outside world than the children he taught.

Walter Webb was lucky in some respects; the fact that his father was a teacher who kept some books in the house and took a newspaper regularly gave him something of an advantage over most of his contemporaries. Though Casner's qualifications were not of the conventional variety, there seems little doubt that he was well educated by the standards of the day: those of his letters that have survived among Walter Webb's papers suggest a careful grounding in composition and a clear, straightforward writing style. Though he was much more of a farmer than a teacher, Casner's modest accomplishments suggest that the home atmosphere that Walter Webb knew as a child differed from the frontier norm to that extent.[1] Most parents in the area expected that the school—when it was available—would train their children to read, write, and make simple calculations; anything else was extraneous and difficult to justify.[2] But Casner knew that intelligence and training gave an individual a competitive edge in a world that was already far more complex than the one he had known as a boy in Mississippi. He had to ask a good deal of the boy, especially when a crippling injury to his foot hampered his own efforts; but Walter found more sympathy for his broadening interests than might have been the case, and his later comments do not suggest that any pressure was put on him to stay on the farm and carry on his father's work.[3]

Walter was also lucky in that he found school a pleasant experience; good teachers were not always easy to find in rural areas, but he was apparently satisfied with those who taught him. One in particular he remembered with special affection—E. Temple Peters, the man who taught him enough to qualify for his teachers' certificate and a good deal more: "how to tip waiters, have our shoes shined, send candy to our dates, wear clean linen, rubber-soled shoes and tailor-made clothes if we could afford it, and to stay at good hotels."[4] For a boy who would have to make the transition from farm to town within a few years, those were useful things to know—and he was not likely to learn them from any other source.

Against all these more positive elements stood a series of practical difficulties that jeopardized his links with the one institution that had something to offer him. When he was quite young the family was always on the move from one school to the next, and, although Casner did not teach outside a three-county area, the frequent changes in school added to the boy's difficulties.[5] Sometimes the school was simply too far from home, especially when he was still quite young, but the more serious interruption came when he had turned thirteen—an interruption that affected his schooling for the next four years. In 1902 his father decided to begin farming on a small tract of land near Ranger, and, since he still needed the income from teaching, Casner came home to the farm at weekends and left his son in charge for the rest of the week. Walter enjoyed being given responsibility, but when the task lengthened into its fourth year he reacted against the tedium and the dirt and made it clear that he wanted to have done with it.[6] There was some satisfaction in seeing the land come into production and knowing that the new smokehouse and the road and well were the results of both their efforts; but, whereas his parents could look on these developments as signs of a growing self-sufficiency and modest comfort, they meant far less to a boy who knew that his future must be something better than the dull routine of a dirt farmer.[7] The more he resented the lack of companionship and the restrictions on his schooling, the more attractive the school and its teachers appeared. During that period, he managed to attend three different schools for as much as four months per year; that experience left him convinced that this was what he wanted to do—to read and perhaps to write, and to let his imagination roam across a world that seemed far more interesting than anything he had seen in the Cross Timbers.[8]

During that period of relative isolation on the farm, he made a small but significant attempt to break out of his restricted world—significant in that it led to an unexpected result that was to have some importance on the development of his later career. He had written a letter to the children's column of a small magazine published in Atlanta, Georgia, explaining his interest in getting a better education and asking if he could contribute a story about his dog.[9] The editor's reply was friendly and conventional, except for a closing suggestion that proved to be quite apt in the light of Webb's later career: if he wanted to learn more, he should try to obtain a good physical geography and study at home.[10] But what was more intriguing was a letter the boy received some time later from William E. Hinds, an elderly businessman in New York who had seen his letter in the Atlanta paper and decided that he would do something to encourage a deserving youngster. Over the next few years Webb received encouragement and practical help in the form of books and magazines from a patron he never saw, and, when he eventually went on to the state university, the loan funds he needed for the first two years came from the same source.

Years later, when he had retired from teaching and had the opportunity to look back over his early life, Webb became fascinated by the chain of events that led to his contact with Hinds. He realized that the whole affair had the ingredients of a fine human interest story of the type that had always appealed to him, and he used it as the basis for a popular article in *Harper's Magazine*.[11] To his delight it proved to be an enormous success, found its way into *Reader's Digest*, and triggered off an extensive correspondence with ordinary people all over the country and even overseas.[12] Many wanted simply to comment on the moral of the story—how the kindly gesture from a thoughtful adult started a poor boy on the road to success without any thought for his own advantage. Others offered information about the mysterious Mr. Hinds, and dozens suggested that under the circumstances Webb could hardly refuse their own requests for financial aid. Bulging files of letters in the Webb papers are evidence of the remarkable response that the article produced in a wide cross-section of the community. For a man who had always wanted to write in terms that ordinary people could understand, that response was especially gratifying.

In the early years of the century, however, Hinds was not the epic figure he would later become for those who were fascinated by the *Harper's Magazine* article; but his intervention was of critical importance in that it gave adult backing for what the boy felt he must do and convinced him that he must not put his ambitions aside as impractical. Significantly, it was advice that came from outside his own community and his family circle—and, ironically, from that section of the country that Webb was always to regard with a certain amount of suspicion. Hinds was the first of three individuals who, at critical points in Webb's life, stepped in and supplied the direction that he could not find from the resources available within his own community.[13] All three were older men who knew the ways of a more complex and sophisticated world and showed Webb how to proceed if he wanted to achieve his ambitions; he learned quickly and put what he learned to good use. There was never any need for an extended relationship with these men, a constant searching for advice; once he knew the direction to take, Webb followed it out in his own way.

The encouragement from Hinds and the practical sympathy of his own parents made it possible for Webb to commence his secondary education at the age of seventeen. The most difficult period was past as far as the farm was concerned, and there was also the education of Walter's two sisters to be considered; eventually the parents made the decision to move into Ranger for a year so that all the children could attend school there.[14] Casner would return to teaching for a time, and would care for the farm on weekends; it was not an easy arrangement, but it would be worthwhile if Walter could qualify for a teaching certificate and his sisters had the opportunity to find a better education. Other farmers were doing the same thing in those years, preparing their children for entry into a way of life that they themselves did not understand or entirely approve.

The year at Ranger was a difficult one, for the boy had to compress as much study as he could into one year and at the same time correct the deficiencies of his erratic elementary schooling.[15] This would be his one chance to break out of the farm existence; the pressure was there, and he needed very badly to succeed. But he found his teachers helpful and well equipped for what they had to do to get their students through the examinations that were the key to the whole exercise; those who passed would be qualified to teach in rural schools, and for most that was the limit of their ambitions.[16] By the spring of the following year Webb had the certificate that he later likened to an emancipation proclamation; for the first time he was free of the farm and had a source of income of his own.[17] He could fend for himself, read what he liked, and yet not move too far from the rural communities that he knew. In 1906, the year following his certification, he taught in three small schools in Eastland County, where his father's reputation and contacts made it fairly easy for him to get work.[18] Though he had virtually no practical training, he survived and earned enough to return to Ranger for another year of full-time study that would qualify him for a first-class certificate.

This time it was much easier; he was now confident that he could handle the work, and he was back among friends he had made during the first year. He had his own money and more time to relax and take a calmer look at the world around him. Ranger was a very small town, but he had friends there and the chance of a social life of the kind he had missed on the farm.[19] By the time he returned to teaching in the following year, he was a much more confident young man and could see that he was beginning to make something of a mark on his own community. He took over the school at Merriman where his father had taught years earlier, earned the highest salary available in the area, and enjoyed the luxury of having an assistant to work with the lower grades. When he attended the county teacher's institute in Cisco, he went as the equal of his old mentor E. Temple Peters; they lived high for a couple of days, and Walter had the chance to experiment with the social graces that Peters had taught him at the Ranger school.[20] Within the three-county area that had been his father's teaching circuit, he was a man of some standing, a local boy who had made good by local standards; it was a comfortable situation and Webb enjoyed it.[21] He knew the odds had been against him and was proud of what he had achieved; it was now time to enjoy the fruits of success, to read and talk—but not to study. For the moment he was comfortably trapped in the rural world.

To the extent that it opened up a limited alternative to farming life and gave Webb access to books and the time to read them, the rural school obviously served a useful purpose. It is more difficult to gauge the effect of his rather spasmodic education on the boy's intellectual and imaginative development and determine how adequately it prepared him for what was as yet an unsuspected career as a writer and an academic. The deficiencies of the average frontier school are well known: indifferently trained teachers, paucity of books and equipment, and the constant tension between the needs of the school and the practical demands of a hardworking and uncultivated community. But there were also less tangible problems arising out of both the curriculum and the teaching materials used, problems which were of little moment to children whose concerns were limited to mastering the rudimentary skills, but of considerable importance to the shaping of a more fertile and restless imagination.

Webb always remembered the schools and the teachers with affection, but he was indirectly critical of what he learned there. Retrospective estimates of the value of education during the early years are naturally suspect, but the emphasis Webb developed in his remarks is possibly more critical than he realized. Writing from the perspective of middle age, with his standing as an interpreter of his region well established, he deplored the fact that it was only as an adult that he discovered the character of the natural world that surrounded him as a child.[22] How much more interesting it would have been to have known the birds by their distinctive notes and markings and the varieties of wild grasses and the fauna of the plains, to have understood why the jackrabbit is built as he is and the reason for "the cycle that went on between the huge solitary wasps that cruised low over the plains late in the afternoon when the tarantulas were out on their spangly legs. . . . I had to read Fabre years later to know that the wasps were hunting tarantulas, that they caught them in their holes."[23] There was so much that he could have learned by the time he was ten if there had been someone to teach him; outside his own doorstep was a local world that was simply a microcosm of the wider universe, "yet we rake all our time in the muck of books without discovering that the things we labor over are there just outside the door."[24] Books were important, but only insofar as they led an individual on to look more closely at his own world; by themselves, they were inadequate.

Clearly his emphasis owed a good deal to his experiences in working on his Plains book and his later concentration on the historical experience of his own state. But the stated preference and the implied rejection of the sort of education he did receive can be understood as part of an unconscious hostility toward cultural assumptions that had no obvious bearing on his own needs as a child. Learning to read was important and certainly exciting; but the content of what one read was equally important, and in a frontier school virtually all that a child read was geared to a world considerably different from the one he saw about him. For a sensitive child, that fact could easily become a source of dissatisfaction and inner tension.

There are a few scattered indications as to the type of reading material Webb encountered as a child, and most of them refer to the items he virtually scavenged to feed what became a marked appetite for books. Like the western novelist Eugene Manlove Rhodes, he acquired some books by saving the labels on Arbuckle's coffee—*Jack the Giant Killer* made its way to the Cross Timbers by that route—and publishers who thought that he was a teacher answered his queries by sending sample copies of standard children's favorites.[25] *The Adventures of Huckleberry Finn* he borrowed from a friend and read on horseback on the way home. At some point he found a volume of Shakespeare and memorized some passages; but his tastes were still quite plastic, for he also memorized parts of Joel Dorman Steele's *Fourteen Weeks in Natural Philosophy*—the rhythmic presentation of the laws of motion, rather than the subject matter, appealed to his ear.[26] His patron in New York sent him accounts of Henry Morton Stanley's travels in Africa, several books on grammar and composition, and a range of magazines—*The American Boy, National Magazine, Outlook, Success Magazine,* and *McLure's.*[27] He liked *Sunny South,* the magazine that had put him in contact with Hinds and which carried articles by Joel Chandler Harris; but adventure stories held most of his attention, with an occasional magazine—and in one instance, an encyclopedia—regarded as a marvelous windfall.[28]

Obviously these titles represent a fraction of the material he must have read in those early years, but the list suggests something of the difficulties confronting a child in an area where there were few books kept in the average home and very few alternative sources. There are even fewer references to the books he used as a part of his formal schooling, and these suggest that the textbooks circulating in his section of Texas were those that had the widest usage throughout the nation during the late nineteenth century.[29] He could recall only one in any detail, and, while allowance must again be made for the intrusion of a later perspective, the emphasis he gave to this book is of some interest.

Speaking to a conference of geographers in 1960, Webb recalled having used a textbook on physical geography when he first started teaching in 1906.[30] If his memory was correct, this was the first time that he had heard either of the book or the subject it covered, but he was impressed by the way it dealt with the physical world around him, "with things I knew about."[31] He found it much more interesting than political geography, which he understood as memorizing details about remote places, and he preferred the book to the other texts he used in the classroom. Apparently he saw this book and the approach it displayed as being much closer to the ideal education he discussed in his draft autobiography, and his admiration for the work throws some light on the value of his schooling. The reference to the value of reading about "things I knew about" is one that recurs in his comments on the writing of *The Great Plains* and, indirectly, in many of his later speeches. Also, the same preference for linking intellectual activity to the immediate natural environment is implied in the way he centered his interests in later years on such issues as conservation and respect for the environment.[32] The ranch he owned near Austin seemed to satisfy both a need for companionship and for a place to explore the natural environment with a care that had not occurred to him in earlier years—a place where he could become familiar with the grasses and the fauna that had been taken for granted in his childhood. The theme is a constant one, and its relevance to his work is obvious—but its roots seem to lie in those early years.

One part of an explanation could lie in his reaction to the textbook on physical geography that he first saw in 1906. His reference to the work gives the author's name as W. E. Davis, but it seems more likely that the text was William Morris Davis's *Physical Geography*, published in 1898—one of the first to expound the new approach to geography that was to dominate the teaching of the subject at the academic level until the end of the First World War.[33] If this was the case, Webb had by a rather curious coincidence made his first contact with the study of geography at the very point when environmentalism, with its Darwinian overtones, was beginning its capture of American geographic thought. He would meet it again in one of its variant strains when he studied under Lindley Miller Keasbey at the University of Texas between 1909 and 1915, and, although he never became either a geographer or a thoroughgoing environmentalist, his cast of mind always remained sympathetic to that approach. Temperamentally, he was never one to follow another man's system; but when he borrowed, it was most frequently from the environmentalists.

If Webb's career had followed a conventional pattern from 1906 on, he might well have been attracted to the study of geography as a discipline and been made aware of the development of thought in that field. But his interest remained potential, and his education from that point on deferred any contact with current trends in geography—although, as will be indicated elsewhere, he did become linked to another brand of geographic thought through his relationship with Keasbey.[34] On the other hand, the new geography with its emphasis on the "control which geographic forces have over life, especially the life of man," reached many who had no direct contact with the discipline.[35] The assumption that was basic to the Davis approach—that there was "an unbroken chain of causation linking the physical phenomena of the earth's surface, the organic realm, and human society"—could be widely accepted in the early decades of the century, even though other branches of the social sciences were retreating from the neo-Darwinian approach.[36] Through the works of Ellen Churchill Semple and Albert Perry Brigham it filtered into the ranks of the historians and found sanctuary there long after it fell into disrepute among the geographers.[37] So although Webb never explored the theory of geographic influences in any systematic way, there was really no great need for him to do so; the idea was already current, and the steady growth of the Turnerian interpretation guaranteed a continued warm reception among American historians.[38]

Accordingly, the spark that Davis's work struck in 1906 did not catch fire as far as Webb was concerned. Webb was not a geographer by instinct, and only one part of the Davis concept really appealed to him—the impact of the natural environment on man; he was not attracted to the detailed study of the environment for its own sake. As a child he wanted to know about the world around him and to establish his own place within that world. It was only later that he realized that a knowledge of local geography might have helped him; until then his only approach to the wider world was through the curious assortment of reading that came his way during those early years. Accordingly, his imagination developed around adventure stories and magazine articles, most of which took older parts of the country as their setting and centered on a way of life that was radically different from anything he could see around him. It was probably this lack of concordance between the imaginative framework built up from his reading and the realities of a rather humdrum existence in Stephens County that lay at the root of his dissatisfaction with his early schooling. The literary quality of what he read did not matter—the same disparity between the real and the imaginative would have applied in the case of both the classics and the low-grade adventure stories.

If this was the case, Webb shared a problem that was common to many of his generation in the West and the midwestern border and that in a sense constitutes a basic difficulty for any sensitive mind in a dependent culture—the question of relating the cultural assumptions and values of an older society to the realities of a raw and undeveloped country. The problem is dealt with so frequently in studies of the general development of American literature that it does not require further comment. What does need to be emphasized is that, by the end of the nineteenth century, eastern cultural assumptions had something of the same relationship to the raw western mind as those of Europe traditionally had to the East. It would not be difficult to translate the novelist Thomas Wolfe's despairing comment into specifically western terms—with the East in place of the civilizations of the Old World: "Around him lay the village; beyond, the ugly rolling land, sparse with cheap farmhouses, hard and raw and ugly. He was reading Euripides, and all around him a world of black and white was eating fried food. He was reading of ancient sorceries, but did an old ghost ever come to haunt this land? The ghost of Hamlet's father in Connecticut,

> . . . I am thy father's spirit,
> Doomed for a certain time to walk the night
> Between Bloomington and Portland, Maine."[39]

The dilemma of an intelligent child trying to expand his or her imagination in the context of a society one remove beyond the provincial and agitated by the discrepancy between literary assumptions and the realities of frontier life is a familiar enough theme in midwestern autobiography. It was graphically portrayed by one child of that generation, a girl brought up on the Iowa prairie and forced to reconcile imagination and reality as best she could. Margaret Lyn, later a professor of English at the University of Kansas, recalled that "it was little less than tragic to read of things that one could never know, and to live among things that had never been thought worth putting in a book. What did it avail to read of forests and crags and waterfalls and castles and blue seas, when I could know only barbed-wire fences and frame buildings and prairie grass?"[40] She could remember that as a child she had been fascinated by the few clumps of trees that grew near her home, for to her they became woods and forests, a link with the images of conventional literature, "a glimpse of dream things, an illustration of poems read, a mystery of undefined possibilities."[41]

> The woods seemed to put me nearer to the world on whose borders I always hovered, the world of stories and poems, the world of books in general. The whole business of my life just then was to discover in the real world of actual events enough that was bookish to reconcile me to being a real child and not

one in a story. For the most part, aside from play, which was a thing in itself and had a sane importance of its own, the realities of life were those that had their counterparts in books. Whatever I found in books, especially in poetry, I craved for my own experience . . . But the two things, books and the visible world that the sun shone in and the prairies spread out in, were far apart, and according to my lights, were incompatible. Who had ever heard of Iowa in a novel or a poem? . . . I wished that life could be translated into terms of literature, but as far as I could see I had to do it if it was to be done.[42]

Webb never thought the problem through as carefully as this, and it seems likely that in his case the dilemma centered more on the element of adventure—of life and movement and drama— than on the aesthetic. As an adult he did gradually confront the problem of adjusting his notions of beauty to the apparently harsh and forbidding landscape that he had come to love, and by the end of his life he had brought the two elements into some sort of acceptable harmony. But this was a secondary problem, one that only became evident when other more urgent difficulties had been resolved. It was more important that he settle the question of his region's historical distinctiveness and give depth to his own existence; only then would it become important that he probe its aesthetic qualities.

Yet there was so little on which a historical imagination could feed, and so few objects that could act as a focus—no great buildings, no state mansions, no obvious grandeur, nothing that was specifically the creation of his own people save the fact of their survival.[43] There were no great incidents outside the domestic realm that men acknowledged as significant and worthy of memory, no battles, no individuals to stand undeniably in the cast of heroes, no legends—only quiet little towns and scattered farms, with ordinary people going about their mundane tasks. None of the books he read told him anything that would suggest a deeper significance for the placid world around him; their frame of reference stood far to the East and even further across the Atlantic, the source and venue of authentic history and dramatic adventure.

Something of this conflict between life and literature lay at the root of the resentment that boiled up in later years and put him at odds with a world that had failed to come up to expectations. Like so many of his generation, he made the journey out to the world "that was described so erroneously in those books."[44] But when disillusionment set in and he turned back to the land that he had too arbitrarily rejected, he found that nothing had changed: the books had still not been written, and the landscape of his father's world was as anonymous as ever. If the life of the Plains was to be put on paper, he would have to do it and do it quickly; much had already been lost, and the survivors were few in number. The impulse was there, but the techniques were lacking; a good deal of raking through the muck of books would follow before he turned back to the rocks and the grasses and the wasps that drifted low over the Plains in the late afternoons of his childhood.

3. A Plainsman and
His College

IN THE LATE SUMMER of 1883, John William Mallet left his home
in Virginia and traveled southwest toward Austin in Central Texas.
His journey almost coincided with that of Casner Webb as the latter crossed from Mississippi and through Louisiana to East Texas;
in a sense, both men were following the path that for generations
had drawn thousands of people out of the older sections of the
South and spread them across the broad acres and the fresh soil
to the southwest. But timing and direction were the only things the
two men had in common; in terms of social background, education,
and future expectations they were poles apart, and exposure to life
in one of the more remote corners of the United States could never
bridge that gap.

At first sight, Mallet's southern credentials were impeccable. A
Confederate brigadier, he had held a post on the staff of General
Gorgas, the chief of the Ordnance Department. He had been the
director of the Alabama Survey, had married the daughter of a
Tuscaloosa judge, and had taught at the University of Alabama,
Tulane, and the University of Virginia.[1] Yet his background was
more varied and complex than even this career outline would suggest; born in Dublin in 1832, he had enjoyed all the benefits that
membership in a talented family and exposure to the best available
education could supply. He graduated from Trinity College and
the University of Göttingen with the promise of a fine scientific career in front of him. A chance visit to the United States in the
1850's lengthened into permanent residence, and in the postwar
years Mallet developed a reputation as one of the finest chemists
in the nation. Despite the handicap of being both an ex-Confederate
officer and a British citizen, he was elected to the presidency of the
American Chemical Society in 1882. A year later he made his journey to the Southwest, to lend his prestige and his administrative experience to the task of founding a new state university at Austin.

The fact that he had been asked to take up such a responsibility
(he was to be the foundation professor of physics and chemistry

and also chairman of the faculty, a post analogous to that of president) underlined certain unmistakable features of the condition of education in Texas at the time. One was the backwardness of the system of higher education compared both to the standards operating in other parts of the country and to the avowed intentions of the founders of the state. Among the grievances cited as justifying the revolt against Mexico was the failure of that government to make adequate provision for a system of general education, and the first constitution of the Republic of Texas had enjoined the legislature to make the necessary arrangements. But both the infant republic and the later state found it difficult to translate intent into action. The disruption of the Civil War and the problems that followed in its wake compounded the situation, and successive legislatures haggled over both means and method.[2] By the last quarter of the century, elementary education throughout the state left much to be desired, and the secondary and tertiary levels were still in the process of emerging. The effects were already evident: a state handicapped by its remoteness and the vast expanses of its own territory was falling behind in professional and technical skills, even though its needs were still those of a predominantly agricultural society. By 1882, one state senator could point to the practical impact of these deficiencies:

> After forty years of independence and prosperity, where are the distinguished linguists, mathematicians, geologists, civil engineers, or learned men of any sort, who have been educated in our state? There is not one. With great resources at our control, a generation has been reared with only such opportunities that the common school can afford. If a strange mineral is found on your land, you must send it out of Texas to be assayed, or import a man to tell you what it is. If water works, gas works or manufactories are to be established in your towns, you must send abroad for the educated brains to construct and operate them. If a railroad is to be built, its course and grades must be determined by engineers educated abroad. Nor is this all: the science and the skilled labor that we need must be imported from a section of the country which has been instructed by demagogues to look on the South with suspicion and distrust . . . Hewers of wood and drawers of water for others we must remain, unless advanced education shall relieve us.[3]

He might also have referred to less tangible deficiencies; many of the founders of the state had been cultivated men who took seriously the eighteenth century's view of the relationship between enlightenment and political virtue. But though their prescriptions were sound enough and a few educated men tried to keep the vision alive in later years, the end result was all too clear—"the gist of what they said was . . . carved in stone and then largely forgotten."[4]

After nearly half a century in which most of the energies of the state had been invested in the task of subduing a large and complex territory, Texas was now moving to erect an institution that would produce the professional and technical skills the community needed. Already the number of students leaving the state each year to further their education was as high as four hundred.[5] Local pride and an unwillingness to see fee money leaving the state economy combined to prod legislators into action. But the lack of trained and experienced staff at the local level forced the planners to look outside the state for the professors they needed. Only two of the foundation professors were Texans, and they were there to teach law, an area where local experience was obviously an asset.[6] As with any other underdeveloped society, Texas in the 1880's looked to older and more experienced communities for the expert assistance it needed to launch a novel and complex enterprise. For obvious reasons, it turned first to the South, and three of the new professors had been officers in the Confederate forces.[7]

The founding of a university in the 1880's had a significance that went beyond the need of an individual state for trained personnel. The timing of the event was in itself important; though a late arrival in terms of local needs, the new institution inevitably rode just a little behind that wave of university building that was to alter the face of higher education throughout the country in the last decades of the century. The decisions made concerning curriculum and organization would necessarily be affected by the new trends in the North and the West as well as by the older precedents of the South. The winds of academic change were moving through the entire system of higher education at an unprecedented pace, and the new university at Austin would reflect their influence.

Yet the very modernity and the relative sophistication that characterized a major university in the 1880's—its secular character, its interest in scientific and technical education, its willingness to develop broad community interests—were sources of heightened frustration as well as pride and confidence. The benefits were obvious enough, the sources of frustration less evident; the latter had their roots in certain disparities between the values to which the new institution bore witness and the unspoken needs of the communities they served, especially if those communities were part of the newly settled trans–Mississippi West.

There can be little doubt that the new-style university brought badly needed skills to the area and that in many ways the institution was a highly successful transplant. But those who entered the new universities differed in one important respect from most of their counterparts to the east: they were the first generation born to their region. They emerged from communities that were themselves curious hybrids and reflected a special kind of homogeneity; though his family traveled over a three-county area in North Central Texas during the 1890's, Webb could remember meeting very few elderly people, one foreigner, hardly any blacks, and only one farmer who could be described as well educated.[8] Built up mainly from the depressed and discontented whites of the South and the border regions, these communities reflected the kind of homogeneity that usually fosters a sense of local identity but in some cases paralyzes or inhibits it, for their children could draw little from the older generation to help them define their own relation to the world around them; there were no traditions to be passed on, no memories that went back more than a few decades.[9]

In an idealized situation, communities of the type Webb had known as a child would have gradually developed that comfortable sense of familiarity with their own past that seems to anchor long-established towns and villages to their cultural landscape. But there was nothing static about the social and economic pressures characteristic of the age that brought them into existence; the tempo of life in the late nineteenth century did not favor the growth of local traditions by the process of slow accretion. The trend was to uproot and supersede, to foster growth in one area and then cut it off abruptly as economic necessity dictated. The speed with which small towns and settlements could disappear, relocate, or wither to a fraction of their former size in a very brief period—depending on changes in economic conditions or the whims of railroad builders—was a feature of development throughout the West in the late nineteenth century.[10] Less obvious was a pressure of a rather different kind—the slow erosion of agriculture as a way of life and the steady flow of young people away from the land and back to the cities in search of the opportunities no longer available in the West.[11] With each departure, the task of defining a local sense of identity became more difficult.

Those who stayed had no alternative but to wait for the passage of time and the eventual inheritance of family land that would confer status and identity through the simple fact of ownership. Those who left, as Webb did, had either to cut their links with the land of their childhood and establish new links with the older urban societies to the east or remain anonymous outlanders, stranded in a wasteland that had no cultural or historical significance. For a time Webb tried to develop the first alternative and found it unsatisfactory; but eventually he became reconciled to the fact "that I had grown up on the frontier, and that I could not rub off the evidence."[12] Yet at the same time he refused to accept the implications of the second alternative, and gradually he moved to establish at least a part of the historical identity that he felt must be hidden beneath the surface of ordinary events.

In a sense, Webb's contact with university study during the period 1909–1915 represented his attempt to fit himself into the cultural assumptions of older societies and to find a satisfying alternative to the way of life he had abandoned. If he had become a lawyer or an engineer, there would have been tangible results to show for the efforts he made to educate himself; he would have a secure and satisfying career that carried its own justification in terms of visible achievement, and the state would have had the benefit of the skills it hoped to produce when it established the university. But neither his inclinations nor his education turned him toward the professions; his interests centered on the humanities—or, more specifically, on literature and history. Of the social sciences he knew very little, and of languages even less. Inevitably his interest in writing drew him to the English department and to the general area of university activity that had the least chance of meeting the needs of a refugee from the Cross Timbers.

The scientific skills that John Mallet represented could be adjusted to the needs of a raw community without too much difficulty; the social sciences were still plastic enough to meet the requirements of a new institution, and education had obvious utility in communities where training of teachers left much to be desired. But the humanities—and especially the study of literature—faced special problems in that their exponents could not disguise under the cloak of utility a commitment to the values of a superior culture. Unlike the agricultural scientists and the educationists, those who taught rhetoric and poetry to the sons and daughters of the western soil could not claim that what they were doing reflected in some way the special needs of the area or that it would fertilize or diversify a local culture. At a time when the existence of an American body of literature was rarely acknowledged at the academic level, it was hardly likely that formal instruction in literature would do anything to help a young man find himself in an isolated and unconventional world.[13] Webb's studies of Beowulf and the classics of English literature did not lead him to that long search for meaning in the human drama that his teachers no doubt expected; both sides failed, and one by-product of that failure was a heightened awareness of being part of a dependent culture.

Webb's reaction was by no means typical; there were other students of that generation who found themselves able to state the case for a regional literature without rejecting the traditions their teachers represented and taught to the exclusion of all else. In later years, the emphases would shift and the western universities would take an active role in defining the cultural needs of the region and in stimulating further development; westerners have in the main become aware of the structure of their past through the medium of formal education rather than through oral tradition or folklore, and their traditions have been explained to them in the language of the educated man rather than of the rustic. During the course of the twentieth century the academic has charted and interpreted the life of the west in much the same manner as his forerunner, the topographer, traced the physical outlines of the region in the nineteenth century. Historians and folklorists have been the bellwethers of the trend, and the state historical agencies have played a key role. Teachers of literature have found the task more difficult; whereas the historian could find his material in the routine and unintentional products of life, the literary critic had to deal with the deliberate reflections of a people still largely inarticulate and hesitant, and the problem of maintaining standards without crushing initiative has not always been easily resolved.

These trends have been slow to develop, and their present scope should not blur the fact that earlier in the century the teacher of humanities came more as a missionary spreading the values of an older and more civilized people among the unsophisticated. Those who came to teach in the West were, in the main, schooled in other regions, and neither their personal interests nor their professional orientation inclined them toward the study of local society. It was unusual for a scholar to make a reputation on the basis of a regional emphasis; only in later decades did the local come into its own as a field of legitimate enterprise.

When Walter Webb first registered at the University of Texas in 1909, he was in his twenty-first year and the university in its twenty-sixth. A young adult, as yet virtually uneducated, confronted an institution that was itself still in its formative period. John Mallet had long since returned to Charlottesville, but the small college he had helped to found survived the difficulties of its earlier years and was now achieving the status its original planners had envisioned. The initial difficulties were real enough—lack of an adequate building, shortages of books and equipment—and caused Mallet to comment that to men "accustomed to the more slowly worked out plans of older societies, the contrast between what we were aiming for and the means we had at hand . . . was at times rather depressing."[14]

When Webb arrived there, the hesitancies and doubts of those early years had disappeared, and the quality of the student population had considerably improved. The first group of professors had found their students a likable group, woefully deficient in formal training but generally more mature than their ages warranted. Allowances had to be made for their deficiencies in spelling and arithmetic, but they showed themselves unusually interested in their own state: references to the Texan contribution to the southern cause brought an immediate response.[15]

By the turn of the century there were signs of marked improvement. Already the university had begun to appoint some of its own graduates to the faculty, though as yet it did not attempt to prepare its students for higher degrees; the better graduates were encouraged to go north for further training at the traditionally strong schools until 1910, when a local graduate school was established.[16] Even then, many departments, including the history department, preferred to see students go on to more experienced colleges. The leading members of the faculty were well regarded by their counterparts in other universities, and visiting faculty found a summer assignment at Austin attractive enough to compensate for its remoteness and the notoriously hot climate. Relations with the political leadership of the state were better than they had been, and far better than they were to become in the next two decades. At the federal level, former President David Houston was to achieve cabinet rank within a few years as a member of the Wilson administration—as were two alumni, Albert S. Burleson and Thomas W. Gregory.

Signs of maturity were evident, but the university catered to a predominantly provincial clientele. Texas was still very much a rural state, and, as late as 1933, most of the students attending the university came from farms and small towns within a hundred miles of the campus.[17] In 1900 only nine states were represented among the student population; by 1933, all states, two territories, and five foreign countries were included—but 96 percent of the students were Texans.[18] According to the only major study of student life during the early decades of the century, the predominant tone was provincial and anti-intellectual; but this assessment has to be measured against the very favorable reactions of a significant number of talented graduates who testified to the value of the training they received there.[19] A considerable number were anxious to return to teach there in later years.

In September 1909, Webb commenced his studies at Austin as a freshman in the College of Arts, the largest division within the university and one that had been undergoing reorganization over the previous three years. Within the college, the humanities were represented by schools of English, history, public speaking, philosophy, Latin, Greek, German, and Romance languages; the sciences by schools of botany, geology, chemistry, physics, zoology, and pure and applied mathematics; and the infant social sciences by the conglomerate School of Political Science, which had until 1906 grouped its courses into three broad divisions—economics, social science, and government/jurisprudence/public law. Within the next few years these divisions became three autonomous departments, a development that was to have a considerable impact on Webb's education: Lindley Miller Keasbey, the former head of the School of Political Science, emerged from this reorganization as the head of the Department of Institutional History, a smaller department created out of the residue left after economics and government had been separated out and given autonomy. Keasbey remained in charge until his dismissal from the university in 1917; his department survived him by only two years, and in 1920 it was designated the Department of Anthropology for the first time.[20] The reasons for the move were obvious because Keasbey's assistant, J. H. Pearce, had been appointed to the vacancy, and his interests lay specifically in the fields of anthropology and archaeology; once Keasbey left the scene, the term "institutional history" became something of a misnomer, and an adjustment was obviously called for.[21] But, as Webb's undergraduate studies extended over the period 1909–1915, they coincided neatly with the period when Keasbey was presenting institutional history as a discipline in its own right and quite distinct from government, history, and economics. At probably no other campus in the United States was such a course being offered at that time.

Webb brought very little with him when he registered for courses in late 1909; the credits built up over the two years in Peters's school at Ranger amounted to three units of English, three of algebra, two each of medieval and modern history, three of algebra and plane geometry, and a half-unit of civics—a meager base on which to erect an academic career.[22] The fact that the College of Arts laid down clear guidelines for the selection of first year courses saved Webb from the embarrassment of choosing among courses whose scope and content were unknown to him. He had very little idea of what to expect from a higher education, but he loved writing and assumed that his English courses would train him to be a more effective writer; his most distant ambition was to become a traveling correspondent or perhaps even a staff member of one of the better quality magazines.[23] So he plunged into the study of English with the kind of interest that he could hardly muster for the other courses that were virtually obligatory for freshmen—physics, mathematics, ancient history, and elementary German. Immediately he ran up against the difficulty of writing in terms that were very different from anything arising from his own experience and at the same time meeting the demanding standards of instructors who valued grammatical accuracy far above individual creativity.

By the time he reached the campus Webb had already learned to use the flowery turn of phrase that an earlier generation had considered the epitome of good writing. An early exercise entitled "Nature" discussed the changing seasons in opulent style, with "February days" being followed by "the blustry March who comes with much noise and blowing and melts the remains of snow from mountain sides and shaded glen"—images that hardly squared with his own impressions as a child in Stephens County. But it was still normal to assume that "when we speak of nature, we are prone to think of singing birds, budding trees, and laughing brooks" and that only rather ideal landscapes were the proper object of literary discourse.[24] So an account of a boat trip, written in early 1910, pictured the setting on the Colorado River near Austin in romantic terms: "I turned the boat up the river. The sun had not set, but was hidden behind greenish golden clouds and piled-up hills. Rough mountains and craggy cliffs flanked the left; the opposite shore, while not so steep, was none the less wild and picturesque."[25] The marginal comment indicated that his instructor was impressed by this passage and by a later image of "boisterous sportive boys" skimming over the water and "throwing the spray with their oars."

But the most striking example of the dislocation which resulted from an attempt to superimpose the conventions of a faded romanticism on the realities of existence in a farming community can be seen in an essay entitled "My Old Homestead," written a little over a month after Webb arrived on the campus in 1909. From an introduction drenched in nostalgia and sentimentality, the essay proceeds to invest the daily routine of the Webb home in Stephens County with the grandeur of an idealized plantation. The sandy fields of the Cross Timbers became green meadows "where we went, at evening, to drive home the cows; where we went at early morning, for the calves. Oh! the joy of chasing those red calves over the dewey grass . . ."[26] Little birds flit about in the bright morning sunlight and twitter joyously; the post oaks around the house become "stately trees," even the pigs exude charm, and the old yard gate "has that look of perfect contentment."[27] But the high point of the picture is the transformation of the frame home that he had helped his father build seven years before: its "high porch and wide hall" present a most inviting appearance, leading the writer to explore further. "I pass up the rough stone steps and place my foot on the worn floor, and my hand on the supporting column of the high roof. How tall and cool and white, the great columns are! How still and peaceful everything is, yet how natural!"[28] In such a setting, it is only to be expected that there will be a great repast prepared for the family, "simple, but fit for a king"; yet the real world asserts itself in the midst of all the gilt splendor—the table groans under "cabbage and baked potatoes, a great bowl of fresh butter, bright goblets of sweetmilk, perfectly browned corn-cakes, baked apples and golden pumpkin with scalloped edges and dishes of berries to be eaten later with cream and cake."[29]

Though this type of writing met with approval, it clearly went against the grain for Webb, for he soon discarded it for the leaner and more straightforward style that was to become his trademark over the years. In more sober moments he spoke of his early life in terms that made it clear that he hated the farm, "the stumps, the bony horses and the squealing pigs"—and everything that went with it. No imaginative gloss could disguise that hatred, and he gave up the attempt to paint over the evidence.[30] But he also came close to discarding his interest in writing as such; after a year of contact with classroom instruction in English, Webb showed unmistakable signs of revolt against what he regarded as the excessive formalism of his instructors, especially of Professor Law. Late in 1910 he wrote a paper which amounted to an attack on the instructors for emphasizing grammatical accuracy and technique at the expense of subject matter; for the average freshman, the effect of this approach was quite destructive: "The rules to which he must submit his work seem to deaden his best efforts, and to take away all spontaneity. He thinks that the rules hinder rather than help him."[31] His instructor's comment simply noted that it was a thoughtful and evidently sincere paper, containing some "surprising grammatical errors." Webb tried again a few months later, this time gently registering dissent from orthodox tastes in poetry; stressing that he enjoyed poetry and collected examples of poems that particularly impressed him, he argued that he was entitled to prefer commonplace verse over that of the masters—at least until someone convinced him that the classics were all that they were claimed to be. Again Law valued his sincerity, asked him to find out why the classics were great, and cautioned him against exceeding the prescribed length—there were, after all, seventy-five other papers to be read.[32]

After two years and three courses in English, Webb's interest in writing had considerably diminished; when he returned to the campus after a year spent teaching, he registered for a course in the new Department of General Literature headed by Stark Young, later a drama critic for the *New Republic* and one of the lesser-known Southern Agrarians in the early thirties. Webb had enjoyed his previous contacts with Young, but there is nothing to suggest that a year spent studying Lord Byron's poetry did anything to revive his interest in literature.[33] After that point he left the English department severely alone.

From the marginal comments on over two dozen class papers that have survived, Webb's disillusionment is understandable; even when allowance is made for the stricter standards of the day, the constant reference to errors of spelling and punctuation does appear to have been rather out of proportion to the number of mistakes detected in his papers, and Webb's comments about the lack of interest in subject matter appear to some extent justified. It seems likely that the prevailing atmosphere in the department reflected the rather severely linguistic preoccupations of the senior professor, Morgan Callaway, Jr., who dominated the department as Eugene Barker dominated the historians in later decades. A product of Emory and Johns Hopkins universities, Callaway's interests focused on formal linguistics and on Old English in particular.[34] With the exception of a selection of the poems of Sidney Lanier issued in 1895, his publications over a thirty-year period included studies of the absolute and appositive participles in Anglo-Saxon, the temporal and consecutive subjunctive in Old English, the infinitive in Anglo-Saxon, and the syntax of the Lindisfarne Gospels.[35] Though his scholarship was widely respected and his name associated with rigorous standards in the teaching of English, those whose interests focused on the possibilities of a local literature regarded him with disfavor; a student with a rather pragmatic approach to the study of English would not find the atmosphere congenial, let alone the curriculum.[36] Two years convinced Webb that he would never learn to write through a college course.

Finding no comfort among the English scholars, Webb let his literary aspirations slide. He was then without any positive goal, and, rather than pursue any other area in depth, he drifted into a series of introductory courses in such subjects as economics and philosophy and struggled to master elementary German. His record remained unspectacular, and there was little to suggest the pattern his later career would take—only two history courses were included in his degree, and both were introductory courses. After 1913, when it seemed that a career in the public schools was the only one open to him, more education courses appeared in his program; by that time he was contemplating marriage and needed to strengthen his case for a teaching position.

There was one other exception to this generally rather drab pattern; in his second year, 1910/1911, he found a course in institutional history taught by Lindley Miller Keasbey, and from that point on his work began to find a focal point. He took a second unit in 1912/1913, a third during the summer of 1914, and a fourth during the long session of 1914/1915.[37] At a time when his grades in English and other courses were disappointing, he found that he consistently did well in Keasbey's courses. Impressed by Keasbey's style and the range of his subject matter, Webb started to become an institutional historian instead of a writer. In the absence of any other source of inspiration, Keasbey's teaching may well have constituted the effective bulk of Webb's undergraduate education and possibly shaped his thinking more profoundly than Webb realized.

4. A Frame of Reference

LINDLEY MILLER KEASBEY

AND INSTITUTIONAL HISTORY

NEARLY FIFTY YEARS after he had first heard Keasbey lecture, Webb still remembered the vivid impression made by a man whose life-style and background stood out in marked contrast to anything he had previously known. Keasbey's family had long been prominent in New Jersey politics, and his tastes were as elegant as his lineage; he maintained a mansion-style home in Austin, dressed in the height of fashion, and generally displayed the kind of dash and aristocratic flair that attracts unfavorable attention in the provinces.[1] Webb admired his independence and his sense of style, and his example probably reinforced the element of rebelliousness in Webb that was never too far below the surface. In Keasbey's refusal to bend to the views of others, Webb may have seen a reflection of his own stubborn streak.

Keasbey graduated from Harvard in 1888 and went on to the School of Law and Political Science at Columbia. He took his doctorate there in 1890 at the age of twenty-three, his thesis being a study of the diplomatic background of the projected Nicaragua canal.[2] Possibly the strong German orientation of the Columbia graduate faculty—and especially of John Burgess—suggested his next move, which took Keasbey to the universities of Berlin and Strassburg. By the time he returned to the United States in 1892 he held a doctorate from Strassburg in addition to his Columbia degree—a formidable academic portfolio for a man of twenty-five.[3] After a brief period of teaching at Columbia, he accepted an appointment as professor of economics and politics at the University of Colorado in 1892; two years later he was selected to fill the vacancy at Bryn Mawr College when Franklin H. Giddings moved to Columbia to take over the foundation chair of sociology there.[4] Given the considerable status of his predecessor, Keasbey's nomination was a tribute to his standing among his fellow scholars; he was already an active member of the American Academy of Political and Social Sciences, and, at a time when rapid changes were occurring in the academic world generally, Keasbey had very rapidly established himself as a man with a bright future.[5] He was to remain at Bryn Mawr until 1905, and then a disagreement with the president of the college resulted in his transfer to the University of Texas, just four years before Webb arrived there to commence his undergraduate studies.[6] Webb did not make contact with Keasbey's work until 1910, but from that point on he began to take a lively interest in the older man's approach to the study of history and of the social sciences in general. Any discussion of the sources of what would later be described as Webb's interdisciplinary approach to the study of the Plains environment must come back at some point to the body of ideas he absorbed during those years as a student in Keasbey's department. A creative and exciting teacher, Keasbey brought with him a distinctive attitude toward the study of human society, one which he had refined and polished over a fifteen-year period and which seemed to Webb to provide precisely the kind of integrated approach he needed at that point.

The nine years Keasbey spent at Bryn Mawr were the most effective of his career; he was already regarded as an expert on the diplomatic history of Isthmian canal projects when he arrived there, and new books on the subject were usually sent to him for review by the major journals. His paper on the projected Nicaragua canal appeared in 1895, and a year later he issued his *Nicaragua Canal and the Monroe Doctrine*.[7] From there he moved on to a study of the Clayton-Bulwer Treaty and canal policy in general; but what had been an extremely topical interest in the late 1890's became a rather academic one after the turn of the century—President Theodore Roosevelt's unorthodox diplomacy took little account of the exigencies of academic life, and expert commentary on the Nicaragua canal became redundant after the decision to build at Panama.[8]

This unexpected development should have taught Keasbey to give more weight than he usually did to the role of the individual in the making of history; but he was not unduly embarrassed by the turn of events, for he had begun to shift away from diplomatic history before the end of the century. As a specialist in political economy, he had taken an interest in the currency and protection debates of the 1890's and had reviewed several books on the subject.[9] But a more substantial achievement had been his translation from the French of Achille Loria's *The Economic Foundations of Society*, which appeared in London in 1899 and was favorably received by reviewers.

Given the size of Loria's treatise and the difficulties in rendering an accurate translation, the work must have occupied most of Keasbey's attention in the late 1890's. In the light of the more recent studies of the impact of Loria's ideas on American economists during that decade, Keasbey's decision to produce the first English translation of Loria's major work was of some significance.[10] Few scholars of the day had both the linguistic skills and the familiarity with economic theory necessary for such a project, and the success of the translation must have added to Keasbey's standing in academic circles.

Diplomatic history and economic theory merged into Keasbey's third area of interest, one that seems to have occupied much of his attention in later years—economic geography. The economist Alvin Saunders Johnson claimed that Keasbey was regarded as the best trained economic geographer in the country when he returned from Germany, and two articles which he published in the *Political Science Quarterly* at the turn of the century were among the first attempts to lay a basis for the serious study of the subject in the United States.[11] Johnson believed that Keasbey had studied under Friedrich Ratzel in Germany, and although this seems unlikely—except on the basis of a limited contact—he was clearly aware of the general trends of German thought in geography and related areas.[12] He reviewed Ratzel's *History of Mankind* when it appeared in an English translation in 1896, praised it as the major work in the field, and entered a few carefully argued objections on points of detail.[13] But he does not appear to have been an outspoken disciple of Ratzel or to have made any attempt to adapt Ratzel's views in the manner later associated with the work of Ellen Churchill Semple.[14]

It seems clear that during the 1890's the relatively young Keasbey ranked as one of the more promising scholars working across the broad spectrum of interests loosely designated as the social sciences. To his basic credentials as a diplomatic historian, political scientist, economist, and economic geographer, he added a reading interest in ethnology, anthropology, and sociology. He appears to have kept in touch with developments in contemporary scientific thought and to have moved rather freely through the fluid intellectual climate of that decade, when old patterns of thought were breaking down and academics had to decide on the institutional arrangements that would best serve the newly emerging patterns.[15]

While it was generally assumed that the time was ripe for the application of intelligence and scientific method to the problems which plagued society, there was a good deal of uncertainty as to how to go about the task; social scientists of Keasbey's generation were virtually free to make their own systems and their own methodology as they saw fit. For most of them, the broader problems were resolved or alleviated by the emergence of virtually independent disciplines—especially sociology, political science, and economics, with geography bringing up a rather uncertain rear. The most important task seemed to be to establish rudimentary lines of demarcation between the disciplines and then get on with the business of collecting and ordering the pertinent masses of data. More esoteric questions about the need to develop an overarching system of thought within which the social sciences could operate were held to be of little immediate concern—the critical task was to get the research started and worry about the wider implications later.

Keasbey appears to have parted company with most of his colleagues on this point and to have carried into the new century the conviction that, without the establishment of firm ground rules, the social sciences would suffocate in their own data. He remained relatively uninterested in research and concentrated on the design of a system of thought that would put the social sciences on the same rigorous basis as the natural sciences.[16] After 1900, he wrote less, but his emphasis on theoretical issues is very evident and in part accounts for his increasing isolation from the general body of research workers and teachers in the field. Eventually he found himself in something of an intellectual cul-de-sac, and he remained cut off from the mainstream of thought among his academic colleagues.

When he left Bryn Mawr for Texas in 1905, his best years were behind him, and he was already something of an isolated figure; by the time of his dismissal from the University of Texas in 1917 (for his opposition to American participation in World War I), he had become less active in academic circles.[17] After that point his career broke down, and, when Webb made contact with him just after *The Great Plains* appeared in 1931, he was living on a small farm in Arizona and breeding dogs. But when Webb first met him in 1910, he was still a highly effective teacher, and the courses he offered were the product of nearly fifteen years of experimentation and refinement of his ideas.[18] By that point he was head of the Department of Institutional History, which had no connection with the Department of History or any other academic unit; with a small staff, he was able to develop his own approaches without any interference from other scholars in related fields. No other teacher had the same impact on Webb: he became a disciple, and to some extent a protégé, and the imprint of Keasbey's ideas was probably deeper than Webb himself realized.

From his scattered publications and from the listings of the courses he taught at Colorado, Bryn Mawr, and Texas, it is possible to get some impression of the ideas that intrigued him in the 1890's and carried over into his undergraduate teaching. He appears to have been committed firmly to the importance of establishing the geographic basis before going on to examine other social phenomena. This emphasis on the geographic framework appears first in his studies of diplomatic history ("diplomatic questions for the most part have their roots in geography and ethnography"), and it was further underlined in his acceptance of Ratzel's view that it is essential "to bestow a thorough consideration upon the external surroundings of the various races, and endeavour *pari passu* to trace the historical circumstances in which we find them today. The geographical conception of their surroundings and the historical conception of their development will thus go hand in hand. It is only from a combination of the two that a just estimate can be formed."[19]

In addition to this concern with the geographical setting—which never seems to have involved a thorough investigation of the geographic environment but only a tracing of an outline that would make later social and political development more comprehensible—Keasbey showed the geopolitician's concern for the global frame of reference.[20] His studies of Isthmian diplomacy, for instance, stressed the importance of a Central American line of communication to the global strategy of the British Empire; with her westward thrust diverted by the emergence of the American republic, Britain needed a new access route through the Western Hemisphere to complete the global circle represented by the line to India and the Pacific through Suez.[21] Keasbey's view of history left little room for the vagaries of domestic politics and the operation of irrational forces; he was interested in the behavior of large power blocs, and he argued that the key to an understanding of international issues lay in the interpenetration of world economics, geography, and grand strategy. It was the total picture that counted, the geopolitical setting; the local and the particular amounted to very little unless seen in terms of the broader frame of reference.

The extent to which Keasbey translated his ideas into practice in the classroom can be seen in the changes that he made in the curriculum of the Department of Political Science at Bryn Mawr

when he took over from Franklin H. Giddings in 1895. Giddings
had given his students a series of introductory lectures on the principles of sociology, then a basic course in political economy, plus
a full semester devoted to the study of the origins and development
of political and legal institutions. On that basis, a student could
then go on to studies of communism and socialism and of political
theory in general. At the graduate level, students could take an advanced course in sociology; in Giddings's last year at Bryn Mawr
this class concentrated on the "descriptive sociology of the State
of Pennsylvania," dealing with such topics as the increase and re-
distribution of the population over a ten-year period, crime, pau-
perism, and insanity—all dealt with from the statistical point of
view, "and accompanied by original maps."[22]

When Keasbey arrived to take over the department, he kept most
of the old courses going for the first year but began to move the
emphasis toward economic geography.[23] By the second year he was
able to introduce his own ideas on a larger scale. Students would
begin their work in political science with one semester devoted to
political economy and one to economic geography and demography;
then they moved on in later years to study the origins, history, and
theory of the state, the history of trade and commerce, public finance, and international law—or, in alternate years, the history of
capital, labor, banking, money, and both administrative and constitutional law. Graduates studied political theory and American
economic history. The study of American institutions was to be
included in the graduate program in the following year.[24] By 1896/
1897, economic geography and demography had pushed political
economy out of the first year curriculum; now "the several races
of man are described in connection with their respective environments, both physical and historical."[25] The scope was global: Europe, Asia, and Australia were dealt with in the first semester, and
Africa and America in the second. The course description set out
Keasbey's approach in some detail:

> In this course the various centres of savagery, barbarism and
> civilisation are taken up in turn, and in their climatic, oro-
> graphic, geonostic and geographic conditions described. The
> several races of man are next considered, and by a study of
> their migrations, colonizations and subsequent amalgamations
> it is shown how each important area of the earth's surface
> came to contain its present population. The reciprocal influ-
> ence of environment and race characteristics is then shown by

a comparison of the various politico-economic institutions of the day. The course is fundamental in character, and is intended both to give the student a general knowledge of the modern politico-economic world, and also to serve as a groundwork for further study of the evolution of institutions.[26]

This course alternated with the course in political theory, while sociology and the study of American institutional and economic history were brought in during later years. The overall emphasis was clear—"the impact of the physical environment on social evolution"—and the methods used showed less concern for the compilation of data at the local level than did those used by Giddings.[27]

Keasbey expected wide reading and he asked his students to make a detailed examination of a selected American institution in the light of the original documentary material available. But he placed less emphasis than Giddings on the statistical approach to social problems; Keasbey's scale was global and national rather than local, and he was concerned to ensure that his students grasped the wider picture before they got down to the study of individual cases. By the late 1890's students in theoretical sociology were involved in the "critical study of the works of Comte, Spencer, Giddings, and Loria," and those taking descriptive sociology were concentrating on "the economic antecedents of society and a comparison of social institutions."[28]

By the time Keasbey reached Texas in 1905, he had had plenty of opportunity to develop his ideas and design a course structure to accommodate them. But over the next four years the university carried out a considerable reorganization of the College of Arts, mostly in the area of the social sciences. Initially Keasbey's responsibilities as professor of political science included the teaching of both government and economics, plus any sociology that he cared to include, but in 1908 Alvin Saunders Johnson was brought in to teach economics and was made head of the new Department of Economics in 1909. At the same time, the university erected the new Department of Government under Charles Shirley Potts, a Texan whose interests centered on local government and the regulation of utilities. With two major teaching areas removed from his control, Keasbey was left with a new creation, the Department of Institutional History. By the time Webb reached the campus in 1909, this reorganization was complete, and Keasbey was offering courses in the philosophy of civilization, the antecedents of civilization, and the geography of both Eastern and Western civilization.[29]

It is possible that the reorganization was part of the national trend to break government, sociology, and economics into separate academic areas. However, there are indications that Keasbey had become a controversial figure and that Webb's later comment that the Department of Institutional History had been created to move both the man and his ideas out of the way without too much fuss was close to the mark; the governor received at least one complaint in 1908 that Keasbey was teaching revolutionary socialism, and the president of the university made it clear that he considered the charge justified. Keasbey, he argued, was not competent to teach economics: he did not concern himself with practical matters, such as money, banking, or taxation, but only with "descriptive and historical economics and government, along idealistic lines."[30]

Whatever the explanation behind the erection of Keasbey's unusual department, it is significant that, at the point when Webb first made contact with Keasbey, the latter had just begun to present his own distinctive approach to history free from any restraint from specialists in economics or government or from members of a conventional history department.[31] The themes presented were very much as they had been at Bryn Mawr; the whole range of human history was dealt with in broad outline, with the rise and fall of civilizations as the organizing principle. The influence of the geographic environment was seen as the key to the explanation of social and economic development, and, as the student came to understand the broad basis that underlay the sweep of history, he was encouraged to study the evolution of his own society and to watch the impact of environment on the institutional development around him.

The only indication as to how Keasbey developed his approach in detail lies in the handful of class papers that Webb wrote for courses in institutional history between 1913 and 1915, plus several written for other courses—but with obvious signs of Keasbey's influence. One of these papers dealt with the influence of geographic factors in American history and was submitted as a paper for a political science course. It clearly reflected a determinist position, arguing that the relation between geography and history was so marked that "history can be foretold in broad outline, though not chronologically, from a knowledge of the topographic, orographic and hydrographic environment."[32]

An examination paper written for an institutional history course in 1913 suggests that Keasbey trained his students to consider both the geographic and economic bases of modern states and to determine the extent to which these elements left their impress on the

social structures above them;[33] but there is also some indication
that Keasbey went even further and erected his own distinctive theory to explain the inner dialectic of European history. Since
he regarded himself as neither a geographer, historian, nor sociologist but as a combination of all three, he felt quite free to go beyond the geographer's concern with the relationship between man
and environment and to proceed to the analysis of the relationship
between social groups. Apparently basing his views on an argument developed by Keasbey in his lectures, Webb devoted one class
paper to an interpretation of European history between the fall of
the Roman Empire and the Crusades in terms of a series of clashes
between two contrasting socioeconomic systems, the collegiate-
communal and the republican-patriarchal. [34] The former system
represented those societies which developed above a line running
from the Pyrenees through the Alps to the Balkans, while the latter
occupied the more temperate lands to the south of that line.[35] The
contrast between the two systems—the one exploitive, arrogant,
and wasteful, the other productive, humble, and conservative—
triggered a dialectic process whose surface events were usually regarded as the data of history. Under Webb's interpretation, the
struggle between the Roman state and the Christian church was
a struggle between the two principles, and, though it ended in a victory for the collegiate-communal church, that victory in turn produced further tensions—between the church and the barbarians,
and between monasticism and feudalism. Though reminiscent of
Marxian thought, this interpretation appears to have regarded the
collegiate-communal system as the successful protagonist in all of
these struggles. Although Webb's paper did not bring the discussion down to the modern era in those terms, other papers suggest
that Keasbey did lead his students to trace through the development of modern political theory the emergence of the modern national, industrial, democratic state, which he may have regarded as
the culmination of the dialectical process.[36]

Apparently Webb later abandoned this interpretive scheme, and
it is quite possible that he may not have taken it very seriously in
the first place. What is more intriguing is the way in which Webb
structured the presentation of the case, with elements that may
have carried over into his later work. Beginning with the assertion
of the general principle that each geographic environment develops
its own distinctive civilization, he postulated that the civilizations
produced by the two broad geographic environments that charac-

terized Europe and western Asia could be designated "communal-collegiate" and "republican-patriarchal," respectively.[37] Then, "having indicated the principle of interpretation, namely, the struggle between the two systems," he moved "to apply it to historical facts. We see that the principle is that of unlikeness or contrast, and contrast will be the keynote throughout."[38] The rapid shift from geographical base to sociological assumption is evident, and this readiness to use the theoretical framework so erected as a key to interpret historical data has an obvious bearing on Webb's later approach to the study of the Plains. Moreover, it seems significant that this approach was later identified and singled out for special criticism.[39] Webb, in turn, was careful to acknowledge in later years that Keasbey taught him a special way of thinking, as well as an attitude toward the impact of the environment on human institutions.[40] It seems likely that Webb retained a respect for that way of thinking long after he lost interest in the underlying processes of European history.

It was a fascinating approach for those who heard it directly from Keasbey—and he was apparently an exciting and effective teacher.[41] For Webb, it had a special attraction: for a man arriving late on the scene as far as intellectual inquiry was concerned and disappointed in his early hopes, the Keasbey approach seemed to provide both a comprehensive vision of how human society had evolved and a superb method of investigation. Since it involved the study of anthropology, economics, folklore, history, and political theory, it amounted to a complete education in its own right, and it had the additional attraction of being organized around a set of central ideas—something that was conspicuously lacking in the education Webb received outside Keasbey's department. There is nothing to indicate that Webb saw any dangers in Keasbey's stress on the need for a unifying theory or that he thought carefully about the method of formulating a central principle. In 1915, for example, Webb noted in a class paper that he intended to present "a theory of the relation between ethnology and folklore" and described his approach as being that of "*giving attention to the general principles involved and leaving the details to be worked out in later studies which I hope to make*" (emphasis mine).[42] Since he had no critical apparatus with which to test Keasbey's approach, Webb accepted it enthusiastically. He was to remain convinced of the general value of Keasbey's ideas long after he had forgotten the details used to buttress the argument.

To all this should be added the element that in the long run probably did more than any other to ensure Webb's acceptance of the environmental approach—its apparent confirmation by experience. When Keasbey argued that physical environment was the major determinant of the institutional framework within which social activity occurred, he did so on the basis of extensive reading in the works of the German geographers and a close familiarity with current trends in the fields of sociology, economics, and ethnology. As a relatively raw undergraduate, Webb had to accept Keasbey largely on his own authority, and apparently this was not difficult to do. But what made it far easier was the fact that Webb was already predisposed to recognize the overwhelming influence environment can have because he had spent most of his life in an area where the impact of the physical environment on human life was unusually striking. Had he been brought up in a humid area and been less aware of the consequences of wind and drought, the point may have made less impact on his thinking. But there could be no avoiding the fact that, in the life of his own people, climate and terrain did mean a great deal—and since they were usually negative influences, the impact was all the more forceful. For Webb, the test of theory always remained its concordance with personal experience. In this case, the test became the basis for the theory itself; Keasbey's formidable scholarly justification for it simply withered away, and the theoretical shell remained.

The similarities between Keasbey's approach to history and the general tone and organization of *The Great Plains* (and of the later *Great Frontier*) are obvious: the stress on the geographic base, the assumption of a direct link between environment and institutional development, and the use of large general structures as a framework for the interpretation of apparently disparate social phenomena. When handled by a mind as nimble and well-stocked as Keasbey's, the approach obviously had many advantages as an interpretive device. On the other hand, if adopted without a full grasp of the very considerable structure of geographic and economic data on which it was based, it could become a dangerously narrow and oversimplified approach, and its impression of breadth and comprehension could easily prove to be an illusion. For Webb, that risk was a very definite one, for though he had inherited from Keasbey what others would later describe as an interdisciplinary approach, he did not maintain that close watch on current developments in the adjacent disciplines that Keasbey took for granted; he simply borrowed what he needed as the occasion demanded, and in so doing ran the risk of being unduly selective and of fitting material into a preconceived pattern of his own making.

Webb on several occasions paid tribute to Keasbey's influence on his early development, but he never discussed his ideas in any detail or tried to place them in their proper context. Once he had made his own reputation with *The Great Plains*, there was little need for him to do so, since he had established his version of those ideas to his own satisfaction and that of his colleagues. Moreover, Keasbey had paid little attention to the special problems of the West, and Webb could regard his own work as distinct and capable of standing on its own merits. He even remained unaware of Keasbey's work in translating Achille Loria's *The Economic Foundations of Society* until Loria's theory came under scrutiny in the late 1950's as one of the possible influences on the development of Frederick Jackson Turner's ideas on the frontier. The possibility of that influence in turn became assimilated into his general view of the relationship of his own work to that of Turner: the fact that they were both in some way linked to Keasbey seemed to fit in with his contention that he had worked out his own ideas independently of Turner and that he should not be regarded as a product of the Turner school.[43]

But there is one other element which may help to account for Webb's tendency to let his old teacher slip into the background. In 1931, when the success of *The Great Plains* was evident and he was enjoying the elation that went with it, Webb made contact with Keasbey to tell him about the book and to thank him for the interest he had shown in a raw undergraduate years before. He found that Keasbey, though broken in health and living in straitened circumstances, had lost none of his propensity for intellectual speculation on the grand scale; in addition to writing short stories and plays, he had been preparing a six-volume work entitled *Three Worlds in One*, which he intended to be the revised and final version of his total system. He now believed that his previous thinking had been superficial and inadequate:

> . . . all I did was to emphasize the material and efficient causes, leaving entirely out of the question the formal, first and final. In other words, I answered only the easiest questions, to wit: When, Where and How. The Harder questions are Why and Wherefore; the hardest questions are Whence and Whither. . . . The way to Why and Wherefore lies along fictions (not theories or hypotheses), ficta, or the Philosophy

of As If. The further way towards Whence and Whither starts
from Relativity and the Quantum theory and extends into the
Fourth Dimension . . .[44]

Webb believed that his old mentor had lapsed into both mysticism
and Catholicism, and he broke off the contact; later he remarked
that he preferred to remember Keasbey as the exciting teacher of
his undergraduate days rather than as the sad figure he had now
become.[45]

But he may also have been disturbed by a curious passage at the
end of the second letter he received from Keasbey, one which frac-
tured most of the basis of their previous relationship:". . . whereas
anyone with any sense can see at once that the environment is essentially passive and could not possibly act as anything further than
an efficient cause of something already formed or in the process of
forming. In our haste we are so apt (historians especially) of taking *post hoc* for *propter hoc*. That was my error, which I passed
on to so many students and now have no opportunity to recall."[46]
Webb could hardly have welcomed a recantation by his old teacher
at that particular point, and he made no comment on the remark.

5. Finding a Career

THE SIX YEARS that Webb applied to the pursuit of a degree saw him move only one step away from the rural setting in which he had spent his childhood. Although the campus at Austin became the focal point of his activities during those years, neither the town nor the university presented any major contrast to the Main Street atmosphere prevalent throughout the state in the prewar years. In any case, much of his attention was absorbed by the struggle to make enough money to continue his studies on a full-time basis and earn his degree. As he moved a little closer toward graduation and built up his teaching experience, he was able to move up from the boredom of teaching in rural schools to the slightly better paid drudgery of the high school; but, although this meant a rather more sociable existence and the pleasantries of living in a small country town instead of a farming community, the fact that his income was never large enough to enable him to retire the debt he inevitably accumulated during his years of study irritated him and drove him to look for some form of escape.

For the first two years after he entered the university in late 1909, Webb financed his studies largely from the funds Hinds had made available. At Hinds's suggestion, he spent the academic year 1911/1912 teaching in Throckmorton County to reduce his debt and make enough to return to his studies. A summer spent as a traveling salesman for a Chicago supplier of stereoscopic slides also added to his funds, and he returned to the campus for another year in 1912/1913—the year in which he studied under Keasbey for the first time.[1] One full year was as much as he could afford, so he returned to teaching and, on the basis of his academic training, managed to find work as a history teacher in a high school in the South Texas town of Beeville at a monthly salary of $100.[2]

The year spent at Beeville was a pleasant one, and in some ways a significant period in Webb's development. He obviously liked the status that went with his new job; the pay was better, the work more interesting, and the responsibilities not too demanding. The local school system, which had been in a parlous condition a few years earlier, had felt the impact of a reforming county superintendent; Webb had no complaints about conditions there and regarded it as a pleasant school.[3] He lived in a boarding house, coached the school tennis team (though it is doubtful whether he knew very much about the game), and went hunting on occasion.[4] Without the pressure of classroom and study, he was free to savor the atmosphere of the rather sleepy country town, to listen to its sounds and note the manners of its people with affectionate good nature.

Throughout his life Webb retained a capacity for acute observation of commonplace incidents and a warm sympathy for ordinary people; he had a good ear for dialogue and retained for many years snatches of conversation that intrigued him. Humble people rarely bored him, and he was sensitive to the quirks and manners that were hints of the individuality that lay beneath an apparently conventional surface. He never became a critic of small town society or the rural community, for he had seen that simpler world when it still had a life and value of its own for those who understood it. The advent of rapid transportation and more direct communications had not as yet destroyed the small towns as effective social units; World War I and the age of mass consumption that followed it were still around the corner, and for the moment these communities lived something of an interim existence. Within years, the highway and the automobile would radically alter their character.

Where others would see only restriction and defeat in a town like Beeville, Webb remembered it as a happy town, slow-paced enough to leave some room for eccentricity of speech and habit.[5] Later, during the Ku Klux Klan era of the early twenties, it would know bitterness and hate; but in 1913 the editor of the local paper could in all seriousness mount a campaign against the efforts of the city fathers to police the local dog ordinance ("Must the city of Beeville declare itself an enemy of the dog?").[6] It was while he was at Beeville that he collected the material that later appeared in an article on Negro folklore, and it was here that he became aware of the importance of the windmill in the life of a dry area.[7] From the porch of his boarding house he could see "a hundred whirling wheels when the Gulf Coast breezes came up in the afternoon," and years later that memory would surface and become part of his picture of the Plains.[8]

That year also saw the beginnings of a considerable change in his personal life; he began to correspond with Jane Oliphant, whom he had met in Austin earlier in the year, and over the next few years interest deepened into firm attachment. Webb was twenty-five when the courtship began, and, although he was anxious to settle down, his financial prospects were so indifferent that there seemed little hope that he would be able to marry for some years. Though he now had the objective and the sense of purpose that had been lacking during his first two years of study, the contrast between the neatly patterned order of Jane's life and the indefinite character of his own served to point up the difficulties confronting him. A member of a long-established Austin family, Jane had taken her degree before Webb began his freshman studies and had become a teacher of the deaf in her home town; while Webb moved from county to county in search of short-term teaching positions, she remained in regular employment in work that she liked. Not surprisingly, some members of her family disapproved of her friendship with a man whose prospects seemed so doubtful, and Webb felt himself at a disadvantage.

Early in 1914 he began to make plans to return to full-time study; he had made a good impression at Beeville and could have remained there, but he was now within striking distance of completing his degree. If he was to make any sort of a professional career for himself, the degree was essential. For once, it seemed that he would be able to finance another year of study without too much difficulty; a cousin at Ranger had agreed to guarantee a loan through a bank there, and a fellow teacher who had loaned him money in the past agreed to extend another loan for an indefinite period.[9] An even more substantial boost came with the award of a university scholarship in institutional history worth $100, largely as the result of Keasbey's recommendation; it was the first academic distinction he had ever achieved, and since only nine scholarships were awarded that year he had some cause to be pleased with the way his plans were developing.[10] One more year of study would take him close to the degree, and with that he could aim for a better-paying position in a high school and ultimately perhaps teach in a state normal school—at this point the height of his ambitions.[11] If he could afford it he would spend the summers taking graduate courses at the more established schools of education in the North; Columbia and Chicago were the most likely targets, and a further degree from either one would make his chances of getting to a state normal much better.[12]

For a time, his plans seemed to be working out as he had hoped; he was back in Austin, working in close contact with Keasbey, and was able to see much more of Jane. In those first weeks he also found a new friend, an Austrian student named Emil Sevario who had been awarded a university fellowship to work under Keasbey; besides their common interest in institutional history, Sevario could help Webb in his long-standing struggle with elementary German. All of this ended abruptly when Webb's financial arrangements collapsed. He later attributed the loss of his loan funds to the uncertainty following the outbreak of World War I just as his studies were getting under way.[13] Whatever the reason, Webb found himself thrown back on his own resources, and when these were almost depleted he found an unusually well-paying job as a bookkeeper at the same San Marcos college that he had tried to join earlier in the year. Three months of keeping the books and teaching education and elementary algebra earned him enough to return to the university at the end of the year; months of concentrated study allowed him to graduate in mid-1915, six years after he first came to Austin as a freshman from a rural backwater.[14]

Now he had a certain amount of leverage that he could use to push himself up in what was at best a difficult profession—depending on the whims of school trustees and the unpredictable nature of local elections, teachers at both the elementary and high school levels needed to be shrewd and resourceful if they expected advancement. Employment was still almost on a seasonal basis, and Webb's correspondence with fellow teachers during this period reflects the uncertainty of the work and the deft touch needed to spy out opportunities and calculate the best approach to a coveted opening. With the degree and a number of education courses behind him, plus the practical experience that he had accumulated over the past nine years, Webb could move one point up the educational ladder; he secured an appointment as principal and history teacher at the high school in the South Texas town of Cuero. However, the work was heavier than he expected, and the income left him with little margin to save.[15] Though Webb and his fiancée had planned to marry at some point in 1916, neither one was very certain whether they could manage on his limited earnings, let alone make the out-of-state journeys that would be necessary if ever he were to break out of the public school system.[16]

Early in 1916 Webb became so impatient with the constrictions of his work that he seriously considered setting up a business of his own in Cuero as one way out of his dilemma; Jane disapproved and convinced him that he should go north during the summer and better his chances for a normal school appointment.[17] Reluctantly

Webb fell into line, but he was determined to get away from Cuero and find a post in either Austin or San Antonio. By watching the situation carefully and making the right contacts, he eventually found an opening in the San Antonio school system, and, confident that he would be able to marry later in the year, he pushed ahead with plans to go either to Columbia or Chicago—while hoping that within a few years he would be able to afford to spend a full year at Harvard.[18]

But, for reasons that are not apparent from his correspondence, the summer found him at the University of Wisconsin at Madison, studying history under George Clark Sellery and Laurence M. Larsen.[19] Although Madison was still associated with the Turner tradition, Webb's letters make no reference to an interest in frontier studies; it seems more likely that he simply intended to build up credits toward a master's degree and to gain the experience that would be useful if ever he had the chance to apply for a post in either a normal school or the University of Texas Extension Division.[20] There is little to indicate that he had any hopes of an academic career as a historian at this point; while at Cuero he had given a paper on the teaching of history of a meeting of the Texas State Teachers Association, but this would be helpful in establishing his credentials for a normal school position.[21] Other than classroom teaching, his main interest was the collection of local folklore; his article on folklore in the Beeville area appeared while he was teaching at Cuero and collecting material from local residents—in one case, from prisoners in the Cuero jail.[22] He appears to have written very little fiction at this time and later noted that his reaction against anything to do with formal literature did not weaken for some years; but he did write on folklore when he found material that interested him.[23]

September of 1916 found the Webbs starting their married life in San Antonio, a city that was far more lively than usual due to the sudden buildup of the military forces in the area and the general excitement that went with the preparedness campaign. The streets were crowded, and the general bustle added to the old-world charm that had been the city's traditional attraction. For a year everything seemed promising; Webb liked teaching in a large city school and had every reason to believe that at last his affairs were in good shape. During the year he met the sister of his old benefactor William E. Hinds; she had written to Webb when she found that her brother's executors were pressing him for the money still owing since 1911, and she made arrangements to have the loans transferred to her name. In 1916 she spent some time in San Antonio, and there are indications that Webb hoped she would be able to help him finance his further studies.[24] But at the end of the school year his plans collapsed again, and all the old uncertainties returned with even greater strength.

The move from Cuero to San Antonio had not meant any increase in salary, but it was understood that after his first year Webb would be entitled to a raise; living costs were higher in San Antonio, and they would rise further when their first child was born. Toward the end of the year Webb confidently asked for an increase and received what he regarded as a brusque and unfair rejection.[25] He reacted bitterly, decided to have done with teaching, and, after considerable searching, found work as a bookkeeper for a local optician. To make sure that he could not return to teaching, he sold all his books save two (one of the survivors being James Bryce's *American Commonwealth*) and then sent Jane back to the family home in Austin to await the birth of their child.[26]

It was a curious move for a man whose family responsibilities were growing and suggests an element of stubbornness and a refusal to accept rejection; but at various times during the previous three years he had rather impulsively threatened to leave teaching, and only Jane's restraining hand had persuaded him to remain. Now he had broken loose, and for a time he felt that he made the right decision; he was astonished to find how much more he could earn as a bookkeeper and even more by his employer's ability to make a great deal of money from a fairly unpretentious operation.[27] If years of study and effort could not yield much more than a subsistence income, then some form of independent business venture might well provide him with the financial security he badly needed. He had no desire to remain a bookkeeper, so he began to study for the qualifications he would need to become an optician. It was difficult to start on a totally different career at the age of twenty-nine, but he had been badly shaken by his treatment in San Antonio, especially as other disappointments crowded in: the war had caused a deferment of plans to open up new normal schools, lessening his chances of breaking into that area, and legislative action had also cut off a possible opening in the Department of History at Austin. To make matters worse, the area around Ranger was on the verge of an oil boom, and Webb did not approve of his father's plans to sell the farm at that point.[28] Everything seemed to conspire against allowing him any peace of mind, and he was demoralized by his inability to find a secure and well-paying job to support his family in the fashion to which he felt his efforts entitled him. Clearly he could no longer fight against the current; it was far better to break out completely and make a fresh start.

Yet in November 1918 he found himself taking up duty with the Department of History at Austin as an instructor, having by-passed the high schools completely and vaulted the normal schools as well. He had heard in 1917 that the department was trying to get approval for an extra position that would involve responsibility for an education course in teaching methods and some work in lower-level courses. The initial move failed, and no funds were appropriated; by mid-1918 the prospects had improved, and eventually Frederic Duncalf, who had presented the methods course for some time, notified Webb that he had been appointed.[29] The salary of $1600 was less than he could make as a bookkeeper, but he could not pass up the opportunity to do the sort of work that had been his hope for so long. The decision proved to be a fortunate one—his employer sold the business shortly after Webb left, and the incoming owner dismissed the rest of the staff.[30]

Stroke of fortune though it was, the new job meant that once again Webb was at the bottom of an unfamiliar ladder. He knew that he had few qualifications for the position, save his experience in the high schools.[31] He had taken only two courses in Barker's department as an undergraduate and had made some tentative moves toward taking graduate work in history while he was teaching at San Antonio. Previously his interests had been centered on Keasbey's area, but Keasbey had now left the campus, and, although his department survived for a few years, Webb showed no interest in following up his earlier interest in institutional history. (Keasbey's successor was by training an anthropologist, and by now Webb probably realized that his old teacher's ideas were rather peculiar to him.) Now Webb had the opportunity to make a name for himself in an orthodox history department, but under difficult circumstances. He had been brought in to satisfy a short-term need and not because he was expected to carve out a bright academic career; he was older than the average graduate student, had some practical experience, and could take some of the load off the shoulders of the senior members of the department. Whether he stayed would be largely up to him: if he worked for higher degrees, he might achieve a permanent niche in the department. For the moment he was useful—but that situation could easily change.

Webb had only to look around him to see the difficulties of his position. Eugene C. Barker, the dominant force in the department since the death of George P. Garrison in 1910, had recruited carefully and had brought in only teachers with solid qualifications and clearly defined research interests; graduate students were encouraged to go elsewhere for further training if at all possible—preferably to the University of Pennsylvania, where Barker had taken his own advanced work.[32] By comparison to those already teaching in the department, Webb's qualifications were indifferent, and he had no definite research interests. Nor was he associated with any particular field: his appointment specified that he was to assist in teaching English history, and for years he worked with Frederic Duncalf in a freshman course in European history. It was almost a decade before he established himself as an Americanist within the department, and then the Plains book fixed his claim to be the resident specialist in western history. But, for the moment, he was at the bottom of the heap, and to survive he would have to discover the ground rules that governed upward movement in a social group that was a good deal more complex than any he had known previously.

Any questions he might have about what was required of him were answered by a glance at Barker's own career. The product of a poor home in East Texas, Barker had worked his way up from blacksmith to college professor; already becoming something of a power within the university, Barker crammed a good deal of activity into what appeared to be an unhurried existence. He administered the department, edited the *Southwestern Historical Quarterly*, wrote school textbooks, and continued his own researches on the colonization of Texas.[33] He had also managed to find time to take a leading role in the clash between the university faculty and Governor Ferguson in 1917: the subsequent impeachment of the governor eased the pressure, but Barker was to remain one of the most active members of the faculty in matters that concerned the survival of the institution and the preservation of academic standards.

It was a formidable performance, and any incoming teacher hardly needed to ask what was expected of him. Neither Barker nor the men around him were likely to make concessions to a newcomer who would in any way weaken the standing of the department within the university or the wider professional circle. Obviously Webb would have to begin the pursuit of the higher degree that was already becoming the badge of respectability and a prerequisite to advancement. In later years Webb was to become a rather acid critic of some features of the methods used to determine academic advancement, but in 1919 he was in no position to complain; either he made the most of his opportunity under the existing rules, or he accepted eventual release. There was no midway position that would satisfy both Webb and his colleagues.[34]

What was more difficult was the choice of a research field, for his earlier work with Keasbey had not focused on any area that would be acceptable in a conventional history department. One obvious approach was to work in the field that Barker and a number of his associates had made their specialty—the history of the Spanish Southwest and the Mexican Borderland. Herbert Bolton had opened up the field a decade earlier, and since his departure Barker had encouraged the collection of relevant archival material. But Webb appears to have shown little interest in the Spanish era. Stephens County had always been an Anglo area, and its links with the Spanish past were minimal; also, the fact that he had no grasp of Spanish made it unlikely that he could move in that direction, even if his motivation had been stronger. Nor did he favor the other major interest within the department, in this case represented by the work of Charles W. Ramsdell; he had heard enough southern history from his parents as a child to kill his interest in that field, and he preferred to focus his attention on the West that he regarded as his own homeland. Whatever the choice, he was even then convinced that it must deal with something that would interest the general public; he had already turned down a suggestion by Barker that he undertake a study of the Texas land office on the grounds that whatever he wrote would be of interest only to specialists.[35] Shy and reserved though he was, Webb was determined that he would have an audience, that whatever he wrote would be read—and by as many as possible; the journalist in him had a way of breaking through the academic overlay at every opportunity.

Eventually he found a topic that blended all of his interests to some degree and became in the long run something of a favorite— the history of the Texas Rangers. Its initial attraction was its topicality; the Ranger force was in the news due to its involvement in the policing of the booming oil towns and the political controversy over its continued existence.[36] It was while Webb was writing some newspaper items about the work of the force in the oil fields that he discovered that no full-scale history of the force had ever been written, despite the fact that such a work would have a wide appeal. At the same time, he suspected that the topic could be developed into an institutional study similar in some ways to the Keasbey approach, though it is not altogether clear how he hoped to adapt that approach to such a limited front.[37] Finally, a study of the Ranger force in the Mexican War would not only make sense in terms of a good starting point in time, but it also tied in to some extent with the departmental interest in Mexican-American relations and the preference for a diplomatic or political framework.

By mid-1920, the work was complete and Webb had overcome the smaller of the two hurdles that blocked his way toward a permanent academic career.[38] But it was only a temporary reprieve; at some point he must obtain the doctorate he needed to guarantee his position in the department. There was no doubt that his reputation in the department was a good one; Barker was anxious to retain him and promised to secure a promotion to adjunct professor in return for Webb's rejection of an offer to teach at Alpine Normal School.[39] To strengthen his case for the promotion, Webb spent the summer of 1920 at the University of Chicago; it was there that he came up against the problem that he did not want to face.[40] C. S. Boucher, a Chicago historian who had previously taught at Austin, warned him that at some point he must take a full year's leave and obtain his degree; until he did so, he would "hibernate as to advancement"—and the longer he postponed the evil day, the lower his credit would sink with his colleagues.[41] It was not a pleasant prospect, but it had to be faced; he would have to study another language to complement his shaky German, teach two summers, and spend the intervening winter in Chicago. The whole procedure would be costly, would disturb his family arrangements, and would yoke him to a treadmill for the next two years—over and above his normal teaching load. He was now thirty-two, and he had spent the best part of eleven years alternating teaching and full-time study, saving enough at one to pay for the other. It was a depressing cycle, even though he had moved upward far beyond his original ambitions; each move made precisely the same demands on him, and he had yet to reach the point where he could make his own decisions as to what he wanted to do with his skills.

In terms of his social background, Webb's career to this point had been something of a success. While he was an undergraduate he made a count of the number of students who had reached the state university from his own county and found there were only nine, including himself.[42] Of those nine, four had graduated, and one had become the dean of the university's College of Arts and Sciences. With all the twists and turns he had had to make since he left Stephens County in 1909, Webb had managed to work his way out of the public school system and into a small professional elite—

but it was an elite whose assumptions and methods of operation were to a large extent governed by rules laid down in the older sections of the country.[43] To gain acceptance by the group, he would have to accept the pressure to go north and complete his training.

Without realizing it, Webb was setting a course that was to involve him in a major disappointment and at the same time start a conflict that would only be resolved by the completion of *The Great Plains* a decade later—and even then it would continue to echo through his later career. It was a crisis composed of many elements, but most of them focused on the clash between the demands of his professional situation and the pressures of his nascent regional identity. It was a clash that might never have become crucial for him had he remained a high school teacher; but once he was thrown into a rather more complex situation, the conflicting pressures came to the surface and demanded resolution. To win the approval of his superiors he had to rehearse the rather arid procedures on which they placed a great deal of store, and, though he respected men like Barker and Ramsdell, their attention to detail and preoccupation with documentary sources must have seemed rather pale and insipid compared to the spectacular flourishes of Keasbey's fertile mind. But they were the arbiters of academic standards, and he had already made one attempt to fall in behind their banner—his master's thesis was an attempt to do what was academically respectable.

Yet, working on the Rangers had one unexpected result: Webb discovered that it triggered the old fascination for writing that had to a large extent remained dormant since his undergraduate days.[44] Once resurrected, the old desire burned more brightly than ever, and Webb was soon experimenting with this rediscovered talent. He began writing small items for newspapers and to his surprise found they were both published and paid for—and Webb had every reason to place high value on payment and the recognition it implied. Now convinced that he had a talent that could be put to good use and whose employment gave him immense personal satisfaction, he was anxious to find the best means of putting it to work. He must find a local theme, one that had life and color and a wide popular appeal; but the difficulty was to find something that would meet these requirements and at the same time satisfy his academic superiors, for there was no tradition of research or even of scholarly interest in the section of the state that interested him most. In the meantime a continuation of the Ranger study seemed the best alternative; perhaps in time it would lead him to something of wider significance.

It was not till some time later that he would accept the full consequences of the advice a friend had given him sometime in 1920, and which in the long run proved to be the best comment on his situation:

> One day . . . Trombly said in effect, "Webb, you are fundamentally a pioneer, a frontiersman, and there is nothing you can do about it." I thought this over for a while and decided that I had been pulling against the stream of my nature. "All right," I said, "If I am still a frontiersman, I'll be one. I'll make the most of it, and go with my nature and not against it." This resolution made things easier and progress more rapid. The West had been settled, and the only pioneering left was of the intellectual sort, in interpreting the land and its people, but as yet I had no idea that I would have any part of this.[45]

Chicago would be his last attempt to see if he could go both with and against his inclinations at the same time.

6. To Chicago—and Back

WEBB ARRIVED in Chicago in late 1922; he was now thirty-four, and unlike many of his fellow students, already held a junior university teaching position. His age was not in itself a problem, as it was still normal for students to spread their studies over a period of some years and to intersperse their work with teaching in state normals or private colleges. In some respects, Webb was in a more comfortable position than most; he had a year's leave, a job to go back to, and enough funds to make it possible for him to take Jane and their small daughter with him to Chicago.[1] Finally, he had the assurance of a friend at court: he had already studied under William E. Dodd, then at the height of his national reputation and an influential member of the Chicago history department; Dodd was on good terms with both Ramsdell and Barker and was sympathetic to Webb's position.[2] If Webb needed advice and help, Dodd was the obvious man to supply both.

Even more important was the fact that Webb knew what was in front of him and had a very clear idea of what he wanted to do—a situation that stood in marked contrast to his uncertainty when he first came to Austin in 1909. His earlier visits to Madison and Chicago had given him an introduction to the mechanics of what was required, and he had been able to observe the operation of a smaller graduate program in his own department. His letters to Dodd and the chairman of the department, A. C. McLaughlin, set out a very clear plan of what he intended to do: European history would be a minor field, and he would present as his thesis the study of the Texas Rangers for which he had already completed a good deal of the research.[3] There were no objections to his plans, and Webb set out for his new venture in a confident mood. It would be the longest period that he had ever spent outside his own state, and there was every indication that he would return with the qualification that would establish him in the eyes of his colleagues. From there, he would be able to develop his own interests as he saw fit.

Twelve months later he was back in Austin, bitterly disappointed and humiliated, in debt, and with his academic future under something of a cloud. It was a severe blow, one that had a profound effect on his work from that point on. The simplest explanation of his debacle was that the whole affair was something of an accident; Webb appears to have been badly advised and probably should have avoided taking the preliminary examination only five months after his arrival in Chicago.[4] It seems likely that those who encouraged him to take the examination assumed that he was a strong candidate and that an early examination would enable him to get to work on his thesis and have the bulk of it completed before he returned to Austin at the end of his year's leave. There are signs that Webb himself may have been overconfident, regarding himself as an experienced student and equal in ability to the strongest in his class.[5] Both Webb and his advisors put more store on the depth of his preparation than was warranted by his undergraduate record and by his experience in teaching an introductory course; five months was too brief a period to correct his deficiencies. In his infrequent references to the incident in later years, Webb pointed to his inability to perform well in an oral examination under any circumstances, and certainly nothing in his experience would have prepared him to handle that type of situation.[6]

Webb reacted bitterly, and even twenty years later the memory of that disappointment was still a sharp and painful one. The situation was not irretrievable, for he still had six months to spend in Chicago, and that gave him time to take the examination again with more thorough preparation.[7] But for Webb the failure marked a sharp dividing line in his career; his accounts of the episode make it clear that after this initial failure he virtually withdrew from any active part in the program. He did not make his revolt an open one, for that would have been difficult to explain to Barker and his colleagues; he attended classes and went through the motions of compliance.[8] But he refused to participate in any other fashion, sitting glumly through his lectures and waiting for the time when he could go home to Austin. Ill health compounded the situation: all three members of the family were ill with influenza in early 1923, and, with the great influenza epidemic so recent in their experience, the psychological effect was probably as severe as the physical.[9] Then it became necessary to search for another apartment, and the irritations associated with locating a landlord who would accept a small child added to the general frustrations of the period. Later Jane and her daughter returned to Austin, and Walter was left to cope with his resentments alone. At one stage he was convinced that his constant moodiness and depression were close to effecting a mental breakdown, and he found it necessary to break out of his general lethargy before he slipped across the edge.[10]

In later years he tended to focus the blame for this black period of his life on the men who taught him and on the system of academic advancement of which they were the representatives. He noted that he had arrived at Chicago at a time when the reputation of the graduate school was on the rise, and he implied that in such a situation the interests of the students tend to be sacrificed to the needs of the institution. On other occasions he suggested that his experience there suggested that it was never worthwhile to take an original idea into a graduate school, though he did not indicate precisely how this had been a factor in his case. This general dissatisfaction with the department, and the apparent failure of any of the courses to stir his interest, appears rather strange when measured against the general reputation of both the department and the individual members of the faculty. Chicago did have one of the strongest history departments in the country at that time, including such well-known scholars as Ferdinand Schevill, James Westfall Thompson, A. C. McLaughlin, Marcus W. Jernegan, and William E. Dodd. It attracted talented graduate students, and those with whom Webb continued to correspond after his return to Austin were anything but critical in their comments on the program.[11] If the work Webb did there made no impact on him, the explanation might just as easily be traced to Webb's own attitude as to any failings on the part of those who taught him. Avery Craven, who was a graduate student at Chicago in those years, and a friend and admirer of Webb, remembered him as something of a maverick "who knew the Western world from which he came better than any professor. So at graduate school he would simply go through the motions while he used up most of his life going his own way towards the ends he had already set for his historical life."[12]

Webb probably resented the fact that there was no opportunity at Chicago to study the history of his own region.[13] He could not take courses on the West, and certainly not on the Anglo Southwest that was becoming his special interest; the emphasis at Chicago was on the traditional areas, on political and constitutional history, and on the older sections of the country. None of these had any special appeal for Webb, and courses on European history had even less; he could see no point in studying nineteenth century German historiography when the area that fascinated him was ignored in the curriculum. "Webb simply refused to prepare himself for the examinations. He did the work that interested him and ignored the rest . . . he had no time to waste on what others thought was history . . . so he failed . . . and was bitter because he knew what he knew as well as others, so it was unfair not to give him the degree that was, after all, just a formal affair."[14]

To make things worse, he was finding himself more at odds with what appeared to him to be the arid methodology of the conventional historians, and though he did not fully realize it at the time, he was well on the way to reverting to the Keasbey approach that had lain dormant since his old professor left Austin in 1917. At least part of the explanation for Webb's bitter reaction to his failure lies in the normal resentment of a proud personality toward any suggestion that he was less than competent in the area he claimed as his specialty; but Webb's reaction also marked something of a confrontation between two different orientations toward the study of history. Webb found that his professional future depended on the opinion of a group of men whose methods and outlook held no attraction for him; when they rejected him, he simply went his own way and refused to pay even lip service to their standards. He was convinced that he knew a better method, and he was determined to prove his point in his own way.[15]

In the late summer of 1923, he made the return journey to Austin. It was very much a homecoming, and the sound of familiar accents and farm talk warmed his spirits and lifted the gloom of many months. Ramsdell had thought that the year away would broaden his thinking and provide the necessary professional gloss; but in Webb's case the usual situation was reversed.[16] If anything, anger and humiliation strengthened his inclination to hunker down in his provincial origins and, at the same time, vehemently defend his right to do so. The only thing that he regarded as a positive gain from his year at Chicago was a new way of looking at his own state, and the indications are that this new viewpoint was based not so much on a fundamental shift in perspective as on a strengthening of already deep-rooted assumptions.[17] He was now more determined than ever to focus his attention on the only type of history that interested him; though others seemed to regard the story of his people as unworthy of attention, he would find some way of convincing them that it was impressive and worthwhile, something that deserved to be told; but as yet he was uncertain as to how he would go about the task.[18]

Coming back to Austin meant a return to familiar places and a comfortable routine. He was in his own home and back on the university payroll; he was in debt, but not to a serious extent, and Jane was again working at the school for the deaf.[19] His teaching load was heavy without being oppressive; it involved working with Duncalf in the familiar survey course in European history and resuming his old course in classroom methods. There was still no place for him among the Americanists, but the extra work he did with the History Teachers' Association gave him the opportunity to indulge his interest in local history. On the surface, Webb seemed to have slipped back into a network of old and comfortable relationships.

But there were some basic problems that could not be ignored. He had suffered a professional setback, and, though his colleagues appeared to regard it as a temporary problem which he could rectify without too much difficulty, his position in the department was still vulnerable. For a man who never felt entirely comfortable about the ways of the academic world, it was an unpleasant situation. It was generally assumed that he would return to Chicago at the first opportunity and complete his degree; as late as 1931, after *The Great Plains* had appeared, Dodd made it clear that he expected Webb to resume his studies. Although Webb was advanced to associate professor in 1925, both he and Barker remained sensitive to the effect of the failure on his academic future. From time to time Webb made perfunctory gestures in the direction of a return to full-time study, and in 1924 and 1925 he went as far as purchasing sets of class notes from a Chicago student, apparently with a view to presenting for examinations in European history.[20] But in private he was adamant that he would not return; he would not face the possibility of another such humiliation and intended instead to wipe out the incident by a major success outside the university framework. If he could go over the heads of his examiners and produce something that would attract wide attention, he would not only retrieve his position but he would also establish some sort of moral superiority over those who had rejected him—and in that way would compensate for the injury to his pride.

The major difficulty was to establish a new approach: how could he turn his frustration back against itself? After a year's absence, he was more conscious of the emotional ties that bound him to the land of his childhood. But anger and a sense of grievance did nothing to clarify the nature of those ties or to dignify their source; he must do something positive, and do it soon. One fact that struck him forcibly during those months in Chicago was the realization that he was no longer young—that he had passed the halfway point in life and that if he was to achieve anything substantial it must be soon.[21] He had a program, a general position, and a powerful incentive—but no immediate answer to the question of how to realize his objective.

Part of the answer lay in the discovery that he was not alone, that there were a few individuals who shared his concerns in a conscious way and a great many more with similar interests but no way of articulating their feelings. Webb had returned to Austin at a time when the tide of disillusionment and resurgent nativism was running strong at both the state and the national level. Calvin Coolidge was in the White House, and Miriam Ferguson in the Governor's Mansion at Austin. Both ruled by proxy—Coolidge as the legatee of Warren Harding's dubious political estate, and Miriam Ferguson as a front for her husband's apparently indestructible ambition. Even more alarming was the return of the Klan to a position of political power and enormous prestige in Texas; though it was to collapse within a few years, its reappearance was evidence of the tensions and frustration that bedeviled a rural society caught between the disintegration of its own social and economic structure and the vaulting promise of the new consumer economy of the twenties. Social fractures were appearing at many levels, and rural Texans felt the strain more severely than most.[22]

Webb had little direct experience of the jolts that shook so many of his generation; academic life insulated him against sudden social change, and, although the presence of a Ferguson at the head of the state administration was a source of constant concern to the university community, the pattern of his own life remained outwardly unaffected by the broader shifts within the social structure. He enjoyed some of the positive gains of the new order; he now had a car, the first he had owned, and he valued the mobility it gave him—especially when it made it possible for him to explore parts of his own state that he had never seen before. In the summer of 1924 he was able to make an extended visit to Ranger camps along the Mexican border, and his first contact with the Big Bend country made an indelible impression: "Though I had never seen such country, I felt it was somehow mine, and many times later, even now, I feel an almost irresistible desire to see it again. . . . There is an indefinable charm about a high arid area with its grotesque forms of desert erosion, which I think appeals much more to men than to women."[23]

By now his parents had sold the farm at Ranger and had moved nearer to the town of Weatherford to settle down to retirement.

Ironically, it had been the Ranger oil boom rather than his own careful husbandry that made it possible for Casner Webb to spend the rest of his life in moderate comfort; in 1918 he had sold out to a syndicate of would-be oilmen for $33,800.[24] It was a fine return on his original investment, especially as no oil was found on the property. Walter had dabbled in speculation during the boom but apparently lost more than he made; before the decade was out he had discovered that the writing of textbooks was a more reliable source of income to supplement his university salary.[25] But his father's retirement made it even more evident that an era of fine achievement on the part of a generation of humble people was coming to a close. As yet it remained unrecognized and unrewarded.

As he settled back into the routine of teaching, the social and economic structures that had sheltered his own generation began to shift, fragment, and reappear in new guises. The emergence of the oil industry as a major factor in the economic life of both the state and the nation was the most obvious source of change; by showering great wealth erratically across the state without regard to existing social patterns or even the facts of geography, the oil boom upset the older social balances and disrupted the orderly processes of change.[26] By the twenties, a large section of what was essentially a rural society found itself fenced into suburbs and overrun by the new technology; the shift from an agricultural world was sudden and unsettling. The obvious boost in confidence and the infusion of unexpected wealth were in themselves gains, but for those whose roots were set in the late nineteenth century the rate of change was unnerving.[27]

In the twenties, dozens of little communities across the state watched the survivors of the pioneer stock go to their graves and realized that before long there would be little to remind them of an era that held a unique significance for their own lives. Most could only note what was happening and bury their sense of loss under the hopeful circumstances of the present. Yet some had a growing conviction that the ways of the new world would leave less room than usual for a connection with the immediate past, and it seemed important to them that the sounds and accepted customs of their parents' world be retrieved and given the kind of permanence that memory alone could not guarantee.[28]

Bernard De Voto later noted the irony of a situation in which humble people made their own effort to retain a sense of the "usable past" without any awareness of the theoretical formulations of professional historians.[29] Every generation places its own valuation on reminiscence, and the rural mind of the twenties preferred to recreate the quality of that post–Civil War era that seemed to be far more heroic and less complicated than anything that had followed it—a golden age, and not simply a gilded one. Across the country a whole fleet of magazines flourished on the strength of this rural nostalgia, and Walter Webb read many of them.[30] Though a refugee from the land, he had moved only as far as the small town and had never shown any inclination to accept the urban style and tastes normally identified with academic life. Moreover, the geographical isolation of a campus in central Texas made it easier for him to wear his small town personality without embarrassment or discomfort.

The attempt to retrieve that segment of the past that stood in the wake of the Civil War had begun—as far as the Southwest was concerned—while Webb was still an undergraduate. John Lomax's collection of cowboy ballads appeared in 1910, although the material had been gathered much earlier; the idea of collecting folklore had already taken hold by the time Webb began his career as a high school teacher, and he was sufficiently aware of the trend to collect some material on his own initiative while at Cuero and Beeville.[31] His later fascination with the Texas Rangers was in part a response to the formidable body of legend that had developed about them in the course of eighty years—or at least that part of the legend known to the Anglo population.[32] Webb valued folklore, helped to collect it, and encouraged others to do so; but it did not fully satisfy his own interests. He wanted to understand the whole rather than collect the particular.

The work that Lomax had begun under such discouraging circumstances early in the century was picked up by others, especially J. Frank Dobie, a native Texan who taught English at Oklahoma A&M College for a short period early in the twenties but then returned to the University of Texas.[33] Webb knew of his work in collecting folklore and recognized the value of what he was doing in terms of locating and preserving the raw material of a regional identity.[34] But Dobie had his own roots deep in the world of ranching in a way that Webb did not, and the fact that he had formal training in literature gave him a clearer notion of what he wanted to do with his talents than Webb possessed at that point. Dobie was well on the way, but Webb was still uncertain as to his proper course of action; working on the Rangers was a fascinating exercise, and the notion that he would write the first major study of the

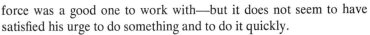

force was a good one to work with—but it does not seem to have satisfied his urge to do something and to do it quickly.

There was one outlet for his energies which met some of the general requirements without providing a complete answer. Webb had become an academic historian just as the wave of interest in the field of local history began to make a definite impression on the profession. Solon J. Buck, himself an active promoter of local history as director of the Minnesota Historical Society, noted in his presidential address to the Mississippi Valley Historical Association in 1923 that the situation had changed radically over the previous decade; professional historians had begun to take the field seriously and were no longer content to leave it to antiquarians.[35] Part of this shift in attitude could be attributed to changing emphases within the profession itself; the growth of social and economic history necessitated a broader view of what constituted source material, while the burgeoning influence of the Turnerian view virtually assured the status of local and sectional history.[36] But Buck also pointed to developments in the wider community, especially in the Mississippi Valley states: "Most of the states of the Mississippi Valley have now reached the stage of comparative stability of their citizenry; and people with more than two or three generations of ancestors who shared in the development of the state naturally have a greater personal interest in its history than those whose family trail leads promptly back to an eastern state or to some foreign country."[37]

Tied in with this element was the considerable impact of World War I in stimulating a wider segment of the general community to value the sources of all that was distinctively American; the willingness of state politicians to vote appropriations for historical commissions and similar projects suggests a shift in attitudes at the grassroots level. Special groups within American society may have had their own reasons for developing a lively interest in the immediate past. In discussing the changing character of the American gentry in the nineteenth century, Stow Persons has suggested that the generation that came to maturity after the Civil War could not define themselves in terms of distinguished family connections as the prewar gentry had done. Instead, "they were content to seek their origins in the autonomous cultural regions of America," but, since many regions could not go back beyond a generation, "memoirs and reminiscence provided a principal source of the gentry's sense of their regional cultural heritage"—hence the flood of autobiographies in the late nineteenth century and the focus on the family as the transmitter of the moral and religious heritage of the region. The interest in local history in the 1920's may well have been an extension of this process.[38]

Other factors may have had some bearing on the new trend: the arrival of the automobile with its impact on the tourist value of historical shrines and museums, the greater activity of women in public life generally, the survival of larger numbers of older people to convert nostalgia into membership subscriptions—all have been cited as part of the explanation for the postwar boom in local history.[39] But the key elements were probably the simple process of maturation described by Buck and the influence of such individual organizers and promoters as Reuben Thwaites at the State Historical Society of Wisconsin: once the model of a widely based and multifaceted operation had been established and its success made obvious, other areas were bound to follow suit.[40]

The organization of historical societies had generally followed several generations behind the initial tide of settlement; with the Northeast in the lead, most of the area east of the Mississippi had been organized by the time of the Civil War.[41] By the same token, proper organization could hardly occur in vast tracts west of the Mississippi until the later nineteenth or early twentieth century. But when it did occur, it was able to take advantage of the innovations being tried out in the older areas of the country. The existence of the Mississippi Valley Historical Association provided those interested in the work at the academic level with a forum and a source of advice; by the early twenties the mechanics of promoting the study of local history and the preservation of likely records were well known in the more recently settled areas to the west, and the rush to form societies, establish journals, and preserve the relics of the recent past was under way.[42]

In Texas the origins of a state historical association went back earlier than in those states erected through the territorial process. Founded in 1897, the Texas State Historical Association could claim to be the oldest learned society in the state, and its links with the Department of History at the University of Texas had always been close; in particular, the main responsibility for editing and gathering copy for its journal had over the years fallen to the academic historians.[43] This in turn meant that the journal reflected to a large extent that department's primary interest in the study of the Spanish phase of the Southwest and the early Anglo period of Texas history; it did not as yet indicate interest in the northern sector of the state and in the post–Civil War period. During the

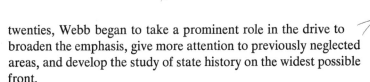

twenties, Webb began to take a prominent role in the drive to broaden the emphasis, give more attention to previously neglected areas, and develop the study of state history on the widest possible front.

From the thirties onward, this interest was reflected in the numerous graduate theses he directed; a high proportion were studies of individual counties or of topics of local interest. A high point came with the publication in 1952 of *The Handbook of Texas*, an encyclopedia of state history that brought together a mass of data, much of it flowing from the local studies carried on throughout the state over the previous quarter century.[44] But in the early twenties, Webb had only begun to develop this approach, and he did not as yet have the Plains synthesis as his base. His role as instructor in teaching methods provided the opening, and he used it effectively; inevitably that assignment carried with it responsibility for the bulletins which the Department of History sponsored as a way of keeping in touch with teachers in the secondary schools, and Webb made sure that both students and teachers were made aware of books that were in any way relevant to the study of local history.[45] By persuading a successful lawyer to provide a substantial prize for an essay-writing contest at the high school level, he laid the basis for what was later to become a remarkably effective project to interest the young in the history of their own localities.[46] At every point his pride in the heritage of his state and his anxiety to rescue the evidence of a recent but already fading past showed through his writing, and there could be little doubt as to the direction in which his own interests were moving.

He was by no means alone, for already other scholars were beginning to fit together the hitherto neglected pieces of the story that Webb had guessed at as a child. Rupert Norval Richardson had begun his study of the struggle against the Indians on the northwestern frontier of Texas, and by the end of the decade J. Evetts Haley had commenced his probing into the ranching records of the area.[47] Later the major studies of the cattle industry by Ernest S. Osgood and Edward Everett Dale would provide an even wider perspective on the cattle industry in the Plains region. The tide had commenced to flow, and Webb was determined to be part of it; for the first time the part of the country that fascinated him was being taken seriously, and for that he was grateful. But there still remained the question of his own role in the new developments; writing reviews was one thing, making a major personal contribution was another—yet the best line of approach still eluded him.

7. The Search for a Medium

NOT LONG AFTER he returned to Austin in 1923, Webb became involved in a minor literary dispute which rather unexpectedly sharpened the issues for him and drew him a good deal closer to the heart of his problem—but without actually solving it.[1] To Webb, the dispute was anything but minor; it aroused him to vigorous activity and allowed him to vent in harmless fashion a good deal of the hostility that had banked up since his reverse at Chicago. When the argument was over, some of the excitement it had generated flowed over into an effort to determine whether he had any talent as a short story writer; and although that experiment convinced him that he had a limited aptitude for fiction, it also took him closer to the answer he was looking for.

The Hough controversy was a curious affair in that the issues involved were far less important than the manner in which they were debated—if that word can be used to describe a situation in which only the more vocal side took part after the initial volley. In November of 1923, the New York–based *Literary Digest International Book Review* included as the last of its major articles a discussion of the elements of distortion that had crept into certain types of popular literature dealing with national groups or types: one section dealt with the stereotyped view of Canada, another with the alleged villainy of the Spaniard, and a third with the romantic view of the American West. It was this latter section, written by Stuart Henry, that caught Webb's attention and touched off the controversy.[2] What irritated Webb was that Henry had chosen to focus his remarks on Emerson Hough's *North of 36*, a saga of the cattle trail which Henry felt exhibited many of the classic defects of fiction dealing with western themes. Webb was an admirer of Hough's work and saw Henry's remarks as a cowardly and defamatory assault on both the man and the vein of literature he represented.[3] He immediately began to organize a counterattack.

The initial move was to contact two men whom he expected would be quick to come to the aid of a western writer under fire—

the novelists Eugene Manlove Rhodes and Andy Adams. Both were former cowboys who had later turned to writing, and, although their fortunes were at the time in something of a decline, their work represented in Webb's eyes the only genuine attempt to produce a literature based on the authentic life of the cattle kingdom. He wrote to each of them for the first time in 1923 and corresponded with them for almost a decade.[4] He found Rhodes equally hostile to the Henry article and anxious to support any campaign mounted against it—though the state of his health and his unwillingness to appear as even an indirect booster of his own work placed some restraints on his participation. Webb had less success in getting aid from Adams; though he agreed in principle with Webb's views, he had his own reservations about the reliability of Hough's accounts of the trail era and clearly resented the fact that Hough had made a good deal of money by introducing the romantic element into his work—a tactic Adams disliked intensely.[5] His disdain for the commercialism involved was enough to prevent him from taking any direct part in defending or promoting the work in the way that Webb expected.

Very soon Webb found himself at the center of the campaign, tapping the two older men for ideas and information, asking their advice as to the best methods of getting a rebuttal into print, and doing most of the organizing work himself. It became an exciting and lively operation, at least from Webb's point of view, and highly beneficial in that it gave him the chance to discuss western problems with men who were actually sympathetic to his position—something to which he was not accustomed.[6]

Two particular aspects of Henry's article aroused the ire of Webb and his western friends—the fact that Henry had challenged the accuracy of Hough's account of the trail era and that he had questioned both the patriotism of some of the men who rode the trails and the attractiveness of their womenfolk. Taken together, these comments amounted in Webb's view to a sneering rejection of the West, its history and its people; the honor of the West was at stake, and those who loved the West should rise up and vindicate their heritage against an eastern interloper.[7]

To the little coterie of westerners, it was all the more galling that the attack should have come from a man long resident in New York, whose published works included studies of Parisian life. That such a man should set himself up as a judge of the work of an authentic westerner like Emerson Hough seemed to them to be the height of impertinence, and that an editor would allow such a mountebank space in a respectable publication was incredible. It was essential that his statements be refuted, and Webb began to collect the necessary evidence. In March 1924 he wrote to Henry, setting out a list of questions designed to establish whether the latter had any claim to be an authority on western matters: Henry never replied, and Webb cited this fact as evidence that Henry was too embarrassed to confess his ignorance—though it is equally possible that he found the tone of the inquiry impertinent and decided to ignore it.[8] At the same time, Webb began to write to survivors of the trail era and collect material that could be used to contradict Henry's assertions and vindicate Hough's reputation as a reliable interpreter of the West. His most useful ally was George W. Saunders of San Antonio, president of the Trail Drivers Association, whose organization could claim to speak for hundreds of men who had personal knowledge of the cattle era, and in the period covered by Hough's book.

It was not hard to find evidence that weakened the force of Henry's illustrations, though the defense of western womenfolk had to be largely a matter of gallant assertion. Unable to goad Henry into a reply, Webb and his allies had to be content with the knowledge that a certain amount of righteous anger had been generated among the hitherto apathetic defenders of the western heritage. Eventually the clamor died down, and Webb and his friends settled back to enjoy the afterglow of an assumed victory.[9]

If Webb had paid much attention to these two aspects of the argument, they would have caused him to hesitate: Henry was by no means the raw easterner all had assumed but had actually grown up in Abilene during the trail era; and, in any case, the main thrust of his comment on western writing was hardly open to question. Henry's unfavorable reaction to Hough's work was based on the view that the history of western expansion deserved better treatment than it usually received at the hands of popular writers, and that much of the authentic story of the trans–Mississippi West had been obscured beneath a layer of inaccurate and romantic cliché. Henry called for a serious study of western history, and, though Webb could hardly have disagreed with that suggestion, he called down the wrath of the West on Henry's head for the deficiencies of his assessment of *North of 36* and failed completely to see the soundness of his overall position. Webb simply overreacted and never managed to get the affair into any proper perspective.

Once stung into activity, Webb found that he had plenty of opportunity to work on the problems that had been at the back of his mind since the Chicago episode. He was now in direct contact with two men who shared his love for the West and who had become in his view the most loyal defenders of its values and its way of life—men who had known it at first hand and had devoted their lives to putting its image on paper. If anyone could advise him as to the proper role of a young man who wanted to do something for the West, these men could.[10] His letters to both men began to raise interpretive questions—what was distinctive about the life and values of westerners, and what place did such qualities have in the overall American amalgam? If the historic West had virtually disappeared from sight, what did this mean for those who still lived in its shadow? Could its values be preserved, and was such preservation essential for the well-being of the nation as a whole? What was the responsibility of the modern westerner to the culture of his own region—especially if he were a writer or a historian? Specifically, what should Webb himself do to carry on the traditions of the West and promote a better understanding of their inherent values?[11]

Both Rhodes and Adams were rather puzzled by this turn of events—a young college professor coming to them for advice on writing techniques, even raising awkward questions about theories of fiction. Though they warmed to their young associate and were flattered by his attentions, they found it difficult to analyze their attitudes toward the West or explain their methods of writing. Both were practical men who wrote for a living and had learned their craft by trial and error and without much reference to theory. Rhodes, always a lively correspondent and a somewhat explosive personality, took up the challenge rather more aggressively than Adams. But in the long run he could do little more than assert values that Webb already took for granted and encourage the younger man to expound them in his turn.

Rhodes felt more comfortable when he could steer away from Webb's problems and mount a frontal assault on what he felt to be detestable attitudes that were becoming rampant in American literature. In his opinion, the Henry article was simply a part of this overall attempt to debase the literary and moral standards of the country and had to be recognized as such.[12] Thus Rhodes's views came to express the old rural way of life and its disgust with many trends in contemporary life. His letters to Webb quickly became salted with attacks on the group of writers he labeled the "Euro-Americans," a term comprehensive enough to cover most of the leading figures in American literature in the early twenties. H. L.

Mencken, F. Scott Fitzgerald, and Sherwood Anderson were among the favorite targets of Rhodes's invective; in letter after letter he blasted the "Euro-Americans" for their willingness to prostitute American literary values for the sake of a brittle sophistication, for deserting American values and American themes and accepting vulgarity and cosmopolitanism as basic criteria in determining literary merit.[13] As long as such writers dominated the literary world, those who tried to capture the authentic essence of American life would be denied a public, and national life would be debilitated both by the lack of access to the sources of its spiritual heritage and the parallel injection of alien and potentially destructive values.

The tone of the discussion was personal, and both Webb and Rhodes were aware that their reaction was as much a question of emotion as of literary judgement. Rhodes pointed up the nature of their personal involvement and saw it as the basic justification for their hostility to modern trends in literature: "It is safe to assume, I think, but just this once, neither of us has no ulterior motive. You *for your father,—I for my friends*—we are trying to give of our best without thought of advantage to ourselves" (emphasis mine).[14] From this sense of a proper veneration for the good name of their forebears, it was a simple matter to identify personal considerations with those of the national culture: "We don't like to have our dead defamed—nor is that all. There is a slow and steady effort—and a slow and steady gain—all along the line—against the attempt to Balkanise the American spirit, to Russianise our politics, to 'Levantise' our business methods, and to Europeanise our letters."[15] It was not just the question of defending Hough that mattered, but the good name of a generation of men; the tendency of the new writers to "belittle them, to belittle all Americans, for that matter," had to be resisted.[16]

Obviously the question of absolute literary values was not central to Rhodes's thinking, and it seems likely that his irritation at the lack of recognition given to his own work and that of western writers in general spilled over into a general hostility toward those elements of the contemporary scene that seemed responsible for his discomfort. This was, after all, the year of the great debate over immigration, and it saw the passage of the act that brought to an end the traditional policy of unrestricted entry. It was also the period of resurgent nativism and the revival of the Klan; the nationalism generated by America's involvement in World War I and the isolationism that followed in the early twenties helped to contract the public mind and encouraged a retreat to the old and familiar guidelines. A later commentator has pointed out that the rural-urban conflict of the period was "at its deepest level a reflection of the cleavage between the native-stock American and the immigrant—a cleavage constantly more distinct than the division between city and country, or between the urban East and the rural West and South."[17]

Rhodes in a sense represented all of these cleavages and added another of his own; while the defenders of traditional American values were inclined to locate them in rural America among the old stock, Rhodes suggested that they were best exemplified in the life of the cattle kingdom and that to ignore the West and its pastoral heritage was something far more reprehensible than the admitted crime of ignoring rural America in general. "This is not merely the petty peevishness of your mind or mine: it concerns the truth of one of the decisive and far reaching adventures in the history of our race. This thing was not done in a corner, the making of the West—and we have a right to have truth told about it."[18]

Rhodes and Webb were both caught up in a mood of resentment that ran through much of Main Street America at that period—Rhodes lashing out with the frustration of a man whose working life was coming to an end without much to show for it in terms of recognition, and Webb with the angry uncertainty of a latecomer in search of his destiny. In one of the few surviving fragments of Webb's letters to Rhodes, something of his mood comes through: he wrote of the need "for someone who will believe in America. I am going to fight these University intellectuals in general and in particular. Fighting, I think, is half the strength of the Mencken crowd. The youth of the country like to see the fur fly, and I believe a little 'intellectual' fur will prove an attraction. I believe Texas and America will make way for an American—no, not Ku Klux, but I can see some things the Ku Klux have in mind."[19] They were brave words, comforting, no doubt, to the aging Rhodes, but generally reflective of Webb's inability to comprehend the literary issues of the day and of the limitations of his provincial background. But in actual fact they meant very little; Webb was not equipped to engage in literary combat at any level, and he was far too reserved to take to the hustings.

Yet Webb's urge to do something positive was, if anything, stronger; Hough and Rhodes had campaigned hard for a national—or more specifically, a western—literature, but their strength had now faded.[20] Hough was dead, and Rhodes was a sick and harried man whose working life was near its end. On the other hand, Webb was alive and healthy and, by comparison, comfortably situated; he could not avoid the responsibility that seemed to be falling in his direction. In a way, he welcomed the load, for it fitted his inclination to cast himself in some sort of western role. He wanted to carry the torch, but where, and how?

The most obvious answer was that he should turn back to his old ambition to be a writer and simply take the historic West as his theme as Rhodes and Adams had done. He had found that his interest in writing had returned, and for some time he had been trying his hand at writing for profit; some of the proceeds had gone into the pool of savings that he took with him to Chicago. So he was by no means a complete novice, though still a long way short of the standard he knew would be needed if he were to establish himself as a leading interpreter of the West. Accordingly he turned to the two older men for practical advice and had them scratching to find the theory behind the techniques they took for granted. Rhodes finally fell back on the idea that writing articles and letters was as good a method of self-training as any.[21] Adams was equally puzzled by Webb's request that he comment on his "philosophy of art, of fiction, of life," and he addressed himself only to the question of fiction: "When I turned to the writing game I found authority for the statement that fiction was only excusable when it gave us a better transcript of life—that it threw off the dross, the sordid things of life, mirroring only the beautiful."[22] Both agreed that fiction must be grounded in the core of familiar experience, that it must be "the reflex of life, hence the homely setting, the fire on the hearth . . . after which the human imagination peoples it with men and women who are fictional but a mirrored reflection of those we know in the flesh."[23] Rhodes stressed that his stories were founded on "remembered facts—not the acts—often imaginary, but the people, codes, traditions."[24] A good story should have its base in the events of an average working life and be topped off with character portrayal that does a little more than justice to the original models: the ordinary, plus a little of the ideal. It was an attractive formula, and in other days it had sold books for both men.

All of this amiable advice could not solve the basic problem for Webb; if anything, it simply exacerbated it. Both his mentors agreed that those who wrote about the West should have firsthand knowledge of it; Adams, Rhodes, and Hough had all qualified without any difficulty, but Webb had only seen what he later called "the hem of the garment of the frontier," as it disappeared from sight.[25] He had not seen the cattle kingdom in its prime, and, although he had personal experience of the life of the Plains, his contact had been with the humdrum of the dirt farmer and not with the colorful world of the cattlemen. Accordingly, if he tried to write about the cattle kingdom, which seemed to him to be the epitome of the West, he could not write from remembered experience or draw his characters from life.

This left Webb with no alternative but to rely on the material yielded by his research and the reminiscences of those who still survived from the cattle era. It was not the most satisfactory answer, for he could never be entirely comfortable about the loss of immediacy and the absence of the authentic note that could only come from personal experience. Yet it was an approach that fit in quite neatly with the demands of his academic career; he had to search for material for his thesis, and it was very likely that in doing that he would come across incidents or characters that would serve as a basis for future short stories or perhaps even for the major work whose form still eluded him. In the interim he could polish his style and perhaps master the techniques of writing; he would soon know whether he had the talent for fiction, and if he failed he still had a livelihood.

In his search for the sense of purpose and direction he needed after his return from Chicago, Webb had one other important source of advice—one that presented a viewpoint radically different from that developed by the older western novelists. Soon after joining the faculty at Austin, Webb became friendly with a young instructor in Romance languages and budding poet, Albert Trombly.[26] Trombly had moved to Missouri shortly after, but the two corresponded regularly until the early thirties, when the contact became intermittent. It was an important association for Webb in that Trombly was the only academic of his acquaintance—with the exception of J. Frank Dobie—who was interested in creative writing rather than in scholarly articles. He was an obvious source of advice and encouragement, and the friendship was close enough to allow Webb to drop some of his reserve and discuss his plans quite frankly. Moreover, Trombly's training and natural inclinations as a writer ensured that the advice he offered was very different in tone and emphasis from that presented by Rhodes and Adams. Since his views were those of a formally trained and well-read poet, his comments developed into a sort of counterpoint to those of the western veterans and had the effect of heightening Webb's dilemma.

In the early months of 1924, Webb apparently sought Trombly's views on the issues raised in his discussions with Rhodes and Adams, and, in particular, asked about the relative importance of the subjective and the national elements in literature. The answer pinpointed the gap that separated Trombly from Rhodes: "As for American or any other local art, I have no patience with it. Ideas and the best possible way of expressing them are the only things which concern me artistically; and they belong to no one time and no one place. That does not mean that place and time cannot furnish basic material; in a sense they furnish it all; but art must fuse them so that they become timeless and homeless."[27] Against Webb's preference for a literature that spoke for and to the ordinary man, Trombly advanced his concept of poetry as an expansion of the individual spirit, a "personal cry, and uttered for my solace alone. . . . It cannot be American or French or anything of the kind."[28] As Webb tried to work out his problems by a process of trial and error, Trombly encouraged his efforts and approved of his decision to take the history of his own state as his theme ("Texas lies before you, what more should you want?"), but he had doubts about the value of the short stories Webb produced—Webb was too prone, he felt, to assume that his ability to write stories that would sell was some sort of guarantee that he had found his true medium. Whatever Webb wrote must be "the best possible expression of the thing that is YOU."[29] It would be "a pity to have a man who could make a substantial contribution to American history spend himself in second rate stories."[30]

To Webb, however, personal expression was not enough; he would not be satisfied unless what he wrote was read by the widest possible audience. Years earlier he had rejected a research topic suggested by Eugene Barker because he knew that the result of his efforts would be an article that only specialists would ever read. The same desire to reach an audience wider than the purely academic accounted for his preference for writing articles for newspapers or large circulation magazines rather than learned journals.[31] He showed little inclination to win the respect—or court the criticism—of his professional colleagues in the conventional manner. A full-scale book was another matter, especially if the field was still virgin territory and would lend itself to the large-scale treatment he preferred. If he had room to work in, he was confident that his book would stand up to attack: individual segments might be called into question, but the overall structure would compensate for such difficulties.

Late in 1924, Trombly startled Webb with a severe critique of his role in the Hough affair; Trombly had just read *North of 36* for the first time and found himself in general agreement with Henry's review. Though he had liked Hough's other books, he found this a hopeless hodgepodge of characters and situations borrowed from his earlier successes and given a new coat of paint. What puzzled him was Webb's enthusiasm for the book and the vigor of his reaction to Henry's comments, which Trombly felt had been if anything charitable to the book.[32] Webb apparently took the reproof to heart, and Trombly had to restate his case: granted the few inaccuracies in Henry's illustrations, was the work really worth all the excitement? And why should anyone resent a reference to the gauntness of the pioneer women? "I wasn't there to see for myself . . . I am inclined to believe with poor Henry that pioneer women were not stunners. They were country-folk, good substantial stuff, but not of the brood of Helen . . ."[33]

As the echoes of the Hough controversy receded, the two friends began to discuss the possibility of collaborating on a novel. Webb was eager to get the project under way, but Trombly was more inclined to regard it as a distant prospect, to be attempted only when current work was out of the way.[34] Nothing came of the idea in the long run, though they continued to discuss it intermittently for another two years. By late 1925, Webb had submitted a scenario that he felt might provide the basis for a book; apparently it dealt with an aspect of the Texas revolution and carried the suggested title *Liberty*. Trombly was not impressed, and argued that a scenario could not be satisfactorily turned into a novel of the type he had in mind; besides, Webb's plot seemed far too reminiscent of those used by Emerson Hough. He liked Webb's background material and his description of the setting, but he felt there was no interaction between the setting and the development of the characters involved; Webb could build the stage, but as yet he could not people it or invite action.[35] So the joint venture died a gentle death; given the gulf that separated their attitudes toward writing, it seems unlikely that there could ever have been a successful collaboration.

To the end, Webb remained determined to write for the ordinary reader and to regard commercial acceptance as the best indicator of success; Trombly held out for purely literary standards, noting that some of Webb's comments on a ballad he had written sounded like "the editor's instructions for writing a story that will sell."[36] He found Webb's approach to literature too mechanical and too orderly to leave much room for inspiration: ". . . poetry begins where non-poetry leaves off. Even in a narrative the poetry will be in what is not said. But dammit, you ask for all the sub-titles and the cross references, and the footnotes, before you get started. Don't tell me that you are putting yourself in the place of the 'average reader'; that creature never reads poetry, much less mine . . ."[37]

But Trombly's advice, and the literary tradition he represented, had very little hope of prevailing over Webb's inclination toward the Rhodes point of view. Webb had now made contact with the men who, however crude their notions of the literary craft might be, stood closer to the sources of his emotional life than any avant-garde easterner; there was never any doubt which road Webb would follow. There is some possibility that Trombly's strictures confirmed Webb's growing suspicion that fiction was not the medium he was searching for, but he could not accept the view that the local element was incidental and that art was more important than acceptance. His sympathies lay with the literary populism of the older westerners, and this was the vein that he must work out in some way or other.

Taken as a whole, the discussions triggered by the Hough affair suggest a very rudimentary grasp of current literary issues on Webb's part. But they also reveal the extent to which he had been caught up in the rural backlash of those years, that sense of anger and frustration in the face of falling incomes and declining social status that plagued rural America and for once failed to find a safety valve in political agitation. Though the plight of the farmers did not affect him directly, some of their complaints were similar to his: he, too, was irritated by the readiness of urban Americans to relegate the land and its people to a position of permanent inferiority, and by the assumption that urban values and urban interests had already prevailed and that those who elected to stay close to the land were foolish and benighted. While others vented their frustration by railing at immigrants and radicals, Webb's irritation flowed along channels more appropriate to his calling and his immediate social milieu, focusing especially on the sins of the educated elite and the literary injustices they perpetrated on the rest of the country.

Nearly twenty years later, Bernard De Voto discussed the literature of the twenties and made the same indictment that Rhodes and Adams tried to make as they thrashed around in futile pursuit of Stuart Henry's misdemeanors.[38] De Voto argued that it was absurd for literary men to inform a hundred and twenty million people "that their ideals are base, their institutions corrupt, and . . . their civilisation too trivial to engage . . . respect."[39] Because the writers of the period were "isolated or insulated from the common culture," there was no room for a literature that was "organically part of American life."[40] When it came to suggesting what might have been advanced as an alternative, De Voto remained very much in the vein of the earlier discussion and argued against the assumption that American life could be adequately assessed through a study of its literary remains: culture meant far more than "the writing of books and associated matters" and should be taken to include the broadest range of national experience:

> Rejection, the attitude of superiority, disdain of the experience of ordinary people, repudiation of the values to which the generality of a writer's countrymen devote their lives—the literature of my generation tried that path and found that the path ended in impotence and death . . . Either literature deals honestly with the basic experiences in which all men may see themselves, or else it is only a mannered diversion practised by the impaired and of interest only to the leisure moments of those who are whole.[41]

De Voto admired Webb's work on the Plains and based some parts of his counterargument on material that Webb had brought to light; his most detailed attack on the ignorance of the front rank of American writers of the period centered on their failure to recognize the existence of John Wesley Powell's *Report on the Lands of the Arid Region of the United States*, a work to which Webb was heavily indebted.[42] Webb in turn retained a long-standing affection for De Voto, recognizing that the latter had developed more effectively and with less anger the case that he had tried to argue in 1923–1924. The raw nerve that Stuart Henry touched in those years was still exposed two decades later, a striking witness to the extent to which a sense of discouragement and alienation had marked off the small group of western writers from the mainstream of literary activity.

Yet Webb's sense of alienation was not of the conventional literary kind: though the discussions with Rhodes were at times couched in literary terms, the basic impulses at work were quite different in character. Webb's antipathy toward current trends in literature did not reflect a well-developed critical standpoint but stemmed rather from pressures inherent in his own cultural context. Like Margaret Lyn in Iowa, he had become familiar enough with the possibilities of creative intelligence to want to have it operating in his own world and making explicable that body of experience that for the moment lay disorganized and shapeless around him; like Margaret Lyn, he had grown to maturity without seeing any evidence of the operation of mind on his familiar world. But, unlike Hamlin Garland and others who fled the vacuum, Webb had not developed intellectual tastes and values that could only be satisfied by a retreat to a denser culture. He was prepared to stay, as were many of his generation who chose to teach and write close to their own communities; for these men and for those who decided to stay for more pragmatic reasons, it was important to prove that they were justified in doing so. The search for the raw material of an indigenous culture—the gathering of folklore and the preservation of the local historical deposit—was in part a response to this need, and in some respects the unrelated efforts of geologists, anthropologists, and sociologists broadened the range of material available and helped to thicken the cultural context.

But in the course of this process of collection and preservation, Webb and his contemporaries also discovered something they had not quite expected: without being fully conscious of what they were doing, a few men like Adams, Rhodes, and Hough had already begun to lay the foundations of a western literature that had the marks of authenticity and was directly grounded in the experience of the region. It was by no means a large body of material, and in many ways it was unsophisticated—but in Webb's view it deserved to be taken seriously and used as a basis for future development. But the arbiters of national literary taste had not simply rejected the work of men like Adams; they ignored it entirely and encouraged contemporary writers to indulge in what appeared to the westerners to be fantastic explorations of the individual psyche that were the very antithesis of the frontier viewpoint. It was bad enough that the new writers seemed preoccupied with an urban milieu that in itself was incomprehensible to the western mind, but the processes involved ran counter to a deep-rooted assumption that there was something indecent about excessive introspection and the public display of intimate concerns. The cultural climate of the West was still heavily masculine, and although the existence of cultural values was readily conceded, their affirmation was not so much a matter of personal statement as of veiled and indirect gesture. The finer qualities of human life were rarely discussed in the abstract; one pointed rather to the conduct of ordinary people and let that stand witness to their greatness.

By the mid-twenties, Webb found himself straddling a cultural

fence between the rural world that he had known as a child and
the world of intellect and imagination that he had found through
books and that owed much to the cultural heartland in the East
and abroad. On the one hand lay a set of experiences that he valued, on the other a method of definition that refused to extend
itself across the gap. Not all his contemporaries felt the pull so
acutely; a man like De Voto could build his own bridges and defend them vigorously, and his friend Dobie was aware of both the
strengths and weaknesses of the regional preoccupation. While
acknowledging that it was vital for communities "to see significance
in the features of the land to which they belong, to make their environments more interesting to them, their past more alive, to bring
them to a realization of the values of their own cultural inheri-
tances . . . ,"[43] Dobie had few illusions about the quality of what
passed for a regional literature. Even as late as 1942, many books
seemed "to explore only the exteriors of life . . . the land is often
pictured as lonely, but the lone way of a human being's essential
self is not for this extrovert world. The banners of individualism
are carried high, but the higher individualism that grows out of
long looking for the meaning in the human drama is negligible . . .
these books . . . are not the stuff of life, not the distillation of mankind's 'agony and bloody sweat.' "[44] For Dobie, it was an easier
matter to move in both worlds and enjoy the benefits of both, and
that ease in turn made it likely that he would keep his literary
perspectives in order.

Webb, on the other hand, was far less convinced that the peaks
of achievement in his craft had already been scaled in other centuries and in other places; for him there was less reason to accept
warnings about the dangers of viewing a provincial setting from a
provincial standpoint. For his purposes, nothing could be better
than an outlook solidly grounded in the local context; that was the
world he understood, and throughout his life he was to remain
convinced that no easterner could ever know it in the way he did.
It was very much the kind of reservation which Walter Van Tilburg Clark tried to convey in a comment made just a few years before Webb's death:

> . . . most reviewing and critical comment, even when it strikes
> closest to my philosophical and technical intentions, somehow
> still has that urban and eastern quality, leaves the impression
> of coming from a mind that doesn't quite . . . believe in the

reality of a world in which man is so small on the landscape, and so aware of the fact, consciously or unconsciously, that the purely human elements of social complications and a sense of the traditional and historical—in the Jamesian way—can't seem to matter very much, though he often wants it to.[45]

8. Writing The Great Plains

BETWEEN LATE 1923 and mid-1927, Webb continued to experiment with short story writing and to work on his Ranger project; as he expected, the research for the one provided him with material for the other.[1] But the Ranger book that was to salvage his reputation after the setback at Chicago began to drift into the distance. Barker at first assumed that it would be finished in June 1924 and noted that it had already been accepted by Henry Holt and Company.[2] But, in July 1924, Webb reported that he was working hard on the project and that the end was in sight; two months later Barker expected the book to appear sometime in 1925.[3] In fact it was not to appear until 1935, and in the intervening period Webb had collaborated with Barker and William E. Dodd in producing a successful school textbook and had written *The Great Plains*; his interest remained constant, and he continued to collect material— but he had no strong desire to draw it together.[4] He regarded the original thesis as "a straight job of investigating and compiling which required no originality at all. Any historian could have done it, and it would have been pretty much the same regardless of who did it."[5]

But in studying the Rangers he gradually came across the elements that were basic to the Plains study. By mid-1927 he had worked out the general structure of *The Great Plains*, and by the end of the year he had a contract with Ginn and Company of Boston; the last months of 1927 and the first half of 1928 were devoted to writing, and a tentative first draft was ready in October of 1928. A completed first draft emerged nine months later, and the book was published in 1931. It is clear that the critical period was between 1923 and 1927, when the general thesis was developed and the approach was decided upon; what followed was the detailed elaboration and expansion of the argument. No major changes occurred between 1927 and the final publication in 1931.

Webb's own account, as given in the preface of the book and repeated on a number of occasions, places the origin of the work

rather earlier than this and emphasizes an incident in early 1922—
nearly six months before he went to Chicago. He had written some
articles on the activities of the Rangers in policing some of the
more riotous of the booming oil towns, and these were published
in an oil-promotion magazine.[6] It was easy enough to put the material together, given his interest in the Rangers and his rediscovered urge to write for popular journals and newspapers. But in the
course of preparing the articles he read Emerson Hough's *Way to
the West* and stumbled across the idea that he believed set him
thinking about the distinctive qualities of the Plains experience:

> . . . I came across his statement that the conquest of the West
> had been effected by four instruments, the horse, the boat, the
> axe, and the long rifle. It was a simple enough statement, and
> I knew enough to see its significance. I saw more, and saw
> that Hough had missed something. My study of the Texas
> Rangers had shown me that these men loved the sixshooter,
> used it constantly, and depended on it at all times. The cow-
> boys and the miners had done the same thing. Why had Hough
> missed it? He with all his knowledge of the West should have
> recognised it as an important factor. My background of wide
> reading came to my aid as I thought of the subject while the
> cold February rain pounded on the roof above. Then I saw
> something very clearly, the great western country, arid and
> treeless, as distinguished from the East with its rich forest of
> trees. The horse, yes, he was the mainstay of the pioneer peri-
> od. I had lived in the horse country. The plainsman was a
> horseman, and the sixshooter was the natural horseman's
> weapon. Of course, it was all clear, even the sharp line separat-
> ing forest and plain.[7]

Characteristically, Webb closed his account of the incident with a
reference to the problem of his identity as a professional: "I went
to the front of the house and told Jane 'I have been an imitator
and a copycat all my life, but now I have seen a truth, something
that no-one else that I know has seen.' "[8]
    One result of this revelation was the research into the history of
the Colt revolver and its impact on warfare on the Plains that provided the basis for an article which he sold to *Scribner's Magazine*
in 1922; Barker had seen and approved of the article and suggested
that it be placed with a general magazine rather than with a scholarly journal.[9] But it was five years before the article appeared, a fact
that became a source of continual embarrassment to Webb as his

friends asked for news of its fate.[10] Webb later regarded this article as the nucleus around which the larger Plains book began to grow, and in a very general sense this was probably true: the concept of technical adaptation that was to be central to the book had its first airing in the *Scribner's Magazine* article, and it provided a natural point of departure for the later studies of fencing and water supply.[11] But Webb was still some way from realizing the full range of the argument, much further than his later comments would suggest. The segments came together in bits and pieces rather than in the flash of intuition that Webb liked to stress.

The concept of adaptation was crucial, and by his own account Webb had begun to see its possibilities in early 1922; the concept of the Plains as a distinct environment supporting a culture of its own was equally crucial, but it took longer to coalesce. Hough's book had alerted him to what now seemed to be obvious physical differences between East and West and evoked for the first time a vision of a "sharp line separating forest and plain."[12] The image foreshadowed his later emphasis on the line of demarcation between East and West that he was to liken to a geological fault line; and it may have reminded him of the element of contrast that Keasbey had used to anchor his interpretation of European history.[13] But as yet he had only a limited impression of the distinctiveness of the Plains as a region, one that went no further than the generally accepted view of the Plains as unusually dry, treeless, and flat.[14] As yet he had no geological or geographical basis for his attitude toward the area, beyond those general assumptions, and he had only just begun to explore what the impact of such an environment on human institutions might be. If anything his starting point was a sociological one—a suspicion that there must be something important about the experience of his own people that marked them off from the general pattern of American life. The revolver gave him the idea of adaptation, and adaptation in turn led to further explorations of individual examples of change. But he had not yet reached the point of regarding the Plains as a total environment, one which had a massive impact on the social groups that came in contact with it.

The interest was there, but it was largely unfocused. In the months that followed his return from Chicago in late 1923, the Ranger study and the Hough controversy were uppermost in his mind; much of his thinking was concentrated on the need for a distinctive Texas literature and the possibility that he might be able to do something to help create it. His emotional attachment to his own state was never more acute—due in part to his reaction against his experience at Chicago and in part to the irritations produced by the Hough affair. In a letter to Rhodes in March 1924 he stressed the special qualities of the Texan experience:

> ... Texas not the West? It is the original West. It is also the North and the South. In Texas four cultural areas meet. That is why, in my opinion, this state offers such tremendous possibilities for fiction. . . . I have never been interested in East Texas, but that is possibly because I know so little about it. Those early Texans were the first Anglo-Americans to break into the Plains corridor. They were solving problems of cattle, horsemanship and horse Indians when the rest of America was still in the woods, and they did it while fighting Mexicans on the South and Indians, the Comanche devils, and at a time when they were dead broke.[15]

Although the notion of problem solving and adaptation was still in his thinking, his preoccupation with Texas and the Rangers tended to keep him from exploring the wider implications of the notion of the Plains as a corridor. His own account suggests that his discovery of Andy Adams's *Log of a Cowboy* not long after he had returned from Chicago set him thinking of the Plains in this context; by making him watch the movements of the cattle herds northward from Texas, Adams's account provided him with a rather different perspective on the area and strengthened the corridor concept. Whereas older treatments of the Plains had generally concentrated on the east-west crossing and tended to look on life there as something of an interlude or an aftermath of a wider pattern of development, Webb was now beginning to look at the area from the point of view of the north-south axis—and, from that perspective, the Plains began to take on a more distinctive character and a life of their own, independent of that of the East or the Midwest.[16]

It seems likely that by late 1924 Webb had a broad notion of the Plains as a region or corridor and an awareness that those who settled there found it necessary to make modifications to their way of life if they were to survive. He was already gathering information about fencing, and soon after he returned from Chicago the chance comments of an old friend reminded him of the windmills at Beeville and raised the whole question of the importance of water in making settlement possible. Again, the element of adaptation became evident, and the growing list of instances made it obvious that he had found a line of inquiry that would yield more useful material: between 1921 and 1924 he had opened up studies on the revolver, barbed wire, and windmills, arguing that in each case the peculiar problems of life in the Plains region had forced a distinctive technical response.[17] But it was not until early in 1927 that he began to make inquiries about the geological structure of the Plains and request information about weather conditions. This would suggest that his notion of the Plains as a complete environment with a uniform impact on social institutions developed during 1925/1926, and that it was during that period that he went back to Keasbey's idea of the dominating influence of the geographic base.

This expansion of the regional concept, with its emphasis on the Plains as an environment instead of simply a locale, provided Webb with the interpretive key he needed. His own account suggests that, after he found the first three instances of modification, he was confident that he would find the same degree of shift in any institution he cared to follow as it made the journey from the East to the Plains.[18] But he was anxious to find some single explanation that would account for the patterns he had noticed.

> In assembling the institutions and running the surveys out on the plains, I kept seeking for a solid foundation, something more substantial than documents, some compelling force that caused the modifications and adaptations I had noticed. This search took me to physical geography and geology and the precepts of environment that Keasbey had taught. . . . After all, the Plains was one, a whole, and if the region was to be understood, it must be understood as a whole. It was geography, climate, vegetation, zoology, anthropology, and finally the Anglo-American civilization and culture which had erected peculiar institutions on these foundations.[19]

The reference to Keasbey was no mere gesture: the eagerness to find a single interpretive key was reminiscent of Keasbey's outlook rather than of the multicausal approach of more orthodox historians—as was the implied comment on the value of documentary sources. But the shift toward the physical environment as the factor which compelled social institutions to bend to its demands was even more suggestive of Keasbey: the very categories Webb chose were those he had been taught to use as an undergraduate in institutional history.[20] Once he had found his "compelling force," his discovery of Willard D. Johnson's study of the geology of the

Plains provided him with the base he needed: "Johnson put the good earth of the Plains under my feet, and from him I went on to vegetation and strange animals, Indians and Spaniards, and finally to Anglo-Americans."[21] When he came to the latter, he found that John Wesley Powell's *Report on the Lands of the Arid Region of the United States* confirmed his suspicions regarding the inhibiting effects of climate and terrain.[22] By now there was no turning back: Webb was committed to the environmental emphasis, and everything he looked at from that point on took its place within the general framework.

At some point after the summer of 1924—and possibly as late as 1926—Webb made a number of entries in a notebook which suggest that he had worked out the outline of the argument that was later to appear in *The Great Plains*. He noted that what was novel about his approach was not its factual basis but the framework used—"the natural frame of environment."[23] Arguing for a full-blooded environmentalism just when geographers were abandoning the idea, he noted that "there is a law in human affairs higher than the law of man—it is the law of nature. It is the law that will—in the end—be obeyed."[24] In recent years historians had been too much bound by "the man made laws of documents" and had ignored the operation of natural forces; but the history of the trans–Mississippi West simply could not be written without reference to the land and its impact on human affairs.[25] "I do not mean to contend that writers have not recognised the land as a factor, but they have not followed the factor through or made the senthesis [*sic*] of all the phenomena, a synthesis which makes the life and story of the Plains essentially unified and harmonious."[26] Webb was careful to stress that the material he examined to verify and elaborate his view of the Plains was not in itself novel or unusual; much of it came from government reports of the type generally neglected by historians preoccupied with political and constitutional issues, and it was so accessible that he lived in fear of being beaten into print. Moreover, there was a good deal of discussion of the problems of pioneering in the popular magazines of the period, and a number of these articles came very close to developing Webb's notion of the impact of environment and the modification of technology.

Among those which Webb clipped and retained for reference as early as 1922 was George F. Parker's "Pioneer Methods," which stressed the importance of technology in the advance of the frontier. According to Parker—who seems to have been concerned mostly with Iowa—the pioneer was still "in leash to the forest" when he emerged onto the prairie, and "he could advance only as fast and as far as he and his followers were able to carry with them those cognate industries that would in due time enable him to add another mile strip to its occupied predecessors."[27] The prairie soils needed different plows and different methods of fencing, and the pioneer had to modify the skills he had perfected in the forest and to "utilize every machine whether it was old or so new that it had been hurriedly designed to meet some particular emergency."[28]

The same stress on the woodsman's ability to adapt and turn technology to his advantage appeared in Herbert Quick's *One Man's Life*, which appeared in serial form in *Saturday Evening Post* in 1925.[29] Webb admired Quick's work and quoted from it in *The Great Plains*, but though it was far more perceptive than many of the autobiographies and reminiscences that began to make their way into the magazines in those years, it stopped short of the full-scale treatment that Webb planned for the Plains area.[30] Others were making the right kinds of generalization, usually based on personal experience; but Webb knew where to find the data to support them and make them applicable to the entire region, and he had the one central generalization clear in his mind since his days as an undergraduate—in those two elements lay his advantage.

By early 1927 the urge to demonstrate that there was something distinctive and worthy about the Plains experience had found an outlet; geography had become the key that brought many disparate elements into focus and provided a satisfying framework for their display. Once he was sure of the essential unity of the Plains, Webb could move his theory out of the social fabric in which he found it and ground it on the firmer basis of physical geography; from there he could trace the evolution of human society on the Plains, using the findings of ethnology and anthropology to buttress the argument for the molding of social forms by their physical setting, and eventually establish the truth of the assumption that had been his original starting point. Now there was unity and cohesion: the main theory had been blocked in, and it remained only to fill in the confirmatory detail.

If this is an accurate representation of the germination of Webb's interpretation of the Plains experience, it does not necessarily explain the evolution of the book itself. Webb recalled that by chance he met Ginn and Company's college representative, George H. Moore, in early 1927, that he discussed with Moore his plans for a study of the Plains, and that a contract was signed shortly after.[31]

If Webb's recollection was correct, Moore did not fully understand what was involved; he apparently reported to his superiors that Webb was engaged on the Ranger book and that he was planning a series of monographs dealing with aspects of Plains history. In March 1927 Dr. A. C. Thurber of Ginn and Company wrote to Webb to suggest that he defer the Ranger book and concentrate on a one-volume study of the Plains that would bring his ideas together and constitute a major contribution to western history.[32]

It is difficult to determine whether or not Thurber's suggestion was instrumental in turning Webb away from the idea of a series of studies of the Colt revolver type or whether Webb had already decided on an integrated study. In late February 1927 Webb forwarded a copy of the long-delayed *Scribner's Magazine* article on the revolver to William E. Dodd in Chicago, describing it as the first of a series of articles in which he intended to develop his own interpretation of the history of the West.[33] A few days earlier he had written to Clark Wissler, curator of anthropology at the American Museum of Natural History in New York, describing an article he had prepared on the use of the horse in the western regions; apparently Webb hoped to have this published in *Scribner's Magazine* also.[34] In late June he raised the possibility of a series of biographies with Dodd and received the promise of a couple of short sketches by the end of the summer—plus a reminder that it was time that he came back to Chicago and finished his degree.[35] Apparently Dodd had no idea that Webb was planning a major book on the Plains, for he devoted some effort to convincing his former student that he should write a major study of the cattle kingdom.[36] By October, another magazine article had appeared, this time dealing with a buffalo hunt in Texas; though less pertinent to his overall view of the Plains than his earlier study of the revolver, it indicated his interest in bringing out a series of articles on topics related to the Plains.[37]

Under the circumstances it seems likely that Thurber had been given a fairly accurate account of Webb's plans; after years of work on the Ranger book, Webb could hardly drop that project and begin work on a new book without some indication that it would be published—especially since the Ranger book was also to be his thesis for the degree at Chicago. Each year his failure to complete the work and regularize his position in the department became more of a problem, and it would have been tactless for him to have dropped abruptly a long-standing project. The suggestion by Thurber may have encouraged him to think in terms of a book rather than a se-

ries of smaller studies—or Webb may have been shrewd enough to
bait the hook in the hope of getting such an invitation and the contract it implied.[38] There can be little doubt that he was anxious to
have a major work published, and the eagerness with which he took
up Thurber's proposal suggests that he had already given the idea
a good deal of thought.

Thurber's argument was a shrewd one, stressing both the professional and commercial advantages of a single volume over a scattered series of articles; the latter approach would simply make it
easy for others to capitalize on the results of his work and divest
him of a good deal of the credit. On the other hand, once the major
work had appeared, sections of it could be used for popular magazine articles. If Webb accepted the proposal, Thurber would undertake to promote the work as "one of the most significant contributions to Western history since Turner's memorable book."[39] A
month later Webb apparently raised the possibility of completing the Ranger book first, and Thurber argued against it; by July
Webb had agreed that the Plains book should take priority and
mentioned that he hoped to use William G. Sumner's *Folkways* as
something of a model.[40] By late August Webb had received a draft
contract and the project was underway.[41]

During the discussions with Thurber, Webb sought the advice of
his friend Albert Trombly and apparently outlined the form the
book would take. Judging by Trombly's reply, very little of what
was eventually to appear in the book was missing from the outline:
the most obvious omissions were any reference to the Plains Indians and to the problem of water law.[42] It was not until the following year that Webb began to seek information on Indian sign language, and the relevance of changes in water law was the last aspect
of the work to catch his attention, in 1928.[43] Similarly, the attempt
to relate the development of western literature to the problems of
the physical environment did not come until 1928, though there
can be little doubt that he had been interested in the idea for a
much longer period. It was only after the larger work was under
way that he hit upon a method of approaching this segment of the
argument.

The last months of 1927 and the first half of 1928 were devoted
almost exclusively to research and writing. He had been relieved of
some of his teaching responsibilities, the Ranger project was defi-
nitely shelved, and he was now able to devote his full attention to
the Plains study. His working methods appear to have been rather
unusual; he did not accumulate the extensive system of note cards

and files of material that Frederic L. Paxson or Turner took for granted, and there are virtually no research notes as such in his papers. His method was to have the books he needed sent to him en masse from the university library and to mark the sections he needed by inserting pieces of paper in the volumes. When he was ready to draft a chapter, he followed his system of markers around the room and took what he needed. Then the cycle was repeated as he moved on to the next chapter, collected the books he needed, made the insertions, and then after some weeks got down to writing again.[44]

In five months he had a tentative draft complete, and it was presumably this draft that he sent to G. H. Moore at Ginn and Company in October 1928 with the stipulation that it be regarded as a guide for marketing purposes only and not used as a basis for appraisal by the editorial staff.[45] Nearly a year after he had signed the contract, he was opening up new material on water law and irrigation—topics that had not caught his attention until after he had commenced the first draft. Then the progress of the work slowed down; he had hoped to have a first draft ready by March of 1929 and became alarmed when he heard that Louis Pelzer at the University of Iowa was working on a similar book which might pre-empt the field.[46] Despite the fact that his manuscript was still incomplete, Webb began to press his publishers for assurance that the book would receive priority treatment as soon as it was submitted. Moore did his best to calm his nervous author and stressed the need for thorough work rather than speed. The first complete draft reached Boston in either June or July of 1929, and the book was published in the summer of 1931.[47]

The writing of *The Great Plains* was obviously a therapeutic experience for Webb, allowing him to release many of the emotional pressures that had irritated him for so long and to enjoy the satisfaction of knowing that at last he had found both his subject and the medium to explore it. But it was also an imaginative exercise that gave full play to his creative instincts and his urge to identify with the life of his father's generation—as he had when he first read Adams's *Log of a Cowboy* in late 1923. He stated: ". . . few books have touched my imagination as this one did. I had seen these men, the trail drivers, eating, drinking and making merry in San Antonio, and now I saw them as young men starting the herd from the Rio Grande . . . For days I lived with the herd, swam the river, travelled by moonlight and suffered with them on the dry drive, a miniature of which I had seen in Stephens County. All the time, with the tunes of San Antonio in my ears, the snatch of cowboy song rang through my head."[48]

From Adams's vivid depiction of an individual cattle drive, Webb's imagination branched out rapidly to recognize "the sweep and magnitude of the Great Plains, that 'broad floor of the world,' " aware that here was a vast and exciting panorama that cried out for graphic portrayal—and, until now, in vain.[49] By late 1927, with his contract signed and a leave of absence in sight, he was ready for the plunge into a theme that for the first time provided his creative urge with a full measure of substance:

> I was living in imagination on the Plains. Never before or since have I worked with such intensity and joy. I lived in a mental cocoon which I had spun about myself through imagination, *building a world into which all the pieces seemed to fit.* I was working creatively as well as historically, breaking a lot of precedents. . . . The people around me were not the real people. The real people were those who were hunting buffalo, fighting Comanches, going up the campaign trails, migrating to the Pacific by the Oregon, California and Santa Fe trails, dry farming, and hunting for water.[50] (Emphasis mine.)

This romantic identification with his Anglo forebears developed a deeper mood when he began to explore the physical environment that preceded them and against which they and others had struggled: "The whole country took on all its dimensions and I could range over it at will both chronologically and geographically from the time Coronado first saw it and before down to the present time, *and I felt at home at any time and at any place*" (emphasis mine).[51]

The same note of high excitement dominated Webb's descriptions of that period in late 1927 when the book began to take shape, and at no other point in his writing career did the exhilaration show through to such a degree. His later books gave him satisfaction, but they did not yield that sense of having found himself, of having seen imagination and intellect harnessed together to produce something that pacified inner tensions and enriched his own sense of identity. For it was not just the ability to let his imagination run freely that fascinated him but the realization that he had circled back to the events and impressions of his childhood, and that in doing so he had found meaning for the elements that had formed his own personality and framed his awareness of the world around him. In later years he was fond of remarking that he began his research for the book at the age of four, and constant repetition made that comment an accepted starting point for discussions of the genesis of the work. Yet the implications of the remark are perhaps wider than they appear at first sight, for Webb had realized that he had at last found the element that had eluded him in his earlier attempts to find himself as a western writer—the element of personal experience that seemed so essential if he were to capture the spirit of an age and render it in authentic tones. Now imagination and intellect, memory and personal experience were working in harmony. "I had seen the things that I now studied, the land, the vegetation, and the animals . . . I had seen the covered wagons go west, and return, . . . broken by drought and disaster and knew how the sound of rain on the roof made men so happy that they had to shout and laugh and go out in it to be drenched to hide the fact that they were almost crying."[52]

Though he had caught only a glimpse of that era as it passed into oblivion, that glimpse was enough to sear his consciousness and establish his credentials as a commentator on the age and its values. The balding, bespectacled academic at his desk in Garrison Hall had found himself a place in the history of the West—though the need to underline that point for the benefit of others would lead him to make constant reference to his childhood experiences in speeches and lectures for years after. Just as the question of the environment provided the key to his interpretation of the Plains, the same concept provided the answer to his own problem of identity: the environment was constant, and he had lived in the same setting and under the same influences as those of the pioneering generation—and it was that fact that gave him a claim to authenticity. Now he had found the link between his experience of life and the formal patterns of research, and the two aspects of his existence blended together harmoniously: "Thus it came about all through my youth that I absorbed by experience bits of isolated knowledge of the country and came to understand the spirit of its people. When I approached it through books, I found myself dealing with familiar things which now took on integral meaning and made an integral part of the whole."[53]

9. Raising the Flag

THE FINAL VERSION of *The Great Plains* appeared in print in the summer of 1931, and Webb waited to see whether the work that had so caught his own imagination would meet with the approval of a wide audience. For a man whose academic prospects had been under a cloud for nearly a decade, the critical test would be the reception the book received in the key national journals, the *American Historical Review* and the *Mississsippi Valley Historical Review*. In both cases he had cause for immediate satisfaction. Frederic L. Paxson reacted favorably to the work, describing it as the first detailed study of one of Turner's sections, and, while the historian Robert G. Caldwell described the earlier parts of the book as largely a synthesis of existing materials, he saw the treatment of the more recent transformation of the Plains as breaking new ground.[1] Webb could take heart from the tone of both reviews and those which eventually appeared in the smaller periodicals and the daily press; invariably, commentators seemed to have been attracted by the sweep of the book and the deftness with which its major thesis had been argued. After so much frustration and uncertainty, Webb now found himself in the happy situation of having his first book cited as a distinctive and important contribution to the writing of American history.

Apart from anything else, the structure of the book was certain to attract attention. Webb had an argument to present, one which was very close to his personal concerns, and he pressed it on the reader with unusual persistence and a good deal of skill. Time and again the reader was taken back to the central thesis and reminded of the line of argument being pursued and buttressed at every turn. Very little material which was not relevant to the basic proposition managed to find its way into the book, and—as Caldwell noted with some puzzlement in his review—Webb ignored or cut back many of the themes that one would have expected to find in a regional history: there was no really systematic treatment of the exploration of the Plains, or of the establishment of settlements, or even the development of territorial and state political sysems within the region. When any of these topics did enter into Webb's account, they did so not on their own merits but because they contributed some element to the overall environmental emphasis. Party politics, the careers of influential citizens, and the economic history of individual states were virtually ignored. Webb's framework of investigation was so markedly different from the conventional patterns that a new designation seemed to be required; even Paxson was uncertain as to how to classify *The Great Plains* and, after deciding that it was neither history nor sociology, opted for geography as the most likely parent.

Webb's basic concern was to demonstrate that in broad terms the United States could be divided along the line of the ninety-eighth meridian into two major regions, each with a distinctive geographic environment and supporting a cultural edifice which reflected the special qualities of that environment. The march of American civilization westward during the first two hundred and fifty years of settlement had taken place within the context of a geographic setting characterized in the main by adequate supplies of water and timber. The techniques needed to master the wilderness and bring new lands into cultivation were developed within that framework and were entirely appropriate to it; but when the westward movement reached the vicinity of the ninety-eighth meridian, it encountered an environment so radically different that it hesitated, drew back, and then bypassed the entire region to establish bridgeheads in more amenable locations along the Pacific coast. Only in the years following the Civil War was a second attempt mounted against this vast central region. The obstacles were so formidable that success depended on the capacity of individuals and groups to adapt their techniques of pioneering to the new situation and on the availability of a new technology to assist that adaptation and counteract specific environmental hazards.

It was a remarkably bold and sweeping thesis, which made serious inroads into prevailing assumptions about the nature of the western experience and required a considerable playing down of the obvious contrasts and variations within each of these very broad regional designations. At the same time, the element of contrast between the two great regions on either side of the ninety-eighth meridian had to be heavily emphasized to give greater force to the concept of major changes in institutional patterns once that midway point had been reached, for it was the degree of divergence from eastern norms which provided Webb with his measure of a distinctive Plains experience. Here the elements of Webb's early training under Keasbey merged neatly with his concern to establish a special place for his own region and its people within—but distinct from—the overall American experience.

To present the vast area from the line of demarcation to the Pacific coast as one homogeneous environment obviously meant taking some liberties with accepted geographical concepts, and in the early chapters of *The Great Plains* Webb tried to establish the strengths and limitations of his definition. Arguing that for his purposes the three critical elements which defined the region were the presence of comparatively level terrain, the absence of forests, and a subhumid climate, Webb conceded that only in the High Plains were all three factors operating; but flanking this core were marginal areas extending as far east as parts of Illinois and Wisconsin, and as far west as the southern portion of the Pacific slope.[2] In these areas, at least two of the three defining characteristics were present in combination, and the effect was to produce virtually the same environmental pressures as in the central core. To Webb, this in turn justified the incorporation within his definition of the Plains environment of extensive tracts of relatively humid prairie in the east, together with the mountainous areas to the west. Areas which were both forested and humid—in particular, parts of the Pacific slope—were obviously excluded.

Although each of these elements was significant in its own right, it was the question of their combined impact on living forms which related most directly to Webb's special concerns. The animal life of the Plains seemed to provide specific evidence of adaptation of a kind quite different from that of the woodland region. The great speed of the antelope and its method of signaling danger to its fellows suggested special adjustments to the risks of life in open and level country; similarly, the habits of the jackrabbit and the prairie dog suggested adaptation to open space and a shortage of surface water. Even the grasses, which sustained most of the animal life on the Plains, reflected in their makeup the distinctive nature of the environment and at the same time characterized the entire region: "Grass is the visible feature that distinguishes the Plains from the desert. Grass grows, has its natural habitat, in the transition area between timber and desert . . . the history of the Plains is the history of the grasslands. Civilization develops on level ground."[3] But European civilization had developed in forested regions and lacked the techniques to cope with a Plains environment. On the other hand, the Plains Indians had learnt by hard experience not only how to survive but also how to build a flourishing culture by integrating their social and economic system with their physical setting; so successful did they become that in time they themselves constituted an element of the Plains environment, the one which more than any other stood in the way of white penetration. The fact that their culture differed so markedly from that of their counterparts in the woodland region amounted to one more indication of the way in which the Plains forced groups to alter their patterns of living and conform to new and difficult pressures.[4]

Again, it was not the Indian culture that attracted Webb's attention but the evidence from within that culture of successful adaptation and innovation. Here he could point to the transformation of a nomadic, nonagricultural people, eking out an existence by hunting and using dogs as beasts of burden, into a proud and formidable aristocracy of the Plains. The introduction of the horse in the sixteenth century was the key to that transformation; made mobile and independent by the ease with which they could now exploit the vast herds of buffalo, the Plains Indians developed a military system which entitled them to be ranked with the great horse cultures of Europe and Asia through the centuries.[5] Their physical conformation, their weapons, and even their value system—all reflected the preeminence of the horse in their culture, and it was because the animal fitted so precisely into the requirements of Plains life that the Indians valued it so highly. Finally, Webb could point to a very specific instance of adaptation within the Indian culture: sign language, which the Plains tribes had developed to a high degree of effectiveness, provided a method of communication over distance which suited the special problems of a flat and open landscape.

The fact that the Plains Indians were able to utilize the resources of their region so effectively meant that they were able to deny access to the Plains until their techniques were matched and then overcome by superior technology. The Spanish, who made the first challenge, were unable either to modify their institutions or to produce mechanical devices to help counteract the military superiority of the Plains Indians. Although it had a long record of conquest and exploitation behind it, the Spanish imperial system failed to master the Plains because it was designed to probe for mineral wealth and utilize the labor of subjugated Indians in its extraction; realizing their limitations, the Spanish were content to rest their boundary at the very edge of the Plains.[6] The task of confronting and dispossessing the Indians eventually fell to the new wave of invaders driving west from Anglo-America in the first half of the nineteenth century. Even then, however, the Indians outlasted the Spanish and were still very much in command of the situation when the first thrusts from the east began to test their defenses.

According to Webb, the development of the revolver eventually reversed the balance of power in favor of the white man by countering the highly effective use of the bow and arrow by skilled and resourceful warriors; but the fact that technical superiority had been achieved even before the Civil War did not mean that the Anglo-American had easy access to the region.[7] Apart from its Indian defenders, the Plains environment still presented formidable resistance, and Webb placed considerable emphasis on the way in which the Cotton Kingdom, which had carried all before it in its decades of expansion into the Old Southwest, stalled abruptly when confronted by the difficulty of coping with the terrain and climate beyond the ninety-eighth meridian.[8] Only in the North did one variant of the Anglo-American civilization make any inroads into the Plains environment, and that movement was in turn something of a departure from the norm: the line of advance was not uniform, and some had already recoiled from the task when they realized that they faced problems which could not be resolved with the resources at their disposal.

For nearly fifty years, the flow of westward settlement had circled around and beyond the Plains to concentrate on expanding the communities established on the Pacific coast. Only in the decades following the Civil War did established farming communities —the nineteenth century's measure of the conquest of the wilderness—begin to spread across the Plains. Before they could do so, Anglo-American civilization had already managed to develop a special fragment peculiarily suited to the penetration of the Plains environment and to mesh into it special characteristics. The cattle kingdom, though ephemeral, displayed precisely the kind of adaptation and ingenuity that had served the Indian so well. By learning to manage cattle in a way that conformed to the realities of climate and terrain, the white man evolved "the most natural economic and social order . . . yet developed in his experiment with the Great Plains."[9] To Webb, the cattle kingdom was more than simply a stage in the economic history of the West; all his nostalgia for the masculine world of horses and cattle drives, and the value system that went with it, welled up in his account of the "rise and fall of what might have been a Plains civilization, the happy epi-

sode in the history of the Great Plains . . ."[10] Short-lived though it
was, the cattle kingdom proved that the Plains environment was
bound to produce a civilization "unlike anything previously known
to the Anglo-European-American experience."[11] Even in decline,
it stood as a witness to the contrast between East and West: the inability of lawmakers in the East to comprehend the special needs
and problems of the cattlemen meant that the cattle kingdom would
be undermined and unable to survive the impact of the industrial
revolution.

Up to that point, the only groups to achieve a satisfactory adjustment to the demands of life on the Plains—the Indians and the
cattlemen—had succeeded because they altered their mode of life
and learned to exploit more efficiently existing resources, such as
the buffalo and the longhorn cattle. Any attempt to change the
basis of occupation and exploitation of the Plains from a pastoral
to an agricultural framework required the prior development of a
technology capable of circumventing specific environmental hazards. Just as the Colt revolver reduced the military effectiveness of
the mounted Indian before the Civil War, technical innovations
made possible by the growth of industry in the postwar period
made it possible for the farmer to function without the need for
timber fencing and assured supplies of surface water. Barbed wire
and the windmill rectified these deficiencies and reduced at least
some of the risk associated with farming in a dry climate. Technology had already made possible the railroad system which
spanned the Plains in the decades following the Civil War and
brought settlers direct to their parcels of land; but without water
and fencing, no amount of hard work and self-discipline could
make large tracts of the Great Plains productive. Moreover, those
who hoped to take advantage of the new technology had to modify
their social institutions to bring them in line with changing circumstances; in particular, the whole question of the acquisition and
tenure of land, together with the legal arrangements relating to
water rights, came under review.[12] Wherever social institutions de-
vised to meet the needs of a civilization operating in a forested and
humid region proved inappropriate to the Plains situation, those
most affected began to press for change; shifts in government attitudes toward the control of water resources and the alienation of
the public demain were to be regarded as the result of such pressures. By the end of the nineteenth century adaptation had become
a conscious and deliberate activity, involving both those who lived
in the region and knew its problems at first hand and the specialists

who were now beginning to collect the data needed for the development of policy at the national level.

By this stage, Webb had taken his account of the Plains experience up to the point where it began to intersect with his boyhood years in the Cross Timbers, the area which he used as an example of the line of demarcation between his two great regions.[13] By emphasizing the enormous difficulties generations of would-be settlers had faced in trying to establish themselves on the Plains, he invariably heightened the impact of their eventual success. Those of Webb's generation who had firsthand experience of life in the region could now identify with a process that had been working itself out over several centuries and which appeared to owe little or nothing to either the East or distant Europe. Its roots were close at hand, in the earth and sky they had known since childhood, and it invested the apparently drab lives of their forebears with historical importance and meaning. In a region as extensive and as sparsely populated as the Plains, the group experience had inevitably become fragmented and isolated; Webb's achievement had been to pull this experience together again and establish it as a coherent and distinct phase within the broader American framework.

But even with that task completed to his satisfaction, there remained one loose end to be taken into account. During the half-century which separated Webb from those early years in the Cross Timbers, a considerable body of literature had accumulated around certain facets of the pioneering experience in the West, and both his early training under Keasbey and his long-standing interest in literature made it unlikely that Webb would exclude the imaginative element from the discussion. He had always resented the way that the life of the cattle kingdom had been distorted by pulp novelists and film producers; yet, at the same time, he found it intriguing that easterners were eager to use the West as a form of escape from the drab routine of urban life. So in the final stages of *The Great Plains* he took pains to stress that the cattle kingdom was in reality the kind of social experience that deserved to be enshrined in an authentic literary tradition and that, if easterners would only look past the insipid and romantic fiction of Zane Grey and his kind, they would find the core of such a literature already in existence in the work of Rhodes, Adams, and Hough. These writers would then at last receive the recognition to which they were entitled.[14]

By emphasizing the literature of the cattle kingdom, Webb did concede that there was as yet no substantial body of literature focused on the experience of the arid Plains—with the notable exception of Ole E. Rölvaag's *Giants in the Earth*. On the other hand, there was already a great deal of fiction based on the experience of communities in the Prairie Plains, most of it emphasizing the brutal tedium of farm life and realistic in the extreme. Hamlin Garland's novels evoked the memory of a common farming background which lay not too distant from many city dwellers; but by contrast, across the ninety-eighth meridian, lay a region whch had become a source of romantic legends, a kind of medieval world with its mounted knights and tales of valor—all far removed from the contemporary world of factories and urban living. In the contrast between the two literary traditions, Webb had one more example of the way in which cultural responses differed according to the physical setting in which they were grounded.[15]

Contrast, difference, change at the ninety-eighth meridian—the theme which was hammered home at every opportunity—stood at the core of Webb's argument. This way of looking at history went back to his days as an undergraduate under Keasbey, when his class papers asserted that each geographic environment produced its own civilization and that, in probing the conflicts between such civilizations, it was critical to remember that the basic principle was "unlikeness, or contrast . . ."[16] In the final stages of *The Great Plains* he came back to the point and tried to give it a broader theoretical basis: "In history the differences are more important than the similarities. When one makes a comparative study of the sections, the dominant truth which emerges is expressed in the word *contrast*."[17]

It was an important doctrine for a scholar determined to find the roots of a culture in the local soil and to minimize the element of continuity with the parent civilization; yet, in spite of his emphasis, reviewers were slow to see the point. By placing *The Great Plains* broadly within the Turner approach to the history of the West, Frederic Paxson unwittingly imposed a label which Webb would almost certainly have preferred to avoid.[18] Throughout his career Webb insisted that his own approach to the study of the West had developed quite independently and that he owed little or nothing to Turner's ideas. On at least one occasion, he claimed that he had not read Turner's essay on the significance of the frontier until after he had written *The Great Plains*—although as far back as 1924 he had made reference to the frontier essay in a review of Paxson's *History of the American Frontier*, and a set of typewritten notes on Turner are filed with his lecture notes as a student.[19] But the point that he wished to make, without appearing to be ungracious toward a scholar who had done so much to make the study of the West respectable, was simply that the experience of the Anglo-American beyond the ninety-eighth meridian was not merely a continuation of the processes Turner had discussed but something qualitatively different.[20]

Any automatic identification of Webb with the Turner school seemed to indicate that the basic thesis of *The Great Plains* had not been adequately grasped and that his efforts to distinguish the Plains frontier from the woodlands frontier had miscarried. From the perspective of the Plains, Turner's theories were highly appropriate to the experience of the pioneers as they pushed their way through the humid east; but once the forest zone had been left behind and settlement moved into an area of rainfall deficiency, new conditions prevailed, and these in turn required a new framework of explanation. The very imagery Webb chose to introduce his account of the American approach to the Great Plains suggests something of the distance he wanted to place between the general view of western history and his own approach. In a scene reminiscent of Turner's observer at the Cumberland Gap, Webb placed his reader on the ninety-eighth meridian, at the intersection with the thirty-first parallel, and asked him to visualize a nation of people emerging from the humid forest region and advancing toward the Plains; inevitably they failed at the first attempt to enter the Plains environment and fell back to lick their wounds and devise the modifications in their pioneering techniques which the new situation made necessary.[21] It was an image that stressed a unique process of adaptation and innovation which would not simply be subsumed within Turner's general commentary on the frontier experience.

If Paxson was a little wide of the mark in this respect, he came rather closer in trying to place the work within the context of current trends in the study of geography. Noting that it was difficult to know whether the book should be classified as either history or sociology, he wondered if it owed something to "that new form of geography that embraces the human occupant as well as the land upon which he lives."[22] If this remark referred to the concept of geography as human ecology developed by Harlan Barrows in the 1920's, Paxson had linked Webb to the wrong strain of geographic theory. Barrows' concept amounted to a revolt against the environmental emphasis in which Webb had been schooled; yet it could be argued that Webb had unwittingly moved a good deal closer to the new approach, with its stress on man's adjustment to his environment rather than on the impact of the environment on man.[23]

However, there is nothing to indicate that Webb was aware of the shifts in geographic theory in the 1920's or, for that matter, in developments in geographic thinking at any other point. Accordingly, he could straddle several points of view without realizing it and remain unaware of any inconsistency. One consequence of his rather eclectic approach to theory was that other scholars were to be as puzzled as Frederic Paxson when it came to locating Webb along any scale in terms of geographic thought: an approach to history which the sociologist Read Bain would characterize as within the geographic determinist school could be cited by the historian Allan Nevins in later years as a significant departure from the Ratzel/Huntington tradition and a demonstration of man's ability to break down geographic controls.[24]

But it was for others to quibble over such technicalities; the task was now complete, and the last months of 1931 found Webb at the threshold of what was to be one of the most satisfying periods of his life. His book was on sale, the early reactions were favorable, and the memory of his early disappointment was fresh enough to make vindication all the more enjoyable. He had been teaching summer school in North Carolina when the book came off the press, and before returning to Austin he took his family north to Boston; he drove through Virginia to Washington and then on to New York—a city which, against all odds, was to become one of his favorites. Though he had visited Baltimore and Washington on his way home from Wisconsin in 1916, he had not traveled to any extent in the upper South or the Northeast, so the trip was something of a novelty. Then in Boston he met Dr. Thurber for the first time and found himself enjoying the fruits of success: a major review of the book appeared in the *New York Times* while he was in Boston, and Webb noted with considerable satisfaction that in conversation Thurber bracketed *The Great Plains* with one of the firm's earlier successes—Sumner's *Folkways*, the book which Webb had used as a model when discussing the format of his own work with Thurber several years before.[25] The family then returned to Austin and settled back into the familiar routine of teaching and what Webb referred to as "the drudgery of straight history."[26]

There was one additional pleasure in store after he returned to his classes, one that Webb was to savor especially: Barker and his colleagues had decided that, rather than try to persuade him to return to Chicago—as Dodd still advised—they would suggest that the book be regarded as fulfilling the requirements of a doctoral thesis at Austin. The proposal was accepted, Webb took a course in anthropology to satisfy the remaining technicalities, and the whole untidy episode was at last closed in 1932—nearly ten years after the journey to Chicago.[27] The last barrier to his promotion was now out of the way, and, although Webb was careful to stress that he had not asked for the concession, the victory was clearly his: by sheer obstinacy he had forced the system to bend as he felt it should, and he had made very few concessions of his own—save the acceptance of delays in promotion.

There was no longer any doubt about his status in the department; the general effect of Paxson's review and those of lesser-known figures was to firmly establish Webb's reputation as a specialist in American history and as something of an innovator in interdisciplinary research. With this new prestige and the seniority he had built up by sheer length of association, Webb could now move up to join the tight-knit group of professors who constituted "the Old Department" during the Barker era. He was already casting about for ways of building on the success of the Plains book; he apparently discarded an earlier plan to write a history of the Texas Grange and then became interested in a biography of John Wesley Powell.[28] He also attempted to obtain funding for a project that would gather material dealing with the Plains and lay the basis for a collection as extensive as the existing holdings of southern and Latin American material in the University of Texas library; now that he had status and a clearly defined field, he could ask for the departmental backing and financial assistance that went with his new position.[29]

The two books that he produced over the next five years were themselves an indication that he was no longer working under the pressure of academic preferment. The first was his long-postponed history of the Texas Rangers, a less ambitious book than *The Great Plains* but one that satisfied the urge to get something into print from the mass of material he had collected over the years—and at the same time fulfilled his obligations to the many people who had supplied him with information and were expecting to see a full-scale account in print.[30] He found it hard to go back to the Ranger book after the excitement of the Plains study; the material seemed "dull and uninteresting," possibly because he could not find the framework that would give it cohesion.[31] The institutional approach simply did not work out as he had hoped years earlier, and eventually he fell back on the only connecting thread he could find—the personal exploits of the Ranger captains.[32] But the book appeared in time for the Texas centenary in 1936 and went on to earn him an unexpected windfall of $11,000 in film rights.[33] His second work from this period, *Divided We Stand*, grew out of Webb's interest in current economic trends as they affected the South; an unusual book in many ways, it reflected his independence of normal academic restraints.

The onset of the Depression did not mean much of a dislocation in Webb's personal life; he had a moderate salary—though subject to the cuts made necessary by the Depression—and an additional source of income from the sale of his textbooks. More important in the long run was the fact that the lean years gave him the opportunity to lay the basis for the substantial holding of real estate that he had accumulated by the time of his death in 1963.[34] In part, he was following a well-established practice among the senior professors of his day; Eugene Barker and others had long supplemented their modest university salaries by investment in real estate and rental property, and some made a considerable amount of money from their operation. Webb quickly became a skilled investor in land, and his success reinforced his belief in the value of local ties and an interest in the world immediately outside one's doorstep. By the time he left with his family for his first overseas visit in 1938, his financial prospects looked good, and he had every reason to be satisfied with his station in life; for a man whose personal life was still basically lonely and restricted, such reassurances of success and good standing were important.

The invitation to teach for a year at the University of London in 1938 indicated that, despite his ill-starred beginnings in the academic world, he had now reached that point where the tangible fruits of success accrue without much further effort. He had earlier been invited to Harvard to teach summer school, and now his reputation had stretched abroad. The effects of the year abroad are difficult to gauge, though it seems likely that they were less marked than they might have been had he gone much earlier; he was now fifty, his intellectual patterns were to a large extent fixed, and, although he could use the impressions he formed in Europe to expand the framework of his ideas, their basic character was no longer subject to modification. But there can be little doubt about the value he placed on the fact that he now received such invitations and the status that went with them.

By the time he resumed his normal routine in Austin, another accolade seemed to have come his way. In 1937 a report presented to the Social Science Research Council by its Policy Review Committee noted that over the years the council had neglected its critical and analytical role and had concentrated too heavily on the promotion of research. To meet this criticism, the council appointed a Committee on Appraisal, and at its first meeting in early 1938 the new committee decided to carry out a systematic probe of selected works in the social sciences in the hope of determining what were the most significant recent developments in research methods. Leading scholars were asked to submit lists of studies in their field that could be regarded as particularly important, and from these lists the committee chose six books for detailed examination.[35] Webb suddenly found *The Great Plains* listed alongside Franz Boas's *Primitive Art*, Adolph A. Berle, Jr., and G. C. Means's *The Modern Corporation and Private Property*, and William I. Thomas and Florian Znaniecki's *The Polish Peasant in Europe and America* and ranked by his professional colleagues as one of the most significant contributions toward interdisciplinary research since the end of World War I.

But his pleasure at the selection was short-lived. The Committee on Appraisal had indicated that it proposed to send each book chosen to a specialist for a detailed appraisal and then to have the appraisal, the book itself, and the author's comments discussed by a relatively small group of scholars drawn from a variety of fields within the social sciences. *The Great Plains* was sent to Professor Fred Shannon of the University of Illinois, and when Webb received his copy of the formal appraisal, the comfortable world he had built up over the past eight years began to disintegrate; the appraisal amounted to a full-scale indictment of the work, and Webb reacted bitterly to both the tone and the method of the critique.

Yet in the long run, he absorbed this reverse much more effectively than the previous one at Chicago; though he resented the attack, his foundations were now far more secure and his sense of accomplishment provided more of a protective shield. Although tempted to have nothing to do with the conference, and having notified the committee that he refused to acknowledge the appraisal as a valid exercise, he eventually agreed to travel into what was now clearly enemy territory and to defend his book against what he felt to be a vicious attack. Given his personal stake in the image of the Plains experience he had so carefully constructed, the confrontation could hardly be a pleasant one.

10. Defending the Redoubt

SHANNON'S APPRAISAL was to become something of a classic in its day, and its echoes were to run through the ranks of the profession for many years afterward. The episode reawakened Webb's suspicion of orthodox historians and strengthened his inclination to have as little as possible to do with them; though he made contact with Shannon again in the late 1950's, when both men were near the end of their careers and could look back on the incident with a certain amount of detachment, the scars of the original encounter took many years to heal.

Given Shannon's background as an agricultural historian with a special interest in the post–Civil War years, it was inevitable that he would find some deficiencies in Webb's treatment of farming techniques on the Plains; but he brought to the task of appraisal a massive respect for factual accuracy and an acid turn of phrase. The hundred-odd pages of criticism he presented began with a careful tribute to Webb's pioneering attempt to apply "a combined geographical and technological interpretation to a phase of American history," and he commended his breadth of approach: the concept Webb had set out to prove was a magnificent one.[1] But the bulk of the critique involved a systematic assault on the book, section by section, and in most cases the effect was to leave relatively little of Webb's argument unassailed. The breadth of the framework Webb had used, and the persistence with which he had stressed the environmental theme, left him open to the charge of selectivity in the use of evidence and of a failure to put his sources under pressure before incorporating material into his argument.[2]

At the detailed level, Shannon contested the validity of Webb's concept of a broad Great Plains environment, arguing that it involved exaggerating the degree of uniformity present and refusing to acknowledge the existence of major variations in terrain and climate within the region.[3] By chipping away at the individual examples Webb used to support his definition of the Plains as a homogeneous environment, Shannon weakened the concept that was basic to the overall interpretation. By pointing to Webb's lack of detailed knowledge of conditions within the broad woodland region east of the ninety-eighth meridian, he tried to undermine the case for elements of contrast between East and West: by exaggerating and oversimplifying his case, Webb had swept aside what Shannon felt to have been the more valid explanation of the process of adaptation—that it had been going on for centuries, and at every stage of the extension of settlement westward.[4] Pioneers had been facing new challenges as they moved across from the Appalachians to the Prairie Plains and had altered their techniques of farming as they did so. Certainly the Plains area presented formidable problems, but the changes needed to deal with them were not as dramatic and novel as Webb had suggested. Moreover, the technological innovation on which Webb had placed such importance usually had its source in the older parts of the country: the Colt revolver, for example, had been developed in Connecticut without any initial reference to its possible use in the Plains situation.[5]

Piece by piece, the segments of Webb's argument were taken apart, examined for accuracy of detail, compared against alternative interpretations, and consigned to an appropriate level on Shannon's scale of reliability. It was a harsh process and difficult to counter; the areas involved were so large that damaging exceptions could be found to undermine any generalization, and Webb could see little point in trying to meet every detailed objection Shannon had raised. On the other hand, he could not ignore the attack, as the procedure which the Committee on Appraisal had established involved a small-scale conference to consider the issues and publish a transcript of its discussions. Webb could hardly accept the good fortune of having his book singled out for praise by those who took part in the poll and then refuse to be a party to the second half of the exercise; eventually he swallowed his anger and headed north to attend the conference.

Despite careful planning and a format which on paper looked quite promising, the conference did not live up to the expectations of those who designed the series of appraisals. There were important issues involved, and under different circumstances they might have been given the treatment they deserved. To a large extent, the failure of the exercise can be attributed to basic contrasts in the approaches of the two men toward their craft, and the assumption that was fundamental to the original concept of the inquiry—that two historians working in the same general area of their discipline would have enough in common to allow them to carry on a satisfactory discussion of methodology—broke down from the start. Those who organized the appraisal were unable to discover any method of dealing with what was to them an unusual and unexpected situation, and the slow collapse of the exercise was inevitable.

Part of the difficulty stemmed from the divergent concerns of the major groups involved in the appraisal. Those who represented the Social Science Research Council or had participated in the two earlier conferences were primarily interested in the basic theoretical problems which had been ignored in the rush to build up masses of data in a multiplicity of fields. What was the value of all this material? Had it led to the formulation of useful generalizations, or were social scientists obliged to dismiss generalizations as irrelevant and impractical? On what basis did specialists discriminate between the success or failure of a particular piece of research? Were there criteria that could be specified, or did most researchers operate largely by some sort of rule-of-thumb procedure?[6] In a sense, the questions being raised confirmed the predictions that Keasbey had made earlier in the century—that the social sciences would find themselves in a state of confusion unless they paid some attention to defining the framework within which they proposed to carry out their empirical studies. Now the council proposed to encourage a critical inquiry into aims and methods; but instead of formulating abstract guidelines of the type Keasbey favored, it would analyze concrete examples of successful research and work back from practice to principle. The end result should be a greater awareness among scholars of what it was that distinguished the significant from the trivial across the broad spectrum of the social sciences.

Since Webb's was the third—and, as it proved, the final—work to come under appraisal, some of those who took part in the conference in late 1939 were conversant with these general problems and had seen them raised during at least one of the previous sessions.[7] In a sense, the discussions of Webb's book were part of a continuing dialogue for those who had attended one or both of the earlier conferences, and their contributions to the debate were couched in those terms. On the other hand, those who were participating for the first time—and this included both Webb and Shannon—had apparently little idea of the nature of the issues raised earlier in the year and tended to work within a much narrower frame of reference. Finally, since many of the new partici-

pants were historians, theoretical questions received less attention
than at the other conferences; traditionally, historians have been
less comfortable than economists or sociologists with the problem
of defining the theoretical basis of their discipline, and at this conference most shied clear of abstraction. But a basic theoretical issue
that had arisen during the first conference—that dealing with
Thomas and Znaniecki's *The Polish Peasant*—emerged as the persistent theme in the examination of Webb's book: the role of the
subjective factor in the interpretation of social phenomena.

Clearly *The Great Plains* constituted an excellent case study for
the examination of this problem, but it is significant that the tone of
the discussion was quite different from that of the earlier conference. There it had been possible to discuss in a dispassionate manner the extent to which "the previous technical training, the experience and personal aptitudes on the part of the preparator and the
clinical researcher" should be ranked in relation to the more formal
mechanisms of research and evaluation.[8] In that instance, the
overall conclusion was that, although Thomas and Znaniecki had
made a brilliant attempt to devise a conceptual framework that
would enable social facts to be handled with some of the precision
characteristic of the natural sciences, in the last analysis a great
deal hinged on the insight and personal background of the interpreter. Their efforts to reduce the subjective element were undermined by the very nature of their material, which was "so subjective, imponderable and evanescent that quantitative procedures
were essentially inapplicable."[9]

To those who felt that the social sciences should progress in the
direction of greater precision in dealing with social facts, this conclusion was inevitably something of a disappointment. But in the
case of the *Great Plains* appraisal, the whole emphasis suddenly
became reversed. By attacking Webb's use of those elements of
historical research which are to some extent subject to formal controls—statements of historical fact, logical consistency, and the
capacity to generalize on the basis of fact—Shannon asserted that
the work did not conform to the few basic rules that the profession
accepted as critical to the proper handling of data.[10] By arguing
that Webb's urge to demonstrate as forcibly as possible a radical
difference in character between the humid East and the arid West
had led him to exaggerate differences and ignore negative evidence,
Shannon indicated that Webb had allowed the subjective element
virtually free rein.[11] The ground of the debate had clearly shifted

since the earlier conference, when the appraiser had conceded that Thomas and Znaniecki had failed to control the subjective factor only after a masterly effort to erect a viable alternative.

Very early in the discussion of the appraisal and Webb's reply to it, the historian Roy F. Nichols pointed to the question of insight versus proof as the unresolved issue carried over from the first conference and noted that for historians in particular the problem was one of special difficulty: traditionally, historians have placed a high value both on the kind of knowledge that resulted from literary insight and that arrived at "by the meticulous accumulation of factual data."[12] In the debate which followed, Shannon clearly represented the latter emphasis, though he was far from advocating mindless factgrubbing as Webb tended to suggest.[13] His concern was with the relationship between data and the generalizations built upon it, arguing for the unexceptionable position that valid generalizations could not be founded on errors of fact, overstatements, or imprecise definitions.[14] Insight could supplement, but never replace, the rigorous application of accepted professional standards in the handling of evidence. Detailed and careful examination of the data must precede the formulation of an interpretation: to interpret first, and then assemble the confirmatory data, was to deny the whole basis of historical inquiry.

Webb, on the other hand, approached the whole problem from the opposite direction. Having objected to the tone and content of Shannon's critique, and refusing to accept it as being in any sense a valid appraisal, he did not feel under any obligation to answer criticism in detail. In some cases it would have been difficult for him to do so; he conceded that there were discrepancies in the work but argued that in a book of its size some errors were inevitable, and that in any case they did not weaken the overall thesis.[15] It seems likely that he was unfamiliar with a good deal of the material Shannon cited, especially that dealing with the humid East, and that he had only a general knowledge of the geographical variations within the area he designated as the Great Plains environment. He conceded that he had not intended the work to be regarded as an exhaustive study, that he had studied only those aspects of the problem that seemed to him to be pertinent to his thesis about the relationship between environment and cultural change, and that in any case he was not disturbed by refutation on points of detail.[16]

But Webb went a good deal further than simply asserting that the mode of presentation was tailored to fit the requirements of the theme and the special objectives he had in mind. He argued that he had not set out to write a history, either of the Plains experience as a whole or of any segment of that experience; the nature of the work was clearly indicated by its subtitle—*A Study in Environment and Institutions*—and as such it was not subject to evaluation by the standards of historical scholarship.[17] There was no need for him to pretend that he had worked "strictly in accord with the Von Ranke tradition" or to deny that he had been emotionally involved in the work; the precedents established by conventional historians had been of very little use to him, and the substance of their work even less.[18] Accordingly, he had followed his own star, and it was now too late for traditionalists to try to force him back into their ways of thinking. Nor was he in any doubt as to the alternative criteria that should be used to evaluate his work, if those of the conventional historians were inapplicable: the personal experience of the author was in itself a guarantee of authenticity, but even more important was the acceptance of the book by those who knew the Plains firsthand—they were the only reliable judges of anything purporting to be an interpretation of their experience.[19]

By this point, the whole appraisal mechanism found itself far behind its original starting point. The subjective element that social scientists found so elusive and difficult to control now emerged as the ultimate test of validity rather than as an uncontrolled variable; insight of a special kind was superior to proof—if by the latter one meant adherence to standardized methods of research and analysis. By embracing his opponent's main line of criticism and converting it to his own use, Webb was not simply carrying through a tactical maneuver designed to divert Shannon's attack on his research procedures, for the whole question of imaginative insight ran through his account of the genesis of the book and its preparation. The flash of insight that had come from his reading of Emerson Hough's *The Way to the West* in 1922 had its basis in personal experience, and his account of its impact underlined his approach to historical inquiry: "Fustel Colanges [*sic*] is supposed to have said, 'years of research for one moment of synthesis.' That night I had my moment of synthesis in which a lot of isolated bits of knowledge united as if in electric current to form the unified pattern. *I had no proof, but I knew I was right.* There was no proof, I did not know where the timber line ran, except in Texas. *All the investigation remained to be done, but that was nothing*" (emphasis mine).[20]

This description was not written until three years after the Shannon appraisal; had it been included in Webb's written reply to the appraisal, it would have confirmed Shannon's worst fears about the basic methodological approach, even if it were conceded that the "isolated bits of knowledge" were a good deal more extensive than that designation would imply. A hypothesis that already bore such a loading of personal conviction could hardly attract the sort of vigorous testing that a conventional historian would demand, and the comment laid Webb open to the charge that he had first formed his conclusion and then went in search of the evidence to support it.

Something of the same emphasis on the subjective element also appeared in a strange passage toward the end of the book, one which Shannon used as the basis for an attack on Webb's concept of historical research: "This study of the Great Plains has thus far . . . been confined to facts which form themselves into what the writer sees as fairly definite patterns of truth. *The facts are available to all, but the patterns they form depend upon the point of view of the observer. Surely the patterns are as valid as the facts themselves, because they make rational and comprehensible a way of life that has too often been considered erratic and strange.* They are merely a diagram of functional processes, a reconstruction of folk ways" (emphasis mine).[21]

Despite its curious logic, this statement underlines Webb's reliance on subjective reaction and the special appeal of the argument to westerners as the ultimate guarantee of the validity of his interpretation. He consistently objected to any attempt to take the work apart and assess its overall value by examining its component parts.[22] It was to be considered as a whole, for it was the total impact that mattered; if the overall effect was to make the experience of the Plains "rational and comprehensible," then the "patterns" were valid and there was no further point in commenting on the quality of the data.[23] The methodological procedures that Shannon took for granted were simply reversed, so that it was not surprising that the two were unable to find any common ground.

Finally, in the rather theatrical conclusion to his written reply to the appraisal, Webb made his appeal to a higher tribunal clear: ". . . now book and critique must travel together to that court from which there is no appeal. Among the scholars of the court must be a Plainsman, representative of that branch of the American people who stood with the forest behind them and gazed at the boundless land . . . If the Plainsman finds there the biography of his own people, a fair story of their heroic and ofttimes tragic struggle with a naked land, he will speak convincingly to the court."[24] He was in fact quite satisfied that the verdict was already in, and that it was a favorable one; after pointing to the wide degree of approval the work had received at the hands of scholars in many disciplines, he emphasized that the judgments he most valued were those of laymen who had found the book a faithful record of their own experience on the Plains: "They have said 'I knew about the things you talk about in there, but I had never put them all together or thought about them in the way you have.' "[25]

As the discussion progressed, it became evident that Webb's hypothetical Plainsman was ably represented at the conference table—if not by his direct descendants, then by men who sympathized with his historical experience. Of the historians present, E. E. Dale was a product of the same Cross Timbers area that had cut deep into Webb's personality.[26] Ernest S. Osgood, though a native New Englander, had spent much of his teaching career in the West and was an acknowledged authority on the cattle kingdom.[27] John D. Hicks had grown up in the West, had studied in the Midwest, and had taught at universities from the Midwest to the Pacific Coast.[28] All were sympathetic to Webb's position and were disinclined to accept Shannon's strictures; like Webb, they tended to assess the work in terms of its fidelity to experience and personal impressions. Dale, for example, made his own position clear by recalling his first reactions to hearing Frederick Jackson Turner lecture at Harvard after World War I; for the first time he became aware of the strangeness of the country that he had taken for granted all through his early life, and he noted the irony of the fact that it was not until he reached New England that he discovered a "new world, . . . a strange and peculiar world" of which he had always been a part.[29] His subsequent experiences, together with the comments of those who lived in the area, convinced him that Webb was correct in his contention that in the broader cultural sense the West was not simply an extension of the East but something distinct and unique. The same note was echoed by other participants, especially when Shannon's detailed criticisms were being reviewed; the occasional lapses in the use of factual data did not outweigh their feeling that Webb's overall thesis made sense in the light of their own experience of the West.[30] The subjective element dominated the discussion as it had dominated the book.

Those participants who represented other branches of the social sciences found it difficult to do much more than comment on the scope and originality of the thesis and its impressive presentation. Webb's long-standing refusal to adopt conventional systems of thought in any discipline made it hard for specialists to relate his work to prevailing trends in their own areas. The geographers present could not accept some elements of Webb's view of the Plains as a region, but, since the criteria he used were not conventional ones and were intended to designate an environment rather than provide a clear geographical description, there was no reason why they could not accept it as a working definition.[31]

The same independence of formal theory presented Louis Wirth with something of a problem in deciding whether Webb's interpretation could be defined as determinist or possibilist, and, though he came down strongly for the latter designation, there was little evidence in the book itself that Webb was aware of the distinction between the two emphases or even felt that such theoretical formulations mattered.[32] Webb was not a theorist by nature, and he went no further than enunciating a few general principles concerning the relationship between environment and cultural change. Since he was interested in only one major example of that relationship, there was no need for him to develop a theory to explain and resolve the variations and apparent contradictions that usually surface when a wide range of phenomena are under consideration.

Free of any loyalty to the systems of other men, and devoid of any ambition to erect a system of his own, Webb gave specialist observers very little opportunity to find a foothold. Even his basic concept linking environment and cultural change could hardly be classified as dogma; though his work clearly revolved around it, Webb refused to claim that it held universal validity. In a comment made many years later, but reflecting an attitude quite compatible with his approach at the time of the appraisal, he noted that "different people have different keys to the half-hidden secrets of a subject. Here was my key, the connection between what men did and the conditions surrounding them, conditions which in some measure prescribe their action and dictate the results. *Not for a moment would I claim that this is the only key, but it is as good as any, better than some, and best for me*" (emphasis mine).[33] In the long run, subjective response was the best guide to the value of a theoretical concept, as well as of the interpretation built upon it.

Over the years western historians have been rather critical of the general tone of Shannon's appraisal and have dismissed his criticisms as petty and irrelevant.[34] Certainly the tone of the analysis was unnecessarily waspish in pia⌣es, and this became a hindrance to the discussion which followed; in this respect, the appraisal fell below the standards set by Herbert Blumer and Raymond T. Bye in the two earlier critiques. It was also in some respects a poorly organized analysis, which lacked a thoroughly worked-out frame of reference and devoted a disproportionate amount of attention to minor issues.[35]

Yet, despite his failure to provide an effective point of departure for the type of discussion the appraisal committee envisioned, Shannon did raise issues that were of interest to the historians present. By highlighting the methodological weaknesses that underlay Webb's attempt to prove the markedly different character of the Plains experience compared to that of the humid East, Shannon forced Webb and his supporters to justify the thesis in terms of personal intuition. Certainly there would be no withdrawal from the forward positions Webb had established in 1931; to the western mind in particular, Webb had achieved his primary objective—"to make rational and logical and natural the story of the Anglo-American civilization of the Plains."[36] To dismantle that interpretation would mean reverting to an unsatisfactory state of historical understanding, and there were few westerners who would accept that alternative once they had seen their heritage made comprehensible.

The conference ended with the basic questions still unresolved, and Webb returned to Austin convinced that he had come out of the whole episode unscathed. Despite his intense annoyance at the way Shannon had treated the book, Webb was far more sure of himself than in the gloomy months that had followed his rejection at Chicago. He was more determined than ever that he would not revise or alter the book in any way, and he made no comment when Shannon's own study of agriculture appeared some years later with a renewed attack on the concept of abrupt cultural change at or about the ninety-eighth meridian.[37] Webb was sure that his reputation as the foremost interpreter of the Plains was still intact, and left it at that.

In the long run, his belief that the book would survive on its own merits seems to have been justified; long after the conference had ended, *The Great Plains* continued to hold its position as the basic study of the region. Nor was its popularity confined to the western sections of the country, where its stress on the special character of life on the Plains would naturally attract favorable attention; its appeal was national, and the views it presented gradually came to be taken for granted. In recent years some vital segments of the thesis have come under critical review, but it still seems likely that Webb's general interpretation of the history of the Plains will persist long after its factual base becomes subject to erosion.

For Webb, the conference marked a temporary and unpleasant reversion to a phase of his career that he had considered completely closed. There was no incentive for him to reconsider his account of the Plains experience; he was satisfied with it, and so were those whose opinions he trusted. But in any case, one event in mid-1940 made him realize that the elements that linked him to the world he had portrayed in the Plains book were fast disappearing. In July of that year he wrote to his old friend E. E. Davis, who years before had set him thinking about water and fencing on the Plains. Davis had just read the published account of the conference and had written to protest against the tone of Shannon's critique. Webb replied with a scathing comment on the waste of money involved and then moved on to add a piece of personal news—the death of his father a few days earlier.[38] With Casner gone, Webb had lost his most direct line of contact with the generation whose experience had gripped him for so long.

Epilogue

WEBB LEFT the conference as totally unrepentant a westerner as when he arrived. Nothing that had happened there induced him to change either his methods of investigation or his interpretation of the Plains; if anything, he became even more solidly convinced that his approach was the right one and that only narrow and conventional minds could fail to appreciate his account of the Plains experience. To underline the point, he refused to alter or revise the book in any way, and in later years he would return again and again to restate its basic propositions. The image of the Plains had been set, and as far as Webb was concerned, it would remain a permanent image. The appraisal had altered nothing.

In any case, the country was soon to be involved in war, and scholarly debates lost any relevance in the face of mobilization and the demands of global conflict. Now in his early fifties, Webb escaped direct involvement; but a year spent in England as a visiting professor gave him the chance to observe the war from whatever perspective life in an Oxford college provided. Puzzled though he was by the conventions of English academic life, he developed a liking for the college system and the opportunities it provided for unhurried discussion and quiet sociability; for once he could put aside his regional identity and concentrate on the problems involved in being the resident American and an interpreter of the American scene.

With the war gone, and with life returning to normal in the universities, Webb settled back to familiar routines. He was now one of the senior members of his department and a figure of some weight in university politics. He enjoyed the rewards of long familiarity with the institution and the wider community outside, and the network of friendships he had carefully built up and cultivated over the years provided him with the warmth and recognition to which he felt he had some claim, and on which he depended. Though a solitary and stubbornly independent thinker, he needed an audience that shared his interest in the historical experience of both the state and the region, and his willingness to write for local publications in preference to scholarly journals ensured that he remained in contact with a broad cross section of his own community.

Yet that continuing concern for the local context went hand in hand with a predilection for grand theory in the Keasbey manner, something that Webb's experience in writing *The Great Plains* had etched even more deeply into his mentality. He was now convinced that he had located what was for him the only effective and creative approach to historical investigation—the slow and patient consideration of apparently unrelated materials, the eventual flash of insight revealing the connecting thread, and the drive to locate the evidence that would confirm the insight. Webb therefore set out in pursuit of one such insight: the concept of Western Europe as "Metropolis," a core civilization transformed over a four-hundred-year period by access to apparently boundless wealth and resources of "the great frontier," the new lands discovered at the opening of the sixteenth century. It was to become the project that would absorb his attention for the next ten years, just as the Plains theme had dominated his thinking in the 1920's. In those earlier years he had worked alone; now he could use his concept as the basis of a series of research seminars, asking his students to join him year after year in the search for new materials and different perspectives on the theme itself. By 1951 he was again in print with *The Great Frontier*. This work met with a more varied reception than had the Plains book in 1931, but, whatever its merits or defects, it stands as the final product of one man's search for the texture and pattern of his own historical environment.

Toward the end of *The Great Frontier*, Webb described his books as stages in the comprehensive investigation of a single theme, one which broadened from a regional to a national—and then to a global—perspective. It was a view that he maintained throughout the twelve years that remained to him, and there is very little to suggest that it was not a valid comment on his long and single-minded interrogation of the recent past. For Webb, that past was not something detached from his own existence and amenable to dispassionate analysis. He took it for granted that his approach to the study of history was shaped by the circumstances of his early life, and he acknowledged that it was only his belated discovery that the two elements were so interrelated that made it possible for him to function as a historian; by retreating to his native soil, he found what he felt to be the most effective way of comprehending both his own region and the wider world beyond. In *The Great Plains* he had stationed himself imaginatively in the Cross Timbers that he had known as a boy and watched the transit of civilizations across the great sweep of country to the north. In later years, he would simply extend the arc of observation both in time and in distance; the vantage point and the method of measurement would remain constant. The professional recognition that came his way in the last decade before his death in 1963 acknowledged an honest and persistent attempt to decipher complex historical movements; but awareness of his standing within the academic community did little to shake him loose from his interest in the web of life that underlay the social and institutional fabric of his own region.

To a generation that has come to recognize that the urge to specify a distinctive cultural heritage and anchor it in a historical framework is part of the mechanism by which both national groups and ethnic minorities define their place within a larger and often hostile world, this account of Walter Webb's preoccupation with the historical identity of the Plains communities should come as no surprise. Many of the same emotional pressures seem to operate in any dependent culture once the practical demands of survival and settlement become less imperative—even when heartland and colony share a common language and common traditions. The desire to establish a satisfactory identity within the larger whole is accentuated when distance and the passage of time provide the opportunity for variations to grow into apparent differences and for assumptions to harden into dogma. Webb's formative years were set in a period when acculturation lagged behind the onward rush of technology; national transportation and a national market could not produce a national outlook overnight, and the generation of which Webb was part resented the fact that a lifetime spent in a large tract of unattractive territory did not qualify one for a place of honor and dignity in the historical consciousness of the nation. For most of that generation, the very circumstances of their lives on the Plains made it difficult for them to see beyond their own experiences to the broader stream of which they felt they must be a part. Webb was to be one of the more respected of their spokesmen, one who knew their story and knew how to shape it into a pattern that they could understand and respect. Webb described *The Great Plains* as the biography of a people; perhaps it would be better described as a backdrop against which a people could set their individual and collective portraits—the kind of backdrop which, by providing a frame and carefully arranged setting, gives balance and order to the human element at its center.

Notes

Introduction

1. Walter Prescott Webb, "Water Conservation as a Private Enterprise," address to the Water Conservation Conference, May 22, 1959, typescript in Walter Prescott Webb Papers, Barker Texas History Center, University of Texas Archives; hereafter cited as "Webb Papers."

1. Family and Community

1. Comer Vann Woodward, *The Origins of the New South, 1877–1913*, pp. 108–110.
2. ". . . my parents . . . left . . . about 1885 at a time when young people had little chance to escape the poverty which had been imposed on them by the Civil War and its aftermath" (Walter Prescott Webb, "Let's Live—and Prosper—in Dixie," address to the Southern Newspaper Editors' Association, Florida, [1960?], typescript in Webb Papers).
3. The northeastern counties of Mississippi had experienced their share of difficulties since 1863; in that year Tishomingo County—directly to the north of Monroe County—had been torn by clashes between Unionists and Secessionists (William C. Harris, *Presidential Reconstruction in Mississippi*, p. 4). The Klan was active in the area after the war, and by the 1880's widespread agrarian discontent testified to the economic and social difficulties troubling the state (James W. Garner, *Reconstruction in Mississippi*, p. 347; Albert Dennis Kirwan, *Revolt of the Rednecks*, chap. 4).
4. Webb, typescript autobiography, Webb Papers, pp. 14, 52. This 231-page account was written while Webb was at Oxford in 1942 and is the most detailed source of information on his childhood. Subsequent citations are to "Autobiography"; a 4-page autobiographical fragment filed with the above is cited as "Autobiography: early text."
5. Webb, Autobiography, p. 3.
6. Homer Lee Kerr, "Migration into Texas, 1865–1880"; table 1: "White, Colored and Foreign Born, 1870–1880," p. 6. Entry under "Panola County" in *The Handbook of Texas*, ed. Walter

Prescott Webb and Horace Bailey Carroll, 2:332. For an account of the operation of a major plantation in adjacent Rusk County, see Dorman F. Winfrey, *Julien Sidney Devereux and His Monte Verdi Plantation.*

7. Webb, Autobiography, p. 6.

8. Interview, Mrs. Ima Wright, Austin, February 1972.

9. Webb, Autobiography, p. 3.

10. Webb, "Let's Live—and Prosper—in Dixie," p. 1.

11. Carolyn Thomas Foreman, *The Cross Timbers*, chap. 1; entry under "Cross Timbers (Western)" in *Handbook of Texas*, ed. Webb and Carroll, 2:885. A class paper prepared by Webb in 1910 gives a firsthand account of the area (Webb, "Do You Want to Invest?" class paper dated February 7, 1910, Walter Prescott Webb Papers, Archives Division, Texas State Library; subsequent citations to this collection, formerly in the possession of Mr. C. B. Smith, Sr., are to the "Smith Collection").

12. Webb, Autobiography, p. 6.

13. Ibid., p. 5.

14. Virdie C. Hodnett, "History of Rural Education in Texas, 1900–1935," chap. 2. Walter Webb began his own career as a rural teacher under the same system (Webb, "The Events of My First School," class paper dated March 25, 1911, Smith Collection).

15. Webb, Autobiography, pp. 6, 7, 46.

16. Loy W. Hartsfield, "A History of Stephens County, Texas," pp. 17–27; entry under "Stephens County" in *Handbook of Texas*, ed. Webb and Carroll, 2:667; Carolyne L. Langston, *History of Eastland County, Texas*; Robert Y. Lindsey, Jr., "A History of Eastland County, Texas."

17. Allen Callaway Bradley, "The History of Education in Eastland County, Texas," p. 2.

18. Hartsfield, "Stephens County," pp. 175–176. For an account of the pattern of migration which brought agriculturalists into the area during the eighties, see Kerr, "Migration into Texas."

19. Woodward, *Origins of the New South*, p. 108; Millicent S. Huff, "A Study of Work Done by Texas Railroad Companies to Encourage Immigration into Texas between 1870 and 1890," chap. 3; Harry Williams, Jr., "'The Development of a Market Economy in Texas: The Establishment of the Railway Network, 1836–1890," chap. 14.

20. Kerr, "Migration into Texas," pp. 27, 28.

21. Entries under "Cisco," "Eastland," "Breckenridge," "Ranger," and "Wayland" in *Handbook of Texas*, ed. Webb and Carroll, 1: 348, 538, 212, and 2:439, 872.

22. Webb, Autobiography, p. 31.

23. Webb, Autobiography, p. 9; interview, Mrs. Ima Wright.

24. Webb, Autobiography, p. 20.

25. Ibid.

26. Ibid., p. 9.

27. Ibid., p. 11.

28. Ibid., p. 10.

29. Ibid., p. 35.
30. Ibid., p. 15.
31. Ibid., p. 35.
32. Ibid., p. 27.
33. Ibid., p. 38.
34. Ibid., p. 29.
35. Ibid.
36. Ibid., p. 81. J. Fred Rippy, *Bygones I Cannot Help Recalling*, p. 44.
37. Webb's mother was a hard-shell Baptist, his father a skeptic (interviews, Mrs. Ima Wright, Miss Mildred Webb, Austin, May 1972; Webb, Autobiography, pp. 24–25).
38. Jay B. Hubbell, "The Great Plains: A Study in Landscape," in his *South and Southwest*, p. 286. Hubbell's comment was based on his first visit to the Texas Plains in 1923.
39. Webb consistently stressed the dominance of his father and contrasted his determination and self-confidence with his mother's excessive caution. Webb's surviving sister and his daughter remember Mary Kyle Webb as a more forceful personality than these remarks would suggest (interviews, Mrs. Ima Wright, Miss Mildred Webb).

2. The Making of an Imagination

1. A rather more exceptional case was that of Harry Yandell Benedict, a product of the same area in West Texas, who later became president of the University of Texas. Despite the frontier conditions, Benedict had access to his father's thousand-volume library and by the age of fourteen "had read Scott, Dickens, Thackeray . . . and most of the standard authors" (Webb, "Life Sketch of Dr. Harry Yandell Benedict," class paper dated December 6, 1912, Smith Collection).
2. Webb, "Recollections of Life in Ranger," typescript dated 1959, Webb Papers.
3. Casner Webb worked at whatever he could find during the summer and the injury to his foot that left him permanently lame occurred while he was employed by the Texas and Pacific Railroad. He won some damages from the company and used the money to help start the small farm near Ranger in 1902 (Webb, Autobiography, pp. 48, 50).
4. Webb, "Recollections," p. 4.
5. Webb, Autobiography, p. 60. The family appears to have moved about eight times in a little more than ten years before establishing a permanent home on the farm near Ranger.
6. Ibid.
7. Ibid.
8. "Here was the spiritual world in which I was living, far removed from the physical and social world around me" (ibid., p. 68).
9. Clipping in Webb Papers.

10. "One can become fairly educated without much school training. Some of the best writers never went to college, and cultivated themselves by reading with care and observation and thinking. Keep your eyes open to all that goes on around you—the ways of men and in the processes of nature. Read books of travel and study physical geography. A good physical geography is crammed full of information and food for thought . . ." (ibid.). Since the study of physical geography had only just begun to replace the older nineteenth-century stress on political geography in the school curriculum, the last piece of advice was a little unusual. William Morris Davis, "Physical Geography in the High School," *School Review* 8 (September 1900): 388–404, 449–456; Albert Perry Brigham, review of *Physical Geography*, by William Morris Davis, *School Review* 7 (April 1899): 248–249. For indirect comments on the presentation of geography in nineteenth century schools, see Ruth Miller Elson, *Guardians of Tradition*, chaps. 4 and 5.
11. Walter Prescott Webb, "Search for William E. Hinds," *Harper's Magazine* 223 (July 1961): 62–69.
12. Webb, "The Search for William E. Hinds," *Reader's Digest* 79 (August 1961): 35–40. In addition to the general correspondence that developed as a result of the articles, the Webb Papers contain the original drafts and discussions between Webb and the editors of *Harper's* and *Reader's Digest* as the story took form. At one stage he hoped to expand the story into a book, but his publishers rejected the idea (Webb Papers).
13. The other two were E. Temple Peters, who taught him at Ranger school, and Lindley Miller Keasbey.
14. Webb, Autobiography: early text, p. 5.
15. "I skipped grades and landed in a miscellany of subjects that approximated the 8th grade, and added all the subjects required for the state examination" (ibid.). Most of his difficulties came in those areas where the lack of cumulative training told against him—particularly mathematics. Literary subjects were less of a problem, though his grasp of vocabulary outran his ability to spell and pronounce correctly.
16. Ibid.
17. Ibid.
18. By the time he left for Austin in 1909, he had taught a total of five schools for a period of about sixteen and a half months (Webb, Autobiography, p. 105).
19. Ibid., pp. 96–99.
20. Ibid., p. 101.
21. Ibid., p. 105.
22. Ibid., pp. 159–161.
23. Ibid., p. 160.
24. Ibid.
25. Ibid., p. 44. Rhodes's widow recalled that her husband used the coffee labels to obtain books for his children; Hans Christian Andersen's fairy tales and *Alice's Adventures in Wonderland*

were among the books that found their way to the frontier by this route (May Davison Rhodes, *The Hired Man on Horseback*, p. 48). Later Webb graduated to *Youth's Companion*, to which a neighboring family subscribed, and sample copies of the Williams's school readers—*The King of the Golden River* and *The Ugly Duckling* were two titles that he could recall.

26. Webb, Autobiography, p. 67. Joel Dorman Steele's book first appeared in 1869 and was reprinted and revised on many occasions during the remaining years of the century. Together with its companion volumes in chemistry and other branches of the natural sciences, it became one of the most popular and widely used school textbooks of the period. In 1889 it appeared as the *Chautauqua Course in Physics* and was one of the required texts for those who took Chautauqua courses in that year (John A. Nietz, *The Evolution of American Secondary School Textbooks*, p. 125; Charles H. Carpenter, *History of American Schoolbooks*, p. 218).

27. Webb, Autobiography: early text, p. 4.

28. In addition to the stories of Joel Chandler Harris and Frank Carpenter, *Sunny South* carried Arthur Conan Doyle's *Hound of the Baskervilles* in serial form at the time Webb first came in contact with it (ibid.).

29. Webb used an arithmetic by George Albert Wentworth and a grammar by Alonzo Reed and Brainerd Kellogg, either as a student or as a rural teacher (Walter Prescott Webb, "Geographical-Historical Concepts in American History," *Annals of the Association of American Geographers* 50 [June 1960]: 85). Wentworth's texts in mathematics were probably the most widely used throughout the country in the second half of the nineteenth century (Nietz, *Evolution of American Secondary School Textbooks*, pp. 56, 70). Reed and Kellogg's *Higher Lessons in English* first appeared in 1877, and it continued to circulate for the next three decades in revised and reprinted editions (Carpenter, *History of American Schoolbooks*, p. 107).

30. Webb, "Geographical-Historical Concepts," p. 85.

31. Ibid.

32. Webb, "Texas Is Our Garden," speech to the Garden Club of Houston, Texas, November 1, 1961, typescript in Webb Papers.

33. John Leighly, "What Has Happened to Physical Geography?" *Annals of the Association of American Geographers* 45 (December 1955): 309–318; William Warntz, *Geography Now and Then*, pp. 144–145. By the early twenties Davis's approach was losing favor among geographers, and attempts were being made to find alternative emphases—for example, Harlan Barrows, "Geography as Human Ecology," *Annals of the Association of American Geographers* 13 (March 1923): 1–14; and Carl Sauer, "The Survey Method in Geography and Its Objectives," *Annals of the Association of American Geographers* 14 (March 1924): 17–33.

34. Webb had no opportunity to study geography as an undergraduate;

no geography department existed at the University of Texas
until 1949.

35. Brigham, review of *Physical Geography*, p. 248.
36. Leighly, "What Has Happened to Physical Geography?" pp. 312–
313.
37. Ellen Churchill Semple, *American History and Its Geographic
Conditions*; Ellen Churchill Semple, *Influences of Geographic
Environment on the Basis of Ratzel's System of Anthropo-
geography*; Albert Perry Brigham, *Geographic Influences in
American History*.
38. In 1907 the American Historical Association sponsored a conference on the relationship between history and geography, with
Ellen Churchill Semple as one of the participants (see Frederick
Jackson Turner, "Report of the Conference on the Relation of
Geography and History," *American Historical Association Report for the Year 1907* 1:45–48).
39. Thomas Wolfe, *Look Homeward, Angel*, p. 423.
40. Margaret Lyn, "A Step-daughter of the Prairies," *Atlantic Monthly* 107 (March 1911): 380.
41. Ibid.
42. Ibid.
43. For a comment on the same kind of problem as it affected Hamlin
Garland, see Percy Boynton, *The Rediscovery of the Frontier*,
p. 161.
44. Walter Prescott Webb with Professor William A. Owens, taped interview in the possession of Professor Owens, Columbia University, dated August 18, 1953.

3. A Plainsman and His College

1. Emmet Bryan Carmichael, "John William Mallet: Scholar-Teacher-
Scientist," *Scalpel* 25 (Winter 1955): 35–42; Frank E. Van-
diver, "John William Mallet and the University of Texas,"
Southwestern Historical Quarterly 53 (April 1950): 421–442;
William Holding Echols, "John William Mallet: Scholar,
Teacher, Gentleman," *Alumni Bulletin of the University of
Virginia*, 3rd series, 6 (January 1913): 4–47.
2. Frederick Eby, *The Development of Education in Texas*, chaps. 5–8.
3. Speech of Senator Terrell, April 19, 1882, in *A Source-Book Relating to the History of the University of Texas*, comp. Harry
Yandell Benedict, p. 270.
4. Harry H. Ransom, "Educational Resources in Texas," in *Texas
Today and Tomorrow*, ed. Herbert Gambrell, p. 55.
5. Benedict, *A Source-Book Relating to the History of the University
of Texas*, p. 662.
6. The two Texan appointees were former Governor Oran Milo Roberts, who had sponsored the establishment of the university during his term of office, and Robert S. Gould.
7. John William Mallet, William Le Roy Brown, and R. L. Dabney.

8. Webb, Autobiography, p. 31.
9. The early chapters of Edmund Wilson's *Upstate* suggest by comparison the special problems of growing up in an area devoid of the memories and the complex family linkages that intersect the growth of personality and intellect. It would be hard to find more contrasting situations, but the comparison has some merit (Edmund Wilson, *Upstate*).
10. The rapid shifts in the fortunes of the cattle towns are best illustrated in Robert Dykstra's *The Cattle Towns*, and those of the mining communities in Rodman Wilson Paul's *Mining Frontiers of the Far West, 1848–1880*, pp. 102–108. The strange career of tiny Dothan in Eastland County suggests something of the uncertainties of the period. It began life as a settlement known as Delmar, founded in 1880 when the Texas and Pacific Railroad reached the area. A year later Delmar was moved to Red Gap, and it changed its name to Cisco in 1882. Later the original site was resettled as Dothan. It reached its maximum population of 50 in 1915, fell to 20 by 1939, and by 1947 had contracted to a store and a railroad station (Walter Prescott Webb and Horace Bailey Carroll, eds., *The Handbook of Texas*, 1: 515. See also Dick King, *Ghost Towns of Texas*).
11. Many of the smaller settlements that Webb knew as a child in Stephens County either stabilized in population or actually fell away after 1890—though, significantly, the school populations continued to rise (Allen Callaway Bradley, "The History of Education in Eastland County, Texas," pp. 56, 58).
12. Webb, Autobiography, p. 134.
13. Jay B. Hubbell, "The Creative Writer and the University, with Special Reference to the 1920's," in *South and Southwest*, pp. 330–363.
14. John W. Mallet, "Recollections of the First Years of the University of Texas," *Alcalde* 1 (1913): 16.
15. Ibid., pp. 15, 16.
16. Thomas Herndon Wolfe, "Dimensions of a Prominent American Graduate School: The Graduate School of the University of Texas in Austin, 1883–1969," chap. 2.
17. Margaret C. Berry, "Campus Culture: A Product of Its Own History," *Journal of College Student Personnel* 8 (January 1967): 4.
18. Ibid.
19. Ibid., pp. 4, 7. By 1932–1933, 44 percent of the degrees held by faculty in the College of Arts and Sciences were awarded by the University of Texas (ibid., p. 6).
20. *Catalogue of the University of Texas*, 1919–1920, p. 121.
21. Helen D. Barnard, "Early History of Research in Texas Archaeology by the Department of Anthropology, and the History of the Anthropology Museum of the University of Texas," pp. 19–21.
22. Webb transcript in the possession of Mrs. Walter Prescott Webb, Austin.

23. Webb, "My Object in Studying English 3," undergraduate theme dated October 20, 1910, Smith Collection.
24. Webb, literary exercise dated March 5, 1909, Smith Collection. The date is puzzling, as Webb did not begin his freshman year until September 1909. But the marginal comments suggest that it was a class paper rather than a private exercise.
25. Webb, "On Deep Eddy," class paper dated April 25, 1910, Smith Collection.
26. Webb, "My Old Homestead," class paper dated October 29, 1909, Smith Collection.
27. Ibid.
28. Ibid.
29. Ibid.
30. Webb, two handwritten pages of an incomplete paper, undated but interleaved with papers from the 1909–1911 period, Smith Collection.
31. Webb, "The Freshman's Attitude towards English 1," class paper dated December 7, 1910, Smith Collection.
32. Webb, "My Love of Poetry," class paper dated March 4, 1911, Smith Collection.
33. Ibid.
34. Webb and Carroll, eds., *Handbook of Texas*, 1: 273.
35. Ibid.
36. The experience of the ballad collector John Avery Lomax is often cited to Callaway's discredit. While a student at Austin, Lomax showed Callaway the collection of cowboy ballads that were to lay the basis for his later career as a folklorist. Callaway advised him to burn them, and it was not until Lomax took the material to Harvard that its value was realized (John Avery Lomax, *Adventures of a Ballad Hunter*, pp. 32–35).
37. Webb transcript in the possession of Mrs. Walter Prescott Webb, Austin.

4. A Frame of Reference

1. The Keasbey family line ran direct from a member who sat in the colonial assembly in the 1770's, another who sat in the general assembly at the turn of the century, and a third who cast a New Jersey vote for Henry Clay in 1844. Keasbey's father had been appointed United States District Attorney by Lincoln and held the position until 1886; two brothers were prominent lawyers in Newark. His mother was a daughter of Jacob W. Miller, Senator for New Jersey from 1851 to 1853 (John James Scannell, ed., *New Jersey's First Citizens and State Guide*, 1:301). Webb commented on Keasbey's elegant tastes in a taped interview, August 18, 1953. Alvin Saunders Johnson, who worked under Keasbey at both Bryn Mawr and Texas, has left a lively sketch in his *Pioneer's Progress*, pp. 147–150, 178–179.
2. *University Record* 6, no. 3 (February 1906): 228; Lindley Miller

Keasbey, *The Early Diplomatic History of the Nicaragua Canal.*

3. A German version of his thesis was published in Strassburg as part of his inaugural dissertation (Lindley Miller Keasbey, *Der Nicaragua-kanal*).

4. *Program of Bryn Mawr College*, 1895, p. 8.

5. Keasbey was a member of the Council of the Academy for a term ending December 13, 1899; the council appears to have numbered about thirteen elected members at the time (*Handbook of the American Academy of Political Sciences* 7 [January 1896]: 52). A list published in 1896 indicated that he presented papers on "The Tabular Standard" and "The Concept of Organic Social Value," neither of which was published ("List of Papers Presented to the Academy since the First Scientific Session, December 20, 1893," *Annals of the American Academy of Political and Social Sciences* 7 [January 1896]: 52–53).

6. Johnson, *Pioneer's Progress*, pp. 149–150.

7. Lindley Miller Keasbey, "The Nicaragua Canal and the Monroe Doctrine," *Annals of the American Academy of Political and Social Sciences* 7 (January 1896): 1–31; Lindley Miller Keasbey, *The Nicaragua Canal and the Monroe Doctrine.*

8. Lindley Miller Keasbey, "The Terms and Tenor of the Clayton-Bulwer Treaty," *Annals of the American Academy of Political and Social Sciences* 14 (November 1899): 285–309.

9. For example, his review of Arthur Kitson's study of the money question in *Annals of the American Academy of Political and Social Sciences* 7 (March 1896): 310–313.

10. Lee Benson, *Turner and Beard*, pp. 1–40, and "The Historian as Mythmaker: Turner and the Closed Frontier," in *The Frontier in American Development*, ed. David M. Ellis, pp. 3–19. The most recent appraisal of Loria's impact on Turner's ideas is Ray Billington, *The Genesis of the Frontier Thesis*, pp. 134–142, 155–156.

11. Johnson, *Pioneer's Progress*, pp. 148, 181. Webb also noted that Keasbey had "trained in Germany, knew Frederick Ratzel and J. E. Reclus, Ellsworth Huntingdon and the other greats, and made us read their books." (Walter Prescott Webb, "Geographical-Historical Concepts in American History," *Annals of the Association of American Geographers* 50 [June 1960]: 85). I have not found any earlier reference by Webb to this connection with Ratzel, and it is possible that he was relying on Johnson's account—though the latter referred only to Ratzel. See also Virginia M. Rowley, *J. Russell Smith*, p. 44; Charles Colby, "Changing Currents in Geographic Thought in America," *Annals of the Association of American Geographers* 26 (March 1936): 22, fn. 58; Lindley Miller Keasbey, "The Study of Economic Geography," *Political Science Quarterly* 16 (March 1901): 79–95; Lindley Miller Keasbey, "The Principles of Economic Geography," *Political Science Quarterly* 16 (September 1901): 476–485.

12. Keasbey studied at Berlin and Strassburg during the two years he spent in Germany, and he may have visited Ratzel at Leipzig—but he does not appear to have studied there. Examples of his familiarity with contemporary German scholarship can be found in reviews in *Political Science Quarterly* 7 (December 1892): 754–757 and 8 (March 1893): 152–154. He had apparently studied under Georg Friedrich Knapp at Strassburg and admired his studies of the evolution of the German peasant class.

13. Lindley Miller Keasbey, review of *The History of Mankind*, by Friedrich Ratzel, trans. A. J. Butler, *Annals of the American Academy of Political and Social Sciences* 9 (May 1897): 447–450.

14. Ellen Churchill Semple, *Influences of Geographic Environment on the Basis of Ratzel's System of Anthropo-geography.* For a discussion of Semple's links with Ratzel, see Harriet Grace Wanklyn, *Friedrich Ratzel.*

15. For a discussion of the problems facing social scientists in only one of the new areas of study—sociology—see Robert K. Merton, "Social Conflicts over Styles of Sociological Work," in *Sociology of Sociology*, ed. Larry T. Reynolds and Janice M. Reynolds, pp. 172–197.

16. Lindley Miller Keasbey, "Civology—a Suggestion," *Popular Science Monthly* 70 (April 1907): 365–371.

17. Keasbey's career is the subject of an investigation being carried out by Miss Mazie Mathews at Southwest Texas State University, San Marcos, on the basis of a collection of Keasbey's papers located in August 1972. Keasbey was dismissed for actively opposing American entry into World War I. His case was quite distinct from that of six other professors whose dismissals were voted on the same day and whose fates became a central issue in a long, drawn-out struggle between the state governor and his critics. The controversy ended in the successful impeachment of Governor James Ferguson, though its shadows hung over the university for many years. Keasbey's dismissal attracted very little comment or sympathy from either faculty or students at the time (Stark Young, "A Texas Program," *New Republic*, August 11, 1917, pp. 45–47).

18. Interview, Mr. Richard Fleming, Austin, February 1972.

19. Keasbey, "The Nicaragua Canal and the Monroe Doctrine," p. 2; Keasbey, review of *History of Mankind*, p. 447.

20. Alvin S. Johnson credited Keasbey with being the first to introduce the concepts of German *geopolitik* to the United States (Johnson, *Pioneer's Progress*, p. 148).

21. Keasbey, "The Nicaragua Canal and the Monroe Doctrine," p. 26.

22. *President's Reports, Bryn Mawr College*, 1893/1894, pp. 400–402.

23. *Annual Report of the President of Bryn Mawr College*, 1894/1895, pp. 475–476; *Program of Bryn Mawr College*, 1895, pp. 90–91.

24. *Annual Report of the President of Bryn Mawr College*, 1895/
    1896, pp. 580–581.
25. *Program of Bryn Mawr College*, 1896, p. 101.
26. Ibid.
27. Ibid.
28. *Annual Report of the President of Bryn Mawr College*, 1898/
    1899, p. 91.
29. *Catalogue of the University of Texas*, 1905/1906, pp. 117–122;
    1906/1907, pp. 109–114; 1907/1908, pp. 105–109; 1908/
    1909, pp. 113–117; 1909/1910, pp. 72–74, 89–90, 97–98; *Uni-
    versity Record* 10, nos. 1–4 (April 1910–April 1911): 199.
30. Webb, taped interview. David F. Houston to Regent T. S. Hender-
    son, May 15, 1908; T. S. Henderson to David F. Houston, May
    16, 1908; G. W. Owens to Governor Campbell, May 8, 1908, in
    folder "Institutional History," in Records of the President's Of-
    fice, University of Texas, Barker Texas History Center, Univer-
    sity of Texas Archives. The quotation is in the letter from
    Houston to Henderson.
31. During 1909/1910, the regular Department of History was also
    undergoing a certain amount of reorganization (Thomas B.
    Brewer, "A History of the Department of History of the Uni-
    versity of Texas, 1883–1951"; William C. Pool, *Eugene C.
    Barker, Historian*, pp. 45–53).
32. Webb, "Geographic Factors as a Factor in the History of the
    United States of America," class paper for political science
    course, no course number or date, Smith Collection. Among the
    texts noted in footnotes were Ellen Churchill Semple's *American
    History and Its Geographic Conditions* and John Burgess's
    Political Science and Constitutional Law.
33. Webb, examination paper for Institutional History 2, dated May
    16, 1913, Smith Collection.
34. Webb, "The Communal-Collegiate System versus the Republican-
    Patriarchal System in the History of Medieval Europe," class
    paper, Institutional History 6, dated January 18, 1915, Smith
    Collection. An untitled paper dated March 16, 1915, examined
    the manner in which each of the different groups which made
    up this system developed capitalist traits (Smith Collection).
35. Webb, "The Communal-Collegiate System."
36. Keasbey devoted some attention to discussions of political theory,
    and a number of Webb's class papers suggest that Institutional
    History 6 traced the evolution of the modern democratic state
    from the Renaissance to the eighteenth century—for example,
    Webb, "The Defence of the Patriarch in England" (a study of
    Sir Robert Filmer's *De Patriarcha*), n.d.; "Machiavelli, the
    Forerunner of the Industrial, Democratic, National State,"
    n.d.; "Locke's Theory of Government," dated February 26,
    1915; "The Democracy of Rousseau," n.d., Smith Collection.
    The last two papers point out that Hobbes was also studied as
    part of this course, but they do not give any indication as to

how Hobbesian thought was dealt with in the light of the overall theme. Webb used the material gathered for the Machiavelli paper for a paper in Government 213, dated March 10, 1915, Smith Collection. It is difficult to determine whether these papers were based on original sources or on secondary accounts, such as William A. Dunning's *History of Political Theories*, which is cited on several occasions. The instructor's comment on the Rousseau paper suggests that the materialist emphasis was consistently applied ("Very satisfactory paper. The economic antecedents are quite omitted, however").

37. Webb, "The Communal-Collegiate System."
38. Ibid.
39. See the criticism by Professor Fred Shannon in chap. 9.
40. Webb, "Geographical-Historical Concepts," p. 85.
41. The late Mr. Richard Fleming, former curator of the Fleming Collection of Texas writings at the University of Texas, Austin, studied under Keasbey and recalled that he was an excellent lecturer and that his course attracted unusually large enrollments (interview, Mr. Richard Fleming).
42. Webb, "The Ethnological Significance of Folklore," paper dated March 5, 1915, Smith Collection.
43. Webb, "History as High Adventure," *American Historical Review* 64 (January 1959): 278–281.
44. Keasbey to Webb, September 14, 1931, Webb Papers.
45. Webb, taped interview.
46. Keasbey to Webb, September 14, 1931, Webb Papers.

5. Finding a Career

1. Webb, Autobiography, p. 112. Webb had apparently considered selling atlases in East Texas as another source of income (George F. Cram to Webb, June 10, 1910, Smith Collection).
2. Two other positions—at Lubbock and Jacksboro—were offered to him, but he preferred to get away from the dust and heat of the Plains and spent the year in South Texas (L. Z. Timmons to Webb, June 5, 1913, Smith Collection).
3. Webb, Autobiography, p. 119; *Beeville Bee*, November 7, 1913.
4. Webb, Autobiography, p. 119; *Beeville Bee*, November 14, 1913.
5. Webb, Autobiography, pp. 119, 121.
6. *Beeville Bee*, September 5, 1913.
7. Webb, "Folklore of Texas," *Journal of American Folklore* 28 (July/September 1915): 290–301.
8. Webb, Autobiography, p. 119.
9. E. H. Webb to Webb, May 20, 1914, August 18, 1914; P. R. Crowley to Webb, February 9, 1914, Smith Collection.
10. Keasbey to Webb, March 22, 1914; Eugene O. Farmer to Webb, April 7, 1914; Keasbey to Webb, April 1, 1914; John Lomax to Webb, April 28, 1914; Dean Harper to Webb, May 12, 1914; clipping, *Daily Texan*, May 6, 1914, Smith Collection.

11. C. E. Evans to Webb, May 18, 1914; Webb to C. E. Evans, May 24, 1914, Smith Collection.
12. Webb to C. E. Evans, May 24, 1914, Smith Collection.
13. Webb, Autobiography, p. 121.
14. Ibid., pp. 122–123.
15. Ibid., p. 123.
16. Webb to Jane Oliphant, January 11, 1915, Smith Collection.
17. Webb to Jane Oliphant, February 3, 1915, Smith Collection.
18. Ibid.
19. Webb, Autobiography, p. 125.
20. Webb investigated the operations of both the extension services and the student loan system at Madison, apparently hoping that he could find work in those areas at Austin; a close friend, E. E. Davis, had worked with the Extension Division at Austin for some time, and this may have turned Webb's thinking in that direction. While at Madison he also considered going into business supplying projection equipment to schools using material supplied by the Extension Division (Jane Oliphant to Webb, July 9, 1916; Webb to Jane Oliphant, July 24, 1916, Smith Collection).
21. Walter Prescott Webb, "Increasing the Functional Value of History by the Use of the Problem Method of Presentation," *Texas History Teachers' Bulletin*, February 15, 1916, pp. 16–40.
22. This material was not published until 1923 (Walter Prescott Webb, "Miscellany of Texas Folklore," in *Coffee in the Gourd*, ed. J. Frank Dobie, Publications of the Texas Folklore Society 2:38–49).
23. Walter Prescott Webb, "Wild Horse Stories of Southwest Texas," in *Round the Levee*, ed. Stith Thompson, Publications of the Texas Folklore Society 1:58–61.
24. "She will help those M.A. aspirations when the time comes. In fact, she has shown her friendship very thoroughly already" (Webb to Jane Oliphant, April 30, 1916, Smith Collection).
25. Webb, Autobiography, p. 125.
26. Ibid., p. 127.
27. Ibid., p. 129.
28. Ibid. He was so depressed at this stage that he consulted a local medium; he later reported that her predictions proved to be remarkably accurate.
29. Ibid., p. 130; Frederic Duncalf to Webb, March 24, 1918, Webb Papers; Barker to Vinson, October 30, 1918, Eugene C. Barker Papers, Barker Texas History Center, University of Texas Archives; Eugene C. Barker, "General Report for the Year 1918–1919," Records of the Department of History, University of Texas, Barker Texas History Center, University of Texas Archives.
30. Webb, Autobiography, p. 130.
31. Ibid., p. 131; Walter Prescott Webb, "The University Professor and the Social Studies," in *History as High Adventure*, ed. E. C. Barksdale, p. 129.

32. Eugene C. Barker, "Future Development of the School of History," typescript in Records of the Department of History, University of Texas.
33. William C. Pool, *Eugene C. Barker, Historian*, chap. 2.
34. Webb, Autobiography, p. 132.
35. Ibid., p. 131.
36. Ibid.
37. Webb, "On the Texas Rangers," outline of thesis, n.d., Webb Papers.
38. Webb, "The Texas Rangers in the Mexican War," Webb Papers.
39. Eugene C. Barker, "Report of the Department of History, 1919–1920," Records of the Department of History, University of Texas.
40. Ibid.
41. Webb to Jane Webb, August 17, 1920, Smith Collection. The same letter has some bitter comments on his experiences in oil speculation; he had apparently lost money and was determined to have nothing further to do with it. Records in the Webb Papers, dated late 1919, indicate some small-scale speculation in oil leases in Parker, Jack, and Wilbarger Counties.
42. Walter Prescott Webb, handwritten draft of an article entitled "Record of Stephens County in the University of Texas," n.d., Smith Collection. Webb published a series of articles around this theme in the *Breckenridge Democrat* in 1915; clippings of these articles are in Webb Papers.
43. In 1922 Charles W. Ramsdell tried to organize an association of history teachers at the college level; his list of the potential members included forty-nine names (file, "Correspondence Relating to Organization of College History Teachers, 1921–1922," Charles W. Ramsdell Papers, Barker Texas History Center, University of Texas Archives).
44. Webb, Autobiography, p. 133.
45. Ibid., p. 135.

6. To Chicago—and Back

1. President Vinson to Webb, April 20, 1922, Webb Papers.
2. Webb to Dodd, January 16, 1922, Webb Papers; Dodd to Ramsdell, February 23, 1922, March 1, 1922, Charles W. Ramsdell Papers, Barker Texas History Center, University of Texas Archives. Dodd and Ramsdell exchanged positions during the summer session of 1923, and Barker taught at Chicago during the summer of 1924.
3. Webb to Dodd, January 16, 1922, Webb Papers; Webb to A. C. McLaughlin, January 2, 1922, Webb Papers.
4. Webb, Autobiography, p. 140.
5. Ibid.
6. Ibid., p. 141.
7. Webb to Ramsdell, July 22, 1923, Ramsdell Papers.

8. Webb, Autobiography, p. 143.
9. Webb to Ramsdell, July 6, 1923, Ramsdell Papers; Webb, Autobiography, p. 142.
10. Webb, Autobiography, p. 143.
11. Webb's contemporaries at Chicago included Avery Craven, Frank Graham, and Mack Swearingen.
12. Avery Craven to the writer, January 4, 1972.
13. Webb to Ramsdell, July 22, 1923, Ramsdell Papers.
14. Avery Craven to the writer, January 4, 1972.
15. Ibid.
16. Ramsdell to Dodd, February 15, 1922, Ramsdell Papers.
17. Webb, Autobiography, p. 146.
18. Ibid.
19. Webb to T. V. Smith, October 28, 1923, Webb Papers. Webb was careful in this letter to disguise his bitterness about the Chicago experience, possibly in deference to Smith's position as a dean at Chicago. At this point he was about $300 in debt, but his salary had increased to $2800 during his absence (Webb, Autobiography, p. 146; Ramsdell to Webb, July 11, 1923, Ramsdell Papers).
20. Barker to Webb, July 13, 1924; Logan Fulrath to Webb, July 24, (1924?); Webb to Fulrath, March 1, 1925; Trombly to Webb, October 28, 1924, February 10, 1926, July 10, 1927, Webb Papers.
21. Webb, Autobiography, p. 146.
22. T. R. Fehrenbach, Lone Star, pp. 644–648.
23. Webb, Autobiography, p. 179.
24. Between 1911 and 1918, the Webbs sold short-term oil and gas leases, a right-of-way, and a half-interest in mineral and gas rights from as low as $1 to as much as $7605. With the aid of the Ranger oil boom, the Webbs had turned an initial investment of about $3 per acre in 1903 into a return of $100 per acre fifteen years later (Stephens County Deed Records, 49:320, 43:234–235, 54:156–157, 60:124, 58:332–333, 59:265–266).
25. Webb, Autobiography, p. 198.
26. Fehrenbach, Lone Star, chap. 35; Emma Jean Walker, "The Contemporary Texan: An Examination of Major Additions to the Mythical Texan in the Twentieth Century," pp. 56–67; Donald W. Meinig, Imperial Texas, chap. 4.
27. Fehrenbach, Lone Star, pp. 633–634; Walker, "The Contemporary Texan," pp. 65–67, 90.
28. Hattie Anderson, "The Panhandle-Plains Historical Society," Mississippi Valley Historical Review 10 (September 1923): 182–185.
29. Bernard Augustine De Voto, The Literary Fallacy, p. 137.
30. During the twenties Webb collected material from such magazines as Adventure, Outlook, Outdoor Life, Wide World, and Farm and Fireside, in addition to the more standard publications— Saturday Evening Post, Collier's, and Harper's Magazine (Webb Papers).

31. John Avery Lomax, *Adventures of a Ballad Hunter*; Walter Pres-
    cott Webb, "Folklore of Texas," *Journal of American Folklore*
    28 (July/September 1915): 290–301; Walter Prescott Webb,
    "Miscellany of Texas Folklore," in *Coffee in the Gourd*, ed. J.
    Frank Dobie, Publications of the Texas Folklore Society 2:38–
    49; Walter Prescott Webb, "Wild Horse Stories of Southwest
    Texas," in *Round the Levee*, ed. Stith Thompson, Publications
    of the Texas Folklore Society 1:58–61.
32. For some comments on the place of the Ranger force in Mexican
    American folklore—of which Webb, like most of his generation,
    knew very little in the 1920's—see Américo Paredes, *With His
    Pistol in His Hand*.
33. Dobie had been brought up in the ranching country of South
    Texas, studied literature at Southwestern University and Co-
    lumbia, served as an artillery sergeant during World War I,
    and then returned to being a ranch foreman before teaching
    English at Stillwater, Oklahoma, and Austin.
34. Walter Prescott Webb, Review of *Legends of Texas*, by J. Frank
    Dobie, *Southwestern Historical Quarterly* 28 (January 1925):
    243–247.
35. Solon J. Buck, "The Progress and Possibilities of Mississippi Valley
    History," *Mississippi Valley Historical Review* 10 (June 1923):
    5.
36. Ibid., p. 6.
37. Ibid., p. 18.
38. Stow Persons, "The Origins of the Gentry," in *Essays on History
    and Literature*, ed. Robert H. Bremmer, pp. 83–117; quotations
    on p. 106.
39. Clifford L. Lord, ed., *Keepers of the Past*, pp. 3, 6.
40. Ibid., pp. 53–66.
41. Ibid., p. 5.
42. Dixon Ryan Fox, later an outstanding promoter of local history in
    New York, regarded the states of the Mississippi Valley as the
    most active and progressive in the nation in the early twenties
    (Dixon Ryan Fox, "State History," *Political Science Quarterly*
    36 [December 1921]: 572–585). The Mississippi Valley His-
    torical Association took an active interest in the field at that
    time, especially in promoting the teaching of state and local
    history in the schools and in publicizing the activities of new
    societies and their publications.
43. Walter M. Whitehill, *Independent Historical Societies*, pp. 326–
    330; Horace Bailey Carroll, "A Half-Century of the Texas State
    Historical Association," *Southwestern Historical Quarterly*,
    extra number, February 1, 1947, pp. 9–17.
44. Walter Prescott Webb and Horace Bailey Carroll, eds., *The Hand-
    book of Texas*.
45. A number of these reviews have been brought together in *Talks on
    Texas Books*, by Walter Prescott Webb.
46. Walter Prescott Webb, "Caldwell Prize in Local History," *Texas*

History Teachers' Bulletin, October 22, 1924, pp. 5–19; C. M. Caldwell to Webb, November 6, 1923, Webb Papers.
47. Rupert Norval Richardson, *The Comanche Barrier to South Plains Settlement;* J. Evetts Haley, "A Survey of Texas Cattle Drives to the North, 1866–1895"; James Evetts Haley, *The XIT Ranch of Texas and the Early Days of the Llano Estacado.*

7. The Search for a Medium

1. Accounts of the Emerson Hough controversy can be found in Wilson M. Hudson, *Andy Adams,* chap. 11, and William H. Hutchinson, *A Bar-Cross Man,* chap. 7. Hutchinson reprinted many of Rhodes's letters to Webb during the controversy; very few of Webb's letters survived. J. Frank Dobie also commented on Rhodes's participation in his introduction to Eugene Manlove Rhodes, *The Little World Waddies.*
2. The article appeared in the *Literary Digest International Book Review* 1 (November 1923): 34–35. The text is printed in Hutchinson, *A Bar-Cross Man,* pp. 190–193.
3. Webb had read Hough's *Way to the West* in 1921, and one of his more pleasant memories of the year spent at Chicago was reading *North of 36* as it appeared in serialized form (Webb, Autobiography, pp. 136, 143).
4. Webb preserved many of the incoming letters from Rhodes and Adams, but he did not keep copies of his outgoing letters. In most cases, Webb's views must be inferred from the replies to questions and the comments made by the two older men.
5. Adams to Webb, February 21, 1925, Webb Papers; Hudson, *Andy Adams,* p. 158.
6. Webb admired Adams's *Log of a Cowboy* and tried to boost his reputation; Hudson credits his efforts and those of J. Frank Dobie as being mainly responsible for rescuing Adams from literary oblivion (Hudson, *Andy Adams,* p. 205). Webb seems to have tried to give the older man some advice about the promotion of his work, but, although he prepared the way carefully, Adams did not react favorably (Webb to Adams, February 18, 1924; Adams to Webb, February 22, 1924; Rhodes to Webb, March 11, [1924?], Webb Papers).
7. Webb quoted in *Chicago Evening Post, Literary Review,* April 18, 1924, clipping in Webb Papers.
8. Draft Questionnaire, March 16, 1924, Webb Papers.
9. Henry replied to his critics in indirect fashion in a review in the *Literary Digest International Book Review* 3 (January 1925): 182–184. His main rejoinder came in the appendix to his own study of the Plains, *Conquering Our Great American Plains.* Although Webb reviewed the book (*Mississippi Valley Historical Review* 17 [March 1931]: 644–645), neither he nor Rhodes wanted to reopen the controversy; the realization that Henry

had lived in Abilene during the cattle era may have inhibited them to some degree (Rhodes to Webb, March 24, 1930; Webb to H. A. McComas, April 17, 1930, Webb Papers). Dobie described Henry's attack on Hough in the 1930 work as devastating, but as late as 1942 Webb referred to the original Henry article as an "unwarranted literary attack of Western people by an Eastern writer in an Eastern literary magazine" (J. Frank Dobie, *Guide to the Life and Literature of the Southwest*, p. 108; Webb, "Commencement Address, New Mexico State College of Agricultural and Mechanic Arts, May 19, 1941," typescript in Webb Papers).

10. Adams to Webb, March 14, 1924, Webb Papers.
11. Rhodes to Webb, December 20, (1923?), March 21, (1924?); Adams to Webb, March 14, 1924, Webb Papers. Webb suggested that Adams organize his views on western literature into an article and suggested the outlet. The result was an article entitled "Western Interpreters," in *Southwest Review* 10 (October 1924): 70–74.
12. Hough had been concerned with similar issues for some time prior to his death in 1923 (see Emerson Hough, "Are Americans People?" *Story World and Photodramatist* 4 [June 1923]: 11–15). In particular, he supported the campaign to limit immigration that culminated in the restrictive legislation of 1924.
13. Rhodes claimed that he had devoted most of his energies over the previous three years to fighting "those who hate *democracy* and who despise—and fear—the workers, the Americans . . ." (Rhodes to Webb, March 11, [1924?], Webb Papers).
14. Rhodes to Webb, January 15, (1924?), Webb Papers.
15. Rhodes to Webb, February 1, 1924, Webb Papers.
16. Rhodes to Webb, December 20, (1923?), Webb Papers.
17. David Burner, *The Politics of Provincialism*, p. 79.
18. Rhodes to Webb, (ca. March 21, 1924), Webb Papers.
19. Webb to Rhodes, (ca. March, April 1924), incorporated in a letter from Rhodes to Webb, March 11, 1924, Webb Papers.
20. Webb apparently suggested a new magazine, but Rhodes thought the idea impractical (Rhodes to Webb, March 11, 1924, Webb Papers). After that the discussion focused more on Webb's attempts to develop his own literary talents; both men provided comments on his story, "The Texas Ranger's Jewellery."
21. Rhodes to Webb, March 11, 1924, Webb Papers.
22. Adams to Webb, February 21, 1925, Webb Papers.
23. Adams to Webb, March 2, 1925, Webb Papers.
24. Rhodes to Webb, March 11, 1924, Webb Papers.
25. Walter Prescott Webb, "History as High Adventure," *American Historical Review* 64 (January 1959): 278.
26. Albert Edward Trombly (b. 1888) taught at the University of Texas from 1918 to 1922, spending the rest of his career at the University of Missouri.
27. Trombly to Webb, February 24, 1924, Webb Papers. As in the

case of the Adams and Rhodes correspondence, very few of
Webb's letters to Trombly have survived.

28. Ibid.
29. Trombly to Webb, February 15, (1924?), Webb Papers.
30. Ibid.
31. Webb, Autobiography, pp. 179, 198.
32. Trombly to Webb, October 28, 1924, Webb Papers.
33. Trombly to Webb, November 3, 1924, Webb Papers.
34. Trombly to Webb, January 8, 1926, Webb Papers.
35. Trombly to Webb, October 21, 1925, October 30, 1925, November 9, 1925, May 3, 1926, July 10, 1927, Webb Papers.
36. Trombly to Webb, December 6, 1925, Webb Papers.
37. Ibid.
38. Bernard Augustine De Voto, *The Literary Fallacy*.
39. Ibid., p. 150.
40. Ibid., p. 17.
41. Ibid., pp. 173–174.
42. Webb's influence on De Voto's thinking appears evident in *The Literary Fallacy*, p. 129. For De Voto's discussion of Powell's work, see ibid., pp. 133–135.
43. Dobie, *Life and Literature*, p. 9 (from the preface to the 1942 edition).
44. Ibid., p. 3.
45. Walter Van Tilburg Clark to Webb, September 16, 1959, Webb Papers.

8. Writing *The Great Plains*

1. Webb, Autobiography, p. 146. For an account of the vicissitudes of the Ranger study, see Llerena Friend, "Webb's Texas Rangers," *Southwestern Historical Quarterly* 74 (January 1971): 293–323. A number of the stories Webb wrote in the twenties were clearly an outgrowth of his Ranger studies: "Border Geometry," "The 13th Notch," "A Rio Grande Rendezvous," and "The Texas Ranger's Jewellery" show the influence of his interviews with veteran Rangers and his combing of the archival material (Webb Papers).
2. Eugene C. Barker, "Recommendation for Salaries, 1923–1924," Records of the Department of History, University of Texas, Barker Texas History Center, University of Texas Archives.
3. Webb to Barker, July 11, 1924; Barker to M. F. Hunt, September 26, 1924, Eugene C. Barker Papers, Barker Texas History Center, University of Texas Archives.
4. Walter Prescott Webb, Eugene C. Barker, and William E. Dodd, *The Growth of a Nation*. Barker initiated the project, brought in Webb to handle the post-1860 material, and added Dodd to help secure the adoption of the work in the South (Barker to Dodd, February 2, 1926; Webb to Dodd, February 1, 1926,

William E. Dodd Papers, Manuscripts Division, Library of Congress, Box 25).

5. Webb, Autobiography, p. 157.

6. For a detailed account of the circumstances in which these articles were written, see Friend, "Webb's Texas Rangers," pp. 304–305.

7. Webb, Autobiography, p. 136. A briefer account of this incident appears in the Preface to *The Great Plains*.

8. Webb, Autobiography, p. 136.

9. Ibid., p. 138.

10. Walter Prescott Webb, "The American Revolvers and the West," *Scribner's Magazine* 81 (February 1927): 171–178.

11. Webb, Autobiography, p. 146.

12. Ibid., p. 137.

13. See chap. 4.

14. Webb had already decided to regard the Plains as his area of special interest. At a dinner in honor of William E. Dodd in Chicago on July 27, 1923, Webb and his fellow southerners discussed their own plans in the light of Dodd's advice to push on with state histories and biographies, and Webb indicated that he intended to concentrate on the Plains; but this probably meant no more than a marking out of areas according to place of origin, with as yet little idea of the type of research to be attempted (Webb to Jane Webb, July 27, 1923, Smith Collection).

15. Webb to Rhodes, March 6, 1924, Webb Papers.

16. Adams's book came as a complete surprise. "No one had read it, no one in Texas knew about it. Literary education still consisted of English and New England classics. Anything Western was likely to be vulgar . . ." (Webb, Autobiography, pp. 146–147).

17. Webb credited his friend E. E. Davis, who had grown up in Erath County in North Central Texas, with the initial suggestion concerning the importance of both the windmill and barbed wire, and he indicated that the discussion took place not long after his return from Chicago (ibid., pp. 147, 148). A number of incoming letters dated early 1924 suggest that Webb had asked for information about fencing and barbed wire (Mack Swearingen to Webb, February 24, 1924; James Westfall Thompson to Webb, January 21, 1924; Rhodes to Webb, March 11, 1924, Webb Papers). Webb wrote to the Library of Congress, the United States Patent Office, and a number of wire manufacturers in January 1924, seeking information about the evolution of barbed wire (Webb Papers). He did not have to look far for contemporary accounts of the significance of barbed wire; his clippings from the *Dallas Morning News* indicate that the topic was discussed on a number of occasions, and, in an interview dated December 25, 1924, an associate editor of the paper gave the main credit for the development of Texas agriculture to the invention of barbed wire, with the introduction of well-drilling machinery as the next most significant factor (Webb Papers). Most of Webb's formal inquiries about windmills are dated early 1927.

18. Webb, Autobiography, p. 148.
19. Ibid., p. 153.
20. In what may have been an examination paper written in 1913, Webb set out in brief note form the characteristics of various European countries in terms of their topographic, hydrographic, and meteorographic advantages: boundaries, river systems, climate, mineral deposits, and animal and plant life were noted and their impact on national development indicated (Webb, examination paper for Institutional History 6, dated May 16, 1913, Smith Collection).
21. Webb, Autobiography, p. 154. Over thirty years later, Webb defended the view that physical geography must be the starting point for the study of evolving cultures, asserting that "land is the matrix out of which culture grows" (Walter Prescott Webb, "Geographical-Historical Concepts in American History," *Annals of the Association of American Geographers* 50 (June 1960): 85–93).
22. John Wesley Powell, *Report on the Lands of the Arid Region of the United States.*
23. An undated entry in a notebook in the Webb Papers. The notebook was apparently purchased while Webb was a student at Chicago in 1922–1923: the last date given before this entry is "summer 1924." It seems likely that the summary of his views on the role of the environment—of which this comment is part—was made in 1925, for it represents a viewpoint that was not fully formed by late 1924.
24. Ibid.
25. Ibid.
26. Ibid.
27. George F. Parker, "Pioneer Methods," *Saturday Evening Post,* June 3, 1922, p. 32.
28. Ibid., p. 36.
29. Herbert Quick, "One Man's Life: An Autobiography," *Saturday Evening Post,* June 20, 1925, pp. 3–4, June 27, 1925, pp. 16–17; July 4, 1925, p. 16; July 11, 1925, pp. 24–25; July 25, 1925, pp. 20–21; August 1, 1925, pp. 28–32; August 15, 1925, pp. 28–30; August 29, 1925, p. 23; September 5, 1925, p. 25.
30. Webb used a quotation from the Bobbs-Merrill edition of *One Man's Life* at the head of the first chapter and cited it again in the final chapter.
31. Webb, Autobiography, pp. 164–165.
32. Thurber to Webb, March 25, 1927, Webb Papers. Only a few of Webb's letters to Ginn and Company have survived among his papers, and the company file cannot be located.
33. Webb to Dodd, February 28, 1927, Dodd Papers.
34. Wissler to Webb, March 4, 1927, Webb Papers.
35. Dodd to Webb, July 1, 1927, Webb Papers. The details of this project are not clear. Various circulars in the Dodd Papers indicate that Dodd was a member of a departmental committee at Chicago concerned with producing a series of biographical

studies. There was also some discussion of the possibility of
founding an institute for research on biography. Since Dodd
was also collaborating with Webb and Barker on the writing of
a school textbook at this point, the whole question may have
come up in the context of that work.
36. Ibid.
37. Walter Prescott Webb, "A Texas Buffalo Hunt," *Holland's Magazine* 46 (October 1927): 10–11, 101–102.
38. By this point Webb had had enough contact with the publishing
business to make him aware of the best approaches to use.
Years earlier he had tried to interest publishers in his—as yet
unwritten—history of the Texas Rangers, and he always remained convinced of the advantages of selling an idea rather
than a completed manuscript (Webb, Autobiography, p. 165).
39. Thurber to Webb, March 25, 1927, Webb Papers.
40. Thurber to Webb, May 4, 1927, July 6, 1927, Webb Papers.
41. Thurber to Webb, August 20, 1927, Webb Papers.
42. Trombly to Webb, August 20, 1927, Webb Papers.
43. Chief Clerk, Smithsonian Institution, to Webb, February 27, 1928;
General Hugh L. Scott, ret., to Webb, March 11, 1928; Capt.
W. S. Rumbough, Signal Corps, to Webb, April 24, 1927; Major
Alfred E. Larabee, Signal Corps, U.S.M.A., to Webb, April 25,
1928; memorandum, Division of Bibliography, Library of Congress, to Webb, April 28, 1928, Webb Papers. Webb discussed
the question of water law with Harbert Davenport—an old
friend and an attorney with an interest in state history—during
1928 (Davenport to Webb, January 26, 1928, November 10,
1928, Webb Papers). Webb's own account of his discovery of
the relevance of the question is in Autobiography, p. 154.
44. Ibid., p. 167.
45. G. H. Moore to Webb, October 20, 1928, Webb Papers.
46. G. H. Moore to Webb, March 23, 1929, Webb Papers. The basis
for Webb's assumption is not clear. Pelzer did present a paper
on ox-team freighting on the Plains at a conference of western
historians at Boulder several months later. Webb also participated and delivered a paper on technological adaptation on the
Plains; both papers were printed in James F. Willard and Colin
B. Goodykoontz, eds., *The Trans–Mississippi West*. Pelzer's *The
Cattleman's Frontier* did not appear until 1936. Webb may have
known of a pamphlet written by Pelzer and Clara M. Daley entitled *Aids for History Teachers by the Department of History*
and suspected that Pelzer was likely to produce a historical
geography of the Plains region.
47. Sections of the work had been published in article form prior to
1931 (Walter Prescott Webb, "The Land and Life of the Great
Plains," *West Texas Historical Association Yearbook* 4 [June
1928]: 58–85; "The Great Plains Block the Expansion of the
South," *Panhandle-Plains Historical Review* 2 [1929]: 3–21;
"Some Vagaries of the Search for Water in the Great Plains,"

Panhandle-Plains Historical Review 3 [1930]: 28–37).

48. Webb, Autobiography, p. 147.
49. Ibid.
50. Ibid., pp. 168–169.
51. Ibid., p. 169.
52. Ibid., p. 157.
53. Ibid., p. 158.

9. Raising the Flag

1. Frederic L. Paxson, review of *The Great Plains*, by Walter Prescott Webb, *American Historical Review* 37 (January 1932): 359–360; Robert G. Caldwell, review of *The Great Plains,* by Walter Prescott Webb, *Mississippi Valley Historical Review* 18 (March 1932): 581–583.
2. Walter Prescott Webb, *The Great Plains*, pp. 3–9.
3. Ibid., p. 32.
4. Ibid., p. 48.
5. Ibid., p. 56.
6. Ibid., chap. 4.
7. Ibid., pp. 167–179.
8. Ibid., pp. 184–192.
9. Ibid., p. 226.
10. Ibid., p. 207.
11. Ibid., p. 206.
12. Ibid., chap. 11.
13. Ibid., p. 160.
14. Ibid., pp. 462–463.
15. Ibid., pp. 476–483.
16. Webb, "The Communal-Collegiate System versus the Republican-Patriarchal System in the History of Medieval Europe," Smith Collection.
17. Webb, *The Great Plains*, p. 507.
18. Paxson, review of *The Great Plains*, p. 359.
19. Walter Prescott Webb, "History as High Adventure," *American Historical Review* 64 (January 1959): 279. The undated set of notes headed "Frederick Jackson Turner: Historian" are filed in the Webb Papers. Walter Prescott Webb, review of *History of the American West*, by Frederic L. Paxson, *Southwestern Historical Quarterly* 28 (January 1925): 247–252.
20. Webb, taped interview, August 18, 1953.
21. Webb, *The Great Plains*, pp. 140–141.
22. Paxson, review of *The Great Plains*, p. 359.
23. Harlan Barrows, "Geography as Human Ecology," *Annals of the Association of American Geographers* 13 (March 1923): 1–14; John Leighly, "What Has Happened to Physical Geography?" *Annals of the Association of American Geographers* 45 (December 1955): 314.

24. Read Bain, in Fred A. Shannon, *An Appraisal of Walter Prescott Webb's "The Great Plains: A Study in Institutions and Environment"*, Critiques of Research in the Social Sciences, 3:223, 232; Allan Nevins, *The Gateway to History*, p. 314. The theories of the late nineteenth-century German geographer Friedrich Ratzel concerning the impact of the physical environment on human social activity were highly regarded by American geographers and historians in the early twentieth century. Ellsworth Huntington's studies of the effect of climate on human behavior represent one the of the best-known strands of American environmentalism.
25. Webb, Autobiography, p. 174.
26. Ibid., p. 176.
27. Webb's account of this development implied that the idea emerged only after the publication of the book in 1931 (ibid., p. 176). But a notation by Barker in the departmental budget request for 1928/1929 indicated that he expected Webb to take his doctorate at Austin in June 1929, using part of the Plains book as his dissertation (Budget of the Department of History for the regular session 1928/1929, Records of the Department of History, University of Texas, Barker Texas History Center, University of Texas Archives). In December 1931 Dodd made it clear that he wanted Webb to spend a full semester and two summer sessions at Chicago and take his examinations—after which the book would be accepted as his thesis (Dodd to Barker, December 31, 1931, Eugene C. Barker Papers, Barker Texas History Center, University of Texas Archives). Webb had no intention of returning unless very heavy pressure was exerted; apart from the question of personal pride, he realized that he was by now out of touch with the material on which he would be examined (Webb, Autobiography, p. 176).
28. Minutes of Department of History meeting, March 9, 1929; report of decisions of a meeting of the Department of History, March 25, 1931, Records of the Department of History, University of Texas.
29. Report of decisions . . . March 25, 1931, Records of the Department of History, University of Texas.
30. Walter Prescott Webb, *The Texas Rangers*.
31. Webb to Dodd, October 4, 1931, William E. Dodd Papers, Manuscripts Division, Library of Congress, Box 37.
32. Webb, Autobiography, p. 184.
33. Ibid.
34. Webb discussed his business methods in some detail in Autobiography, pp. 200–217. He invested shrewdly, selecting areas of the city where values increased rapidly as Austin expanded in the postwar decades.
35. Edmund E. Day, foreword to Herbert Blumer, *An Appraisal of Thomas and Znaniecki's ˜he Polish Peasant in Europe and America"*, Critiques of Research in the Social Sciences, 1:ix–xii.

10. Defending the Redoubt

1. Fred A. Shannon, *An Appraisal of Walter Prescott Webb's "The Great Plains: A Study in Institutions and Environment"*, Critiques of Research in the Social Sciences, 3:10.
2. Ibid., p. 9.
3. Ibid., pp. 121–133.
4. Ibid., pp. 37, 52.
5. Ibid., p. 61.
6. The introductions to each of the three volumes of appraisal published under the auspices of the council, together with the commentary by Read Bain at the end of each volume, provide the best impression of the aims of the project and the extent to which these were accomplished.
7. The panel chosen to examine the appraisal was drawn both from the discipline involved and from some of the adjacent disciplines. At each conference, both the author and the appraiser had the opportunity for further comment, and at the end of each exercise the sociologist Read Bain prepared both the text of the proceedings and an interpretive commentary. Of those attending the Shannon appraisal, three had attended both the previous conferences: Read Bain, the economist Edwin G. Nourse, and the political scientist Frederick W. Coker. Three others—the historian Roy F. Nichols, the sociologist Louis Wirth, and the psychologist Albert T. Poffenberger—had attended the first conference, dealing with *The Polish Peasant* by Thomas and Znaniecki. Arthur M. Schlesinger, who chaired the conference on *The Great Plains*, had attended the second conference as an observer; but, as a member of the Committee on Appraisal, he was familiar with the general purposes of the exercise and almost certainly was aware of the general direction of the discussion of the Thomas and Znaniecki work.
8. Edwin G. Nourse in Shannon, *Walter Prescott Webb's "The Great Plains"*, p. x.
9. Ibid.
10. The attack on Webb's procedures extended through most of the appraisal, but the best summary of Shannon's positions can be found in the blunt comments he made during the afternoon session of the conference (Shannon, *Walter Prescott Webb's "The Great Plains"*, pp. 186–188).
11. Ibid., pp. 6–8, 37, 50–51, 112.
12. Roy F. Nichols, in ibid., p. 142.
13. Walter Prescott Webb, in ibid., p. 115 (see also p. 133). In fairness to Webb it should be pointed out that both his editor and the publisher's readers advised him to reduce the documentation of the book (Thurber to Webb, January 17, 1928, Webb Papers). One referred to the manuscript as "an enlarged doctoral dissertation, with its full minutiae of statistical details, its careful references, and its exhaustiveness of treatment." Both agreed

that, as it stood in 1929, the manuscript was too packed with detail and repetition to be of general interest.

14. Shannon, *Walter Prescott Webb's "The Great Plains"*, pp. 186–187.
15. Webb, in ibid., p. 211.
16. Ibid., p. 210.
17. Ibid., pp. 114, 210.
18. Ibid., p. 114. "It may be of interest to know that the book was written in a state of suppressed emotion. . . . It may be bad form for one who earns his living teaching what may be classed as historical composition. On this point I am utterly shameless, because I believe that deep feeling for a subject makes for harder work and better writing."
19. Ibid., p. 112.
20. Webb, Autobiography, p. 137. In an essay written toward the end of his career, Webb discussed the role of the hypothesis in historical inquiry and stressed the need for the rigorous testing of such tentative propositions. But he was not able to maintain a clear distinction between thesis and hypothesis: in the same article he noted that "I wrote *The Great Plains* defending my first hypothesis in four and a half months" (Walter Prescott Webb, "Hypothesis and History," in *History as High Adventure*, ed. E. C. Barksdale, p. 177).
21. Walter Prescott Webb, *The Great Plains*, p. 485. For Shannon's comment on this passage, see Shannon, *Walter Prescott Webb's "The Great Plains"*, pp. 8–9; and for Webb's rejoinder, see Webb in ibid., p. 127.
22. "In my opinion, he [Shannon] failed to discover the method followed in the book . . . the method . . . was to view the entire round to life in the Great Plains, from the geological foundations of the literary and mystical superstructure" (Shannon, *Walter Prescott Webb's "The Great Plains"*, p. 123). "At no place, in no chapter, does he attempt to look at the whole book" (ibid., p. 131). See also ibid., p. 144.
23. "I did not undertake to examine all the literature. It wasn't necessary. When the picture is finished, it is time to stop" (ibid., p. 213).
24. Ibid., p. 135.
25. Ibid., p. 117.
26. Edward Everett Dale, *The Cross Timbers*. Dale's account of his early experiences in the area shows little trace of the hostility and frustration that dominate Webb's memories of his childhood, and it is not surprising that it was not until he left the area that he became aware of its distinctive character.
27. Ernest S. Osgood, "I Discover Western History," *Western Historical Quarterly* 3 (July 1972): 241–251.
28. John D. Hicks, *My Life with History*.
29. Edward Everett Dale, in Shannon, *Walter Prescott Webb's "The Great Plains"*, p. 172.
30. For example, Dale's comments on the psychology of the Plainsman (ibid., pp. 202–205).

31. Charles Colby, in ibid., pp. 146–147.
32. Louis Wirth, in ibid., pp. 179–182, 207–208. Colby agreed that, from a geographer's point of view, Webb did not belong in the determinist school (ibid., p. 207).
33. Walter Prescott Webb, "Geographical-Historical Concepts in American History," *Annals of the Association of American Geographers* 50 (June 1960): 85–93.
34. For an extended comment on the Shannon appraisal from one who sympathized with Webb's position, see John W. Caughey, "A Criticism of the Critique of Webb's *Great Plains*," *Mississippi Valley Historical Review* 27 (December 1940): 442–444.
35. For a review of the Shannon appraisal, see Read Bain's comments in Shannon, *Walter Prescott Webb's "The Great Plains"*, pp. 215, 233–234.
36. Webb, Autobiography, p. 170.
37. Fred A. Shannon, *The Farmer's Last Frontier*, New Economic History of the United States, 5:19–25.
38. Webb to E. E. Davis, July 3, 1940, Webb Papers.

Bibliography

ARCHIVAL MATERIAL

Walter Prescott Webb Papers

Webb, Walter Prescott, Papers. Archives Division, Texas State Library, Austin, Texas.
  In 1972 this collection of material came into the possession of Mr. C. B. Smith, Sr., of Austin, and has since been deposited with the Texas State Library. The holding was examined prior to archival processing, but its main strengths appeared to be its holding of personal letters and material dating from Webb's undergraduate years. It contains a number of letters from Webb to Jane Oliphant prior to their marriage in late 1916 and over thirty class papers and themes written by Webb during his student years, 1909–1915. As the holding was not organized at the time it was examined, the citations include only the date of the document concerned. To avoid confusion with the holding of Webb materials in the Barker Texas History Center Archives, this second collection has been described in the Notes as the "Smith Collection."
Webb, Walter Prescott, Papers. Barker Texas History Center, University of Texas Archives, Austin, Texas.
  This collection holds some personal correspondence, most of the incoming letters from Eugene Manlove Rhodes, Andy Adams, and Albert E. Trombly, drafts of articles and speeches, a bibliography of Webb's writings by Bruce Hupp, and an unrevised autobiography. It also contains a good deal of routine correspondence and a large amount of material classified as research notes; but, as Webb's research methods were rather unusual, the latter consists mainly of magazine articles, clippings, and letters rather than notes. Webb did not maintain a system of file cards; as a result, it is almost impossible to reconstruct the research procedures he used for *The Great Plains* with any accuracy.

Other Collections

Barker, Eugene C., Papers. Barker Texas History Center, University of Texas Archives, Austin, Texas.

Department of History, Records of the, University of Texas. Barker Texas History Center, University of Texas Archives, Austin, Texas. These papers are awaiting classification, but two boxes containing bound volumes of departmental reports, minutes, and draft budgets for the period 1910–1938 were consulted.

Dobie, J. Frank, Papers. Harry Ransom Humanities Research Center, University of Texas, Austin, Texas.

Dodd, William E., Papers. Manuscripts Division, Library of Congress, Washington, D.C.

President's Office, Records of the, University of Texas. Barker Texas History Center, University of Texas Archives, Austin, Texas. These papers are also awaiting classification, but nine boxes of material were available for examination; these consist mainly of routine correspondence between the President's Office and senior members of the Department of History and the Department of Institutional History.

Ramsdell, Charles W., Papers. Barker Texas History Center, University of Texas Archives, Austin, Texas.

Stephens County Deed Records. Breckenridge, Texas.

Webb, Walter Prescott, File. Ginn and Company, Boston, Massachusetts.
This file was made available by Xerox College Publishing, Lexington. Unfortunately, those sections of the file which deal with the period prior to the publication of *The Great Plains* have disappeared.

THESES AND DISSERTATIONS

ALEXANDER, CHARLES C. "Crusade for Conformity: The Ku Klux Klan in Texas, 1920–1927." M.A. thesis, University of Texas, 1959.

BARNARD, HELEN D. "Early History of Research in Texas Archaeology by the Department of Anthropology, and the History of the Anthropology Museum of the University of Texas." M.A. thesis, University of Texas, 1939.

BERRY, MARGARET C. "Student Life and Customs, 1883–1933, at the University of Texas." 2 vols. Ed.D. dissertation, Teachers College, Columbia University, 1965.

BRADLEY, ALLEN CALLAWAY. "The History of Education in Eastland County, Texas." M.A. thesis, University of Texas, 1939.

BREWER, THOMAS B. "A History of the Department of History of the University of Texas, 1883–1951." M.A. thesis, University of Texas, 1957.

COONS, ROBERT R. "The Life and Educational Achievements of Governor Oran Milo Roberts." M.A. thesis, University of Texas, 1920.

GRAY, JAMES LOUIS. "The Second Generation on the Plains: A Comparative Study of Selected Canadian and American Literature." M.A. thesis, University of Texas, 1964.

HALEY, JAMES EVETTS. "A Survey of Texas Cattle Drives to the North, 1866–1895." M.A. thesis, University of Texas, 1926.

HARTSFIELD, LOY W. "A History of Stephens County, Texas." M.A. thesis, University of Texas, 1929.

HODNETT, VIRDIE C. "History of Rural Education in Texas, 1900–1935." M.Ed. thesis, University of Texas, 1935.

HUFF, MILLICENT S. "A Study of Work Done by Texas Railroad Companies to Encourage Immigration into Texas between 1870 and 1890." M.A. thesis, University of Texas, 1955.

KERR, HOMER LEE. "Migration into Texas, 1865–1880." Ph.D. dissertation, University of Texas, 1953.

LILES, VERNER. "Pioneering on the Plains: The History of Martin County, Texas." M.A. thesis, University of Texas, 1953.

LINDSEY, ROBERT Y., JR. "A History of Eastland County, Texas." M.A. thesis, University of Texas, 1940.

MC KINNEY, MARY E. "The Southwestern Town." M.A. thesis, University of Texas, 1952.

PETERSON, FLORIDE S. "The Changes in the Objectives and Materials in Geography Textbooks since 1850." M.A. thesis, University of Texas, 1935.

RATHJEN, FREDERICK W. "The Texas Panhandle Frontier." Ph.D. dissertation, University of Texas, 1970.

ROSS, MAUD E. "The Early Years of John A. Lomax." M.A. thesis, University of Texas, 1953.

SAWEY, ORLAN L. "The Cowboy Autobiography." Ph.D. dissertation, University of Texas, 1953.

SPRATT, JOHN S. "The Economic Development of Texas, 1875–1901." Ph.D. dissertation, University of Texas, 1953.

WALKER, EMMA JEAN. "The Contemporary Texan: An Examination of Major Additions to the Mythical Texan in the Twentieth Century." Ph.D. dissertation, University of Texas, 1966.

WEATHER, RAYMOND D. "The Great Plains—Zone of Transition." M.A. thesis, University of Texas, 1968.

WEBB, WALTER PRESCOTT. "The Texas Rangers in the Mexican War." M.A. thesis, University of Texas, 1920.

WILLIAMS, HARRY, JR. "The Development of a Market Economy in Texas: The Establishment of the Railway Network, 1836–1890." Ph.D. dissertation, University of Texas, 1957.

WOLFE, THOMAS HERNDON. "Dimensions of a Prominent American Graduate School: The Graduate School of the University of Texas in Austin, 1883–1969." M.A. thesis, University of Texas, 1970.

YOUNG, MARGARET S. "The Social Efficiency of the Texas Small Town in Relation to Its Young People." M.A. thesis, University of Texas, 1930.

YOUNKER, DONNA LEE. "Teacher Education in Texas, 1879–1919." Ph.D. dissertation, University of Texas, 1964.

BOOKS AND ARTICLES

ADAMS, ANDY. *Log of a Cowboy*. 1927. Reprint. Lincoln: University of Nebraska Press, 1968.

————. "Western Interpreters." *Southwest Review* 10 (October 1924): 70–74.

AIKMAN, DUNCAN, ed. *The Taming of the Frontier*. New York: Minton Balch and Co., 1925.

ALLEN, WALTER. *The Urgent West: The American Dream and Modern Man*. New York: E. P. Dutton and Co., 1969.

ANDERSON, HATTIE. "The Panhandle-Plains Historical Society." *Mississippi Valley Historical Review* 10 (September 1923): 182–185.

ANDERSON, SHERWOOD. *A Story Teller's Story*. New York: B. W. Heubsch, 1924.

ANGOFF, CHARLES. *The Tone of the Twenties, and Other Essays*. South Brunswick, N.J.: A. S. Barnes, 1966.

Annual Report of the President of Bryn Mawr College. Philadelphia, 1894–1899.

ARNOW, HARRIETTE L. *Flowering of the Cumberland*. New York: Macmillan Co., 1963.

————. *Seedtime on the Cumberland*. New York: Macmillan Co., 1960.

ATHERTON, LEWIS ELDON. *Main Street on the Middle Border*. Bloomington: Indiana University Press, 1954.

BAKER, O. K. "The Agriculture of the Great Plains Region." *Annals of the Association of American Geographers* 13 (September 1923): 100–167.

BARKER, EUGENE C. "The Changing View of the Function of History." *Social Studies* 29 (September 1923): 100–167.

————. *Speeches, Responses, and Essays: Critical and Historical*. Austin: Eugene C. Barker Texas History Center, 1955.

————. "Three Types of Historical Interpretation." *Southwestern Historical Quarterly* 45 (April 1942): 323–334.

BARKSDALE, E. C., ed. *History as High Adventure*. Austin: Pemberton Press, 1969.

BARROWS, HARLAN. "Geography as Human Ecology." *Annals of the Association of American Geographers* 13 (March 1923): 1–14.

BASS, HERBERT J., ed. *The State of American History*. Chicago: Quadrangle Books, 1970.

BATTLE, W. J. "A Concise History of the University of Texas." *Southwestern Historical Quarterly* 54 (April 1951): 391–411.

BENEDICT, HARRY YANDELL, comp. *A Source-Book Relating to the History of the University of Texas: Legislative, Legal, Bibliographical, and Statistical*. Austin: University of Texas, 1917.

BENSON, LEE. *Turner and Beard: American Historical Writing Reconsidered*. Glencoe, Ill.: Free Press, 1960.

BERRY, MARGARET C. "Campus Culture: A Product of Its Own History." *Journal of College Student Personnel* 8 (January 1967): 3–9.

BILLINGTON, RAY. *The Genesis of the Frontier Thesis: A Study in Historical Creativity*. San Marino: Huntington Library, 1971.

BLEGEN, THEODORE C. "The Twenty-fifth Annual Meeting of the Mississippi Valley Historical Association." *Mississippi Valley Historical Review* 19 (September 1932): 243–254.

BLUMER, HERBERT. *An Appraisal of Thomas and Znaniecki's "The*

Polish Peasant in Europe and America". Critiques of Research in the Social Sciences, vol. 1. New York: Social Sciences Research Council, 1939.

BOBBITT, JOHN FRANKLIN. *The San Antonio School System: A Survey Conducted by J. F. Bobbitt of the School of Education, University of Chicago, January 1915.* San Antonio, Texas: The San Antonio School Board, 1915.

BOYNTON, PERCY. *The Rediscovery of the Frontier.* Chicago: University of Chicago Press, 1931.

BRANCH, EDWARD DOUGLAS. *The Cowboy and His Interpreters.* New York: D. Appleton and Co., 1926.

———. *The Sentimental Years, 1836–1860.* New York: Appleton-Century-Crofts, 1934.

———. *Westward: The Romance of the American Frontier.* New York: D. Appleton and Co., 1930.

BREMMER, ROBERT H., ed. *Essays on History and Literature.* Columbus: Ohio State University Press, 1966.

BRIGHAM, ALBERT PERRY. *Geographic Influences in American History.* New York: Chautauqua Press, 1903.

———. Review of *Physical Geography,* by William Morris Davis. *School Review* 7 (April 1899): 248–249.

Bryn Mawr College: President's Report. Philadelphia, 1893–1894.

BUCK, SOLON J. "The Progress and Possibilities of Mississippi Valley History." *Mississippi Valley Historical Review* 10 (June 1923): 5–20.

BURNER, DAVID. *The Politics of Provincialism: The Democratic Party in Transition, 1918–1932.* New York: Knopf, 1968.

BURT, STRUTHERS. "Crime against the West." *Harper's Monthly Magazine* 152 (April 1926): 608–617.

———. "Dry West." *Scribner's Magazine* 83 (February 1928): 142–150.

BYE, RAYMOND T. *An Appraisal of Frederick C. Mills' "The Behaviour of Prices".* Critiques of Research in the Social Sciences, vol. 2. New York: Social Sciences Research Council, 1940.

CALDWELL, ROBERT G. Review of *The Great Plains,* by Walter Prescott Webb. *Mississippi Valley Historical Review* 18 (March 1932): 581–583.

CALLCOTT, GEORGE H. *History in the United States, 1800–1860: Its Practice and Purpose.* Baltimore: Johns Hopkins Press, 1970.

CARMICHAEL, EMMET BRYAN. "John William Mallet: Scholar-Teacher-Scientist." *Scalpel* 25 (Winter 1955): 35–42.

CARPENTER, CHARLES H. *History of American Schoolbooks.* Philadelphia: University of Pennsylvania Press, 1963.

CARROLL, HORACE BAILEY. "A Half-Century of the Texas State Historical Association." *Southwestern Historical Quarterly,* February 1, 1947, pp. 9–17.

———. *Texas County Histories: A Bibliography.* Austin: Texas State Historical Association, 1943.

——— and GUTSCH, MILTON R., eds. and comps. *Texas History Theses: A Check-list of the Theses and Dissertations Relating to Texas*

History Accepted at the University of Texas, 1893–1951. Austin: Texas State Historical Association, 1955.

Catalogue of the University of Texas. Austin: University of Texas, 1905–1920.

CATHER, WILLA. *O Pioneers!* New York: Houghton Mifflin Co., 1913.

CAUGHEY, JOHN W. "A Criticism of the Critique of Webb's *Great Plains.*" *Mississippi Valley Historical Review* 27 (December 1940): 442–444.

CHAPPELL, JOHN E. "Harlan Barrows and Environmentalism." *Annals of the Association of American Geographers* 61 (March 1971): 198–201.

COLBY, CHARLES. "Changing Currents in Geographic Thought in America." *Annals of the Association of American Geographers* 26 (March 1936): 1–37.

CONNOR, SEYMOUR VINCENT. *West Texas County Histories.* Austin: Archives Division of the Texas State Library, 1954.

COWAN, LOUISE. *The Fugitive Group: A Literary History.* Baton Rouge: Louisiana State University Press, 1959.

CRAVEN, AVERY. "A History Still Unwritten." *Western Historical Quarterly* 2 (October 1971): 377–383.

CUNLIFFE, MARCUS, and WINKS, ROBIN W., eds. *Pastmasters: Some Essays on American Historians.* New York: Harper and Row, 1969.

DALE, EDWARD EVERETT. *Cow Country.* Norman: University of Oklahoma Press, 1942.

————. *The Cross Timbers: Memories of a North Texas Boyhood.* Austin: University of Texas Press, 1966.

————. *Outlines and References for Oklahoma History.* 4th rev. ed. Norman, Okla.: Transcript Press, 1936.

————. *The Range Cattle Industry: Ranching on the Great Plains from 1865 to 1925.* Norman: University of Oklahoma Press, 1930.

————. "The Romance of the Range." *West Texas Historical Association Year-book* 5 (June 1929): 3–22.

DAVIS, WILLIAM MORRIS. "Physical Geography in the High School." *School Review* 8 (September 1900): 388–404, 449–456.

DAVISON, WALTER B. "History in the State Normal Schools." *Proceedings of the Mississippi Valley Historical Association for 1920–1921* 10:506–521.

DE VOTO, BERNARD AUGUSTINE. "Footnote on the West." *Harper's Monthly Magazine* 155 (November 1927): 713–722.

————. *The Literary Fallacy.* Boston: Little, Brown and Co., 1944.

————. "The Novelist of the Cattle Kingdom." Introduction to *The Hired Man on Horseback: My Story of Eugene Manlove Rhodes,* by May Davison Rhodes. Boston: Houghton Mifflin Co., 1938.

DOBIE, J. FRANK. *Guide to the Life and Literature of the Southwest.* Rev. and enlarged ed. Dallas: Southern Methodist University Press, 1952.

————. *Legends of Texas.* Publications of the Texas Folklore Society, vol. 3. Austin: Texas Folklore Society, 1924.

————; BOATRIGHT, MODY C.; and RANSOM, HARRY H., eds. *In the*

Shadow of History. Publications of the Texas Folklore Society, vol. 15. Austin: Texas Folklore Society, 1939.

DONDORE, DOROTHY ANNE. *The Prairie and the Making of Middle America: Four Centuries of Description.* Cedar Rapids, Iowa: Torch Press, 1926.

DRYER, CHARLES R. "Genetic Geography." *Annals of the Association of American Geographers* 10 (1920): 3–16.

DUFFEY, BERNARD I. *The Chicago Renaissance in American Letters: A Critical History.* East Lansing: Michigan State College Press, 1954.

DUGGER, RONNIE, ed. *Three Men in Texas: Bedichek, Webb and Dobie; Essays by Their Friends in the Texas Observer.* Austin: University of Texas Press, 1967.

DUNLAP, LESLIE WHITTAKER. *American Historical Societies in the United States, 1790–1860.* Madison, Wis.: Cantwell Printing Co., 1944.

DYKSTRA, ROBERT. *The Cattle Towns.* New York: Knopf, 1968.

EBY, FREDERICK. *The Development of Education in Texas.* New York: Macmillan Co., 1925.

ECHOLS, WILLIAM HOLDING. "John William Mallet: Scholar, Teacher, Gentleman." *Alumni Bulletin of the University of Virginia,* 3rd series, 6 (January 1913): 4–47.

EDWARDS, GEORGE C. "Texas: The Big Southwestern Specimen." *Nation,* March 21, 1923, pp. 334–337.

ELLIOTT, CLAUDE. *Theses on Texas History: A Check-List of Theses and Dissertations in Texas History Produced in the Departments of History of Eighteen Texas Graduate Schools and Thirty-Three Graduate Schools Outside of Texas, 1907–1952.* Austin: Texas State Historical Association, 1955.

ELLIS, DAVID M., ed. *The Frontier in American Development: Essays in Honor of Paul Wallace Gates.* Ithaca, N.Y.: Cornell University Press, 1969.

ELSON, RUTH MILLER. *Guardians of Tradition: American Schoolbooks of the Nineteenth Century.* Lincoln: University of Nebraska Press, 1964.

EMMONS, DAVID M. *Garden in the Grasslands: Boomer Literature of the Central Great Plains.* Lincoln: University of Nebraska Press, 1971.

FEHRENBACH, T. R. *Lone Star: A History of Texas and the Texans.* New York: Macmillan Co., 1968.

FERRIS, ROBERT G., ed. *The American West: An Appraisal.* Santa Fe: Museum of New Mexico Press, 1963.

FITE, GILBERT C. "The Great Plains: A Colonial Area." *Current History* 40 (May 1961): 280–284.

FOREMAN, CAROLYN THOMAS. *The Cross Timbers.* Muskogee, Okla.: Privately printed, 1947.

FOX, DIXON RYAN. "State History." *Political Science Quarterly* 36 (December 1921): 572–585.

———. "State History II." *Political Science Quarterly* 37 (March 1922): 100–118.

FRIEDRICHS, ROBERT W. *A Sociology of Sociology.* New York: Free Press, 1970.

FRIEND, LLERENA. "Webb's Texas Rangers." *Southwestern Historical Quarterly* 74 (January 1971): 293–323.

FUERMAN, GEORGE M. *Reluctant Empire.* Garden City, N.Y.: Doubleday and Co., 1957.

FUSON, ROBERT H. *A Geography of Geography: Origins and Development of the Discipline.* Dubuque, Iowa: William C. Brown Co., 1969.

GAMBRELL, HERBERT, ed. *Texas Today and Tomorrow.* Dallas: Southern Methodist University Press, 1961.

GARD, WAYNE. *Rawhide Texas.* Norman: University of Oklahoma Press, 1965.

GARLAND, HAMLIN. "The Literacy Emancipation of the West." *Forum* 16 (October 1893): 156–166.

GARNER, JAMES W. *Reconstruction in Mississippi.* 1901. Reprint. Gloucester, Mass.: Peter Smith, 1964.

GARRATY, JOHN. *Interpreting American History: Conversations with Historians.* New York: Macmillan Co., 1970.

GEIGER, LOUIS G. *University of the Northern Plains: A History of the University of North Dakota, 1883–1958.* Grand Forks: University of North Dakota Press, 1958.

GEROULD, KATHARINE FULLERTON. *The Aristocratic West.* New York: Harper and Brothers, 1925.

GIDDINGS, FRANKLIN H. "Sociology as a University Study." *Political Science Quarterly* 6 (December 1891): 635–655.

———. "A Theory of History." *Political Science Quarterly* 35 (December 1920): 493–521.

GITTINGER, ROY. *The University of Oklahoma, 1892–1942.* Norman: University of Oklahoma Press, 1942.

HALEY, JAMES EVETTS. *The XIT Ranch of Texas and the Early Days of the Llano Estacado.* Chicago: The Lakeside Press, 1929.

HAMER, PHILLIP MAY. *Guide to Archives and Manuscripts in the United States.* New Haven: Yale University Press, 1961.

HARRIS, WILLIAM C. *Presidential Reconstruction in Mississippi.* Baton Rouge: Louisiana State University Press, 1967.

HART, JAMES DAVID. *The Popular Book: A History of America's Literary Tastes.* New York: Oxford University Press, 1950.

HART, JOSEPH K. "Out in the Great Empty Spaces." *New Republic,* August 27, 1924, pp. 384–385.

HARTZ, LOUIS. "American Historiography and Comparative Analysis." *Comparative Studies in Society and History* 5 (1962/1963): 365–367.

HAZARD, LUCY LOCKWOOD. *The Frontier in American Literature.* New York: Thomas Y. Crowell Co., 1927.

HENRY, STUART OLIVER. *Conquering Our Great American Plains: A Historical Development.* New York: E. P. Dutton and Co., 1930.

———. "Faults of Our Wild West Stories." *Literary Digest International Book Review* 1 (November 1923): 34–35.

HERBST, JURGEN. *The German Historical School in American Scholarship: A Study in the Transfer of Culture.* Ithaca, N.Y.: Cornell University Press, 1965.

———. "Social Darwinism and the History of American Geography." *Proceedings of the American Philosophical Society* 105 (December 1961): 538–544.

HESSELTINE, WILLIAM B., and MC NEIL, DONALD R., eds. *In Support of Clio: Essays in Memory of Herbert A. Kellar.* Madison: State Historical Society of Wisconsin, 1958.

HEXTER, J. H. *The History Primer.* New York: Basic Books, 1971.

HICKS, JOHN D. *My Life with History: An Autobiography.* Lincoln: University of Nebraska Press, 1968.

HIGHAM, JOHN. *Writing American History: Essays on Modern Scholarship.* Bloomington: Indiana University Press, 1970.

HOLDEN, WILLIAM C. *The Espuela Land and Cattle Company: A Study of a Foreign-Owned Ranch in Texas.* Austin: Texas State Historical Association, 1970.

HOLT, WILLIAM STULL. *The Historical Profession in the United States.* New York: Macmillan Co., 1963.

HOSMER, CHARLES B., JR. *Presence of the Past: A History of the Preservation Movement in the United States before Williamsburg.* New York: Putnam, 1965.

HOUGH, EMERSON. "Are Americans People?" *Story World and Photodramatist* 4 (June 1923): 11–15.

———. *The Covered Wagon.* New York: Grosset and Dunlap, 1922.

———. *North of 36.* New York: D. Appleton and Co., 1923.

———. *The Way to the West and the Lives of Three Early Americans: Boone—Crockett—Carson.* Indianapolis: Bobbs-Merrill Co., 1903.

HOWE, EDGAR WATSON. *The Story of a Country Town.* Boston: J. R. Osgood and Co., 1884.

HOWE, IRVING. *The Literature of America: The Nineteenth Century.* New York: McGraw-Hill, 1970.

HUBBELL, JAY B. *South and Southwest: Literary Essays and Reminiscences.* Durham, N.C.: Duke University Press, 1965.

HUDSON, WILSON M. *Andy Adams: His Life and Writings.* Dallas: Southern Methodist University Press, 1964.

HUMPHREY, SETH. *Following the Prairie Frontier.* Minneapolis: University of Minnesota Press, 1931.

HUTCHINSON, WILLIAM H. *A Bar-Cross Man: The Life and Personal Writings of Eugene Manlove Rhodes.* Norman: University of Oklahoma Press, 1956.

JACOBS, WILBUR R.; CAUGHEY, JOHN W.; and FRANTZ, JOE B. *Turner, Bolton and Webb: Three Historians of the American Frontier.* Seattle: University of Washington Press, 1965.

JAMES, PRESTON E., and JONES, CLARENCE F., eds. *American Geography: Inventory and Prospect.* Syracuse: Syracuse University Press, 1954.

JOHANNSEN, ALBERT. *The House of Beadle and Adams and Its Dime and Nickel Novels: The Story of a Vanished Literature.* 2 vols. Norman: University of Oklahoma Press, 1950–1952.

JOHNSON, ALVIN SAUNDERS. *Pioneer's Progress: An Autobiography.* New York: Viking Press, 1952.

———. *The Professor and the Petticoat.* New York: Dodd, Mead and Co. 1914.

JOHNSON, WILLARD D. *The High Plains and Their Utilization.* Washington: Government Printing Office, 1901–1902.

JOSEPHSON, MATTHEW. "The Frontier and Literature." *New Republic,* September 2, 1931, pp. 77–78.

KEASBEY, LINDLEY MILLER. "Agrarian Unrest in the South." *New Republic,* September 11, 1915, pp. 146–148.

———. "Civology—a Suggestion." *Popular Science Monthly* 70 (April 1907): 365–371.

———. "Competition." *American Journal of Sociology* 12 (March 1908): 649–654.

———. "Co-operation, Coercion and Competition." *Popular Science Monthly* 63 (October 1903): 526–533.

———. "The Descent of Man." *Popular Science Monthly* 60 (February 1902): 365–376.

———. "The Differentiation of the Human Species." *Popular Science Monthly* 60 (March 1902): 448–457.

———. *The Early Diplomatic History of the Nicaragua Canal.* Newark, N.J.: Holbrook Printing Co., 1890.

———. "The Economic State." *Political Science Quarterly* 7 (December 1893): 601–624.

———. "The Institution of Society." *International Monthly* 1 (April 1900): 355–398.

———. "National Canal Policy." *American Historical Association Report for the Year 1902* 1:275–288.

———. "The New Sectionalism: A Western Warning to the East." *Forum* 16 (January 1894): 578–587.

———. "The Nicaragua Canal and the Monroe Doctrine." *Annals of the American Academy of Political and Social Sciences* 7 (January 1896): 1–31.

———. *The Nicaragua Canal and the Monroe Doctrine.* New York: G. P. Putnam's Sons, 1896.

———. *Der Nicaragua-kanal: Geschichte und beurteilung des projekts.* Strassburg: K. J. Trübner, 1893.

———. "The Principles of Economic Geography." *Political Science Quarterly* 16 (September 1901): 476–485.

———. Review of *A Scientific Solution of the Money Question,* by Arthur Kitson. *Annals of the American Academy of Political and Social Sciences* 7 (March 1896): 310–313.

———. Review of *The History of Mankind,* by Friedrich Ratzel, translated by A. J. Butler. *Annals of the American Academy of Political and Social Sciences* 9 (May 1897): 447–450.

———. "The Study of Economic Geography." *Political Science Quarterly* 16 (March 1901): 79–95.

———. "The Terms and Tenor of the Clayton-Bulwer Treaty." *Annals of the American Academy of Political and Social Sciences* 14 (November 1899): 285–309.

———. "Wealth and Its Ways." *American Journal of Sociology* 21 (September 1915): 185–201.

———. "Wealth and Its Ways." *Texas Review* 2 (June 1915): 51–70.

KIELMAN, CHESTER V., comp. and ed. *The University of Texas Archives: A Guide to the Historical Manuscripts Collections in the University of Texas Library*. Vol. 1. Austin: University of Texas Press, 1967.

KINCER, JOSEPH B. "The Climate of the Great Plains as a Factor in their Utilization." *Annals of the Association of American Geographers* 12 (March 1923): 67–80.

KING, DICK. *Ghost Towns of Texas*. San Antonio: Naylor Company, 1953.

KIRWAN, ALBERT DENNIS. *Revolt of the Rednecks: Mississippi Politics, 1876–1925*. Lexington: University of Kentucky Press, 1951.

KRAENZEL, CARL F. "The Great Plains: A Voiceless Region." *Montana, the Magazine of Western History* 8 (January 1958): 42–49.

———. *The Great Plains in Transition*. Norman: University of Oklahoma Press, 1955.

KREY, AUGUST C. *Suggestions for the Teaching of History and Civics in the High Schools*. Austin: University of Texas, 1911.

LAMBERT, NEIL. "Owen Wister—the 'Real Incident' and the 'Thrilling Story.'" In *The American West: An Appraisal*, edited by Robert G. Ferris. Santa Fe: Museum of New Mexico Press, 1963.

LANE, JOHN J. *History of Education in Texas*. Washington: Government Printing Office, 1903.

LANGSTON, CAROLYNE L. *History of Eastland County, Texas*. Dallas: A. D. Aldridge and Co., 1904.

LEIGHLY, JOHN. "What Has Happened to Physical Geography?" *Annals of the Association of American Geographers* 45 (December 1955): 309–318.

LEWIS, G. MALCOLM. "Changing Emphasis in the Description of the Natural Environment of the American Great Plains Area." *Transactions and Papers of the Institute of British Geographers* 30 (1962): 75–90.

LEWIS, R. W. B. *The American Adam: Innocence, Tragedy, and Tradition in the Nineteenth Century*. Chicago: University of Chicago Press, 1955.

LOMAX, JOHN AVERY. *Adventures of a Ballad Hunter*. New York: Macmillan Co., 1947.

———. *Cowboy Songs and Other Frontier Ballads*. New York: Sturgis and Walton Co., 1910.

LORD, CLIFFORD L., ed. *Keepers of the Past*. Chapel Hill: University of North Carolina Press, 1965.

LYN, MARGARET. "A Step-daughter of the Prairies." *Atlantic Monthly* 107 (March 1911): 379–385.

MC CONNELL, WESTON J. *Social Cleavages in Texas: A Study of the*

Proposed Division of the State. Columbia Studies in History, Economics, and Public Law, vol. 119, no. 265. New York: Columbia University Press, 1925.

MC KAY, SETH, and FAULK, ODIE B. *Texas after Spindletop: 1901–1965.* Austin: Steck-Vaughn Co., 1965.

MC VICKER, MARY L. *The Writings of J. Frank Dobie: A Bibliography.* Lawton, Okla.: Museum of the Great Plains, 1968.

MALIN, JAMES C. *The Grassland of North America: Prolegomena to Its History.* Lawrence, Kans., 1947.

MALLET, JOHN W. "Recollections of the First Years of the University of Texas." *Alcalde* 1 (1913): 14–17.

MARBUT, C. F. "Soils of the Great Plains." *Annals of the Association of American Geographers* 13 (June 1923): 41–66.

MARSHALL, THOMAS MAITLAND. *A History of the Western Boundary of the Louisiana Purchase, 1819–1841.* Berkeley: University of California Press, 1914.

MARX, LEO. *The Machine in the Garden: Technology and the Pastoral Ideal in America.* New York: Oxford University Press, 1964.

MEIGS, CORNELIA. *What Makes a College? A History of Bryn Mawr.* New York, Macmillan Co., 1956.

MEINIG, DONALD W. *Imperial Texas: An Interpretive Essay in Cultural Geography.* Austin: University of Texas Press, 1969.

MONAGHAN, JAMES. *The Great Rascal: The Life and Adventures of Ned Buntline.* Boston: Little, Brown and Co., 1952.

MORRIS, MARGARET. "Walter Prescott Webb, 1888–1963: A Bibliography." In *Essays on the American Civil War*, edited by William F. Holmes and Harold M. Hollingsworth. Austin: University of Texas Press, 1968.

NASH, RODERICK. *Wilderness and the American Mind.* New Haven: Yale University Press, 1967.

NEVINS, ALLAN. *The Gateway to History.* Rev. ed. Chicago: Quadrangle Books, 1963.

———. *The State Universities and Democracy.* Urbana: University of Illinois Press, 1962.

NIETZ, JOHN A. *The Evolution of American Secondary School Textbooks: Rhetoric and Literature, Algebra, . . . as Taught in American Latin Grammar School Academies and Early High Schools before 1900.* Rutland, Vt.: C. E. Tuttle Company, 1966.

———. *Old Textbooks: Spelling, Grammar, . . . as Taught in the Common Schools from Colonial Days to 1900.* Pittsburgh: University of Pittsburgh Press, 1961.

NOBLE, DAVID W. *The Eternal Adam and the New World Garden: The Central Myth in the American Novel since 1830.* New York: Braziller, 1968.

———. *Historians against History: The Frontier Thesis and the National Covenant in American Historical Writing since 1830.* Minneapolis: University of Minnesota Press, 1965.

———. *The Paradox of Progressive Thought.* Minneapolis: University of Minnesota Press, 1968.

————. *The Progressive Mind, 1890–1917.* Chicago: Rand McNally and Co., 1970.

NOEL, MARY. *Villains Galore: The Heyday of the Popular Story Weekly.* New York: Macmillan Co., 1954.

ODUM, HOWARD W. *American Masters of Social Science: An Approach to the Study of the Social Sciences through a Neglected Field of Biography.* New York: Henry Holt and Co., 1927.

OSGOOD, ERNEST S. *The Day of the Cattleman.* Minneapolis: University of Minnesota Press, 1929.

————. "I Discover Western History." *Western Historical Quarterly* 3 (July 1972): 241–251.

OWENS, WILLIAM A. *Three Friends: Roy Bedichek, J. Frank Dobie, Walter Prescott Webb.* Garden City, N.Y.: Doubleday and Co., 1969.

PAREDES, AMÉRICO. *With His Pistol in His Hand: A Border Ballad and Its Hero.* Austin: University of Texas Press, 1958.

PARKER, GEORGE F. "Pioneer Methods." *Saturday Evening Post*, June 3, 1922, pp. 32–46.

PARRISH, RANDALL. *The Great Plains: The Romance of Western American Exploration, Warfare and Settlement, 1527–1870.* 3rd ed. Chicago: A. C. McClurg and Co., 1915.

PAUL, RODMAN WILSON. *Mining Frontiers of the Far West, 1848–1880.* New York: Holt, Rinehart and Winston, 1963.

PAXSON, FREDERIC L. Review of *The Great Plains*, by Walter Prescott Webb. *American Historical Review* 37 (January 1932): 359–360.

PECKHAM, HOWARD H. *The Making of the University of Michigan, 1817–1967.* Ann Arbor: University of Michigan Press, 1967.

PELZER, LOUIS. *The Cattleman's Frontier: A Record of the Trans-Mississippi Cattle Industry from Oxen Trains to Pooling Companies, 1850–1890.* Glendale, Calif.: Arthur H. Clark Co., 1936.

————, and DALEY, CLARA M. *Aids for History Teachers by the Department of History: The Correlation of History and Geography.* Iowa City: The University, 1923.

PIERCE, BESSIE LOUISE. *Public Opinion and the Teaching of History in the United States.* New York: Knopf, 1926.

POOL, WILLIAM C. *Eugene C. Barker, Historian.* Austin: Texas State Historical Association, 1971.

POTTER, DAVID M. *People of Plenty: Economic Abundance and the American Character.* Chicago: University of Chicago Press, 1954.

POWELL, JOHN WESLEY. *Report on the Lands of the Arid Region of the United States: With a More Detailed Account of the Lands of Utah,* edited by Wallace Stegner. Cambridge, Mass.: Harvard University Press, 1962.

President's Reports, Bryn Mawr College. Philadelphia, 1893–1894.

Program of Bryn Mawr College. Philadelphia, 1895 and 1896.

QUICK, HERBERT. *One Man's Life: An Autobiography.* Indianapolis: Bobbs-Merrill Co., 1925.

172 | Bibliography

————. "One Man's Life: An Autobiography." *Saturday Evening Post*, June 20–September 5, 1925.

RAINWATER, PERCY L. *Mississippi: Storm Center of Secession, 1856–1861.* Baton Rouge, La.: O. Claitor, 1938.

RANSOM, HARRY H. "Educational Resources in Texas." In *Texas Today and Tomorrow*, edited by Herbert Gambrell. Dallas: Southern Methodist University Press, 1961.

RATZEL, FRIEDRICH. *The History of Mankind.* Translated by A. J. Butler from the 2nd German ed. London: Macmillan and Co., 1898.

REYNOLDS, LARRY T., and REYNOLDS, JANICE M., eds. *Sociology of Sociology: Analysis and Criticism of the Thought, Research, and Ethical Folkways of Sociology and Its Practitioners.* New York: McKay, 1970.

RHODES, EUGENE MANLOVE. *The Little World Waddies.* Chico, Calif.: W. Hutchinson, 1946.

RHODES, MAY DAVISON. *The Hired Man on Horseback: My Story of Eugene Manlove Rhodes.* Boston: Houghton Mifflin Co., 1938.

RICHARDSON, RUPERT NORVAL. *The Comanche Barrier to South Plains Settlement: A Century and a Half of Savage Resistance to the Advancing White Frontier.* Glendale, Calif.: Arthur H. Clark Co., 1933.

RIPPY, J. FRED. *Bygones I Cannot Help Recalling: The Memoirs of a Mobile Scholar.* Austin: Steck-Vaughn Co., 1966.

RISTER, CARL COKE. *The Southwestern Frontier, 1865–1881: A History of the Coming of the Settlers, . . . and the Disappearance of the Frontier.* New York: Russell and Russell Publishers, 1969.

RÖLVAAG, OLE EDVART. *Giants in the Earth: A Saga of the Prairie.* New York: Harper and Brothers, 1927.

ROSENBERG, BERNARD, and WHITE, DAVID MANNING, eds. *Mass Culture: The Popular Arts in America.* Glencoe, Ill.: Free Press, 1957.

ROWLEY, VIRGINIA M. *J. Russell Smith: Geographer, Educator, and Conservationist.* Philadelphia: University of Pennsylvania Press, 1964.

RUDOLPH, FREDERICK. *The American College and University: A History.* New York: Knopf, 1962.

SAUER, CARL. "The Survey Method in Geography and Its Objectives." *Annals of the Association of American Geographers* 14 (March 1924): 17–33.

SCANNELL, JOHN JAMES, ed. *New Jersey's First Citizens and State Guide.* Vol. 1. Paterson, N.J.: Privately printed, 1917–1918.

SCARBOROUGH, DOROTHY. *The Wind.* New York: Harper and Brothers, 1925.

SCHMITT, PETER J. *Back to Nature: The Arcadian Myth in Urban America.* New York: Oxford University Press, 1969.

SEMPLE, ELLEN CHURCHILL. *American History and Its Geographic Conditions.* Boston: Houghton Mifflin Co., 1903.

————. *Influences of Geographic Environment on the Basis of Ratzel's System of Anthropo-geography.* New York: Henry Holt and Co., 1911.

SHANNON, FRED A. *An Appraisal of Walter Prescott Webb's "The*

Great Plains: A Study in Institutions and Environment." Critiques of Research in the Social Sciences, vol. 3. New York: Social Sciences Research Council, 1940.

———. *The Farmer's Last Frontier: Agriculture, 1860–1897.* New Economic History of the United States, vol. 5. New York: Farrar and Rinehart, 1945.

SHINN, CHARLES H. *Mining Camps: A Study in American Frontier Government.* New York: Knopf, 1885. Reprint, 1948.

SMITH, C. B., SR., comp. and ed. *Walter Prescott Webb: From the Great Frontier to the Threshold of Space.* Austin: Walter Prescott Webb Great Frontier Association, 1969.

SPATE, OSKAR HERMANN KHRISTIAN. *Let Me Enjoy: Essays, Partly Geographical.* London: Methuen, 1966.

STEARNS, HAROLD E. *America and the Young Intellectual.* New York: George H. Doran Co., 1921.

STORR, RICHARD J. *Harper's University: The Beginnings; A History of the University of Chicago.* Chicago: University of Chicago Press, 1966.

TAYLOR, THOMAS GRIFFITH, ed. *Geography in the Twentieth Century: A Study of Growth, Fields, Techniques, Aims and Trends.* 2nd revised and enlarged edition. New York: Philosophical Library, 1953.

TRYON, ROLLA MILTON. *Materials, Methods and Administration of History in the Elementary Schools of the United States.* Bloomington: Indiana University, 1912.

———. *The Teaching of History in Junior and Senior High Schools.* Boston: Ginn and Co., 1921.

TURNER, FREDERICK JACKSON. "Report of the Conference on the Relation of Geography and History." *American Historical Association Report for the Year 1907* 1:45–48.

VANDIVER, FRANK E. "John William Mallet and the University of Texas." *Southwestern Historical Quarterly* 53 (April 1950): 421–442.

VEYSEY, LAURENCE R. *The Emergence of the American University.* Chicago: University of Chicago Press, 1965.

WANKLYN, HARRIET GRACE. *Friedrich Ratzel: A Biographical Memoir and Bibliography.* Cambridge: At the University Press, 1961.

WARNTZ, WILLIAM. *Geography Now and Then: Some Notes on the History of Academic Geography in the United States.* New York: American Geographical Society, 1964.

WEBB, WALTER PRESCOTT. "The American Revolvers and the West." *Scribner's Magazine* 81 (February 1927): 171–178.

———. "Caldwell Prize in Local History." *Texas History Teachers' Bulletin*, October 22, 1924, pp. 5–19.

———. *Divided We Stand: The Crisis of a Frontierless Democracy.* New York: Farrar and Rinehart, 1937.

———. *Flat Top: A Story of Modern Ranching.* El Paso: Carl Hertzog, 1960.

———. "Folklore of Texas." *Journal of American Folklore* 28 (July/September 1915): 290–301.

———. "Geographical-Historical Concepts in American History."

Annals of the Association of American Geographers 50 (June 1960): 85–93.

———. *The Great Frontier.* Boston: Houghton Mifflin Co., 1952.

———. *The Great Plains.* Boston: Ginn and Co., 1931.

———. "The Great Plains Block the Expansion of the South." *Panhandle-Plains Historical Review* 2 (1929): 3–21.

———. "History as High Adventure." *American Historical Review* 64 (January 1959): 278–281.

———. *An Honest Preface and Other Essays.* Boston: Houghton Mifflin Co., 1959.

———. "Increasing the Functional Value of History by the Use of the Problem Method of Presentation." *Texas History Teachers' Bulletin,* February 15, 1916, pp. 16–40.

———. "The Land and Life of the Great Plains." *West Texas Historical Association Yearbook* 4 (June 1928): 58–85.

———. "The Last Treaty of the Republic of Texas." *Southwestern Historical Quarterly* 25 (January 1922): 151–173.

———. "Miscellany of Texas Folklore." In *Coffee in the Gourd,* edited by J. Frank Dobie. Publications of the Texas Folklore Society 2:38–49. Austin: Texas Folklore Society, 1923.

———. *More Water for Texas: The Problem and the Plan.* Austin: University of Texas Press, 1954.

———. *Our Nation Begins.* Evanston, Ill.: Row, Peterson and Co., 1932.

———. Review of *Conquering Our Great American Plains,* by Stuart Henry. *Mississippi Valley Historical Review* 17 (March 1931): 644–645.

———. Review of *History of the American Frontier,* by Frederic L. Paxson. *Southwestern Historical Quarterly* 28 (January 1925): 247–252.

———. Review of *Legends of Texas,* by J. Frank Dobie. *Southwestern Historical Quarterly* 28 (January 1925): 243–247.

———. "Search for William E. Hinds." *Harper's Magazine* 223 (July 1961): 62–69.

———. "The Search for William E. Hinds." *Reader's Digest* 79 (August 1961): 35–40.

———. "Some Vagaries of the Search for Water in the Great Plains." *Panhandle-Plains Historical Review* 3 (1930): 28–37.

———. *Talks on Texas Books: A Collection of Book Reviews.* Compiled and edited by Llerena Friend. Austin: Texas State Historical Association, 1970.

———. "A Texas Buffalo Hunt." *Holland's Magazine* 46 (October 1927): 10–11, 101–102.

———. *The Texas Rangers: A Century of Frontier Defense.* Boston: Houghton Mifflin Co., 1935.

———. "Texas Rangers: Riders and Fighters of the Lone Star State. Part III." *Owenwood Magazine* 1 (April 1922): 39–46; "Part IV," 1 (May 1922): 47–54.

———. "The University Professor and the Social Studies." In *History as High Adventure,* edited by E. C. Barksdale. Austin: Pemberton Press, 1969.

————. "Wild Horse Stories of Southwest Texas." In *Round the Levee,* edited by Smith Thompson. Publications of the Texas Folklore Society 1:58–61. Austin: Texas Folklore Society, 1916.

————; BARKER, EUGENE C.; and COMMAGER, HENRY STEELE. *The Building of our Nation.* Evanston, Ill.: Row, Peterson and Co., 1937.

————; ————; and DODD, WILLIAM E. *The Growth of a Nation: The United States of America.* Evanston, Ill.: Row, Peterson and Co., 1928.

————; ————; and ————. *Our Nation Grows Up.* Evanston, Ill.: Row, Peterson and Co., 1938.

————; ————; and ————. *The Story of Our Nation.* Evanston, Ill.: Row, Peterson and Co., 1929.

————; and CARROLL, HORACE BAILEY, eds. *The Handbook of Texas.* 2 vols. Austin: Texas State Historical Association, 1952.

WEDEL, WALDO R. *Prehistoric Man on the Great Plains.* Norman: University of Oklahoma Press, 1961.

WESCOTT, GLENWAY. *Good-bye Wisconsin.* New York: Harper and Brothers, 1928.

————. *The Grandmothers: A Family Portrait.* New York: Harper and Brothers, 1927.

WHITEHILL, WALTER M. *Independent Historical Societies: An Enquiry into Their Research and Publication Functions and Their Financial Future.* Boston: Boston Athenaeum, 1962.

WILLARD, JAMES F., and GOODYKOONTZ, COLIN B., eds. *The Trans-Mississippi West: Papers Read at a Conference Held at the University of Colorado June 18–20, 1929.* Boulder: University of Colorado, 1930.

WILSON, EDMUND. *Upstate: Records and Recollections of Northern New York.* New York: Farrar, Straus and Giroux, 1971.

WINFREY, DORMAN H. *A History of Rusk County, Texas.* Waco: Texian Press, 1961.

————. *Julien Sidney Devereux and His Monte Verdi Plantation.* Waco: Texian Press, 1964.

WINTHER, OSCAR O. *A Classified Bibliography of the Periodical Literature of the Trans-Mississippi West, 1811–1957.* Bloomington: Indiana University Press, 1961.

WISSLER, CLARK. *Man and Culture.* New York: Thomas Y. Crowell Co., 1923.

————. *North American Indians of the Plains.* New York: American Museum of Natural History, 1912.

WOLFE, THOMAS. *Look Homeward, Angel: A Story of the Buried Life.* New York: Charles Scribner's Sons, 1929.

WOODWARD, COMER VANN. *The Origins of the New South, 1877–1913.* Baton Rouge: Louisiana State University Press, 1951.

YOUNG, STARK. "A Texas Pogrom." *New Republic,* August 11, 1917, pp. 45–47.

PERIODICALS

Annals of the American Academy of Political and Social Sciences,
    1896–1899.
Beeville Bee, 1913.
Breckenridge Democrat, 1915.
Chicago Evening Post, 1924.
Handbook of the American Academy of Political Sciences, 1896.
Literary Digest International Book Review, 1923–1925.
Literary Review, 1924.
Political Science Quarterly, 1892–1901.
University Record, 1906–1913.

LETTERS AND INTERVIEWS

Letters

Bain, Read, to the writer, June 23, 1972, July 24, 1972.
Craven, Avery D., to the writer, January 4, 1972.
Shannon, David A., to the writer, February 29, 1972.
Swearingen, Mrs. Mary F., to the writer, March 17, 1972.
Trombly, Albert E., to the writer, January 4, 1972.

Interviews

Fleming, Mr. Richard, Austin, February 1972.
Webb, Miss Mildred, Austin, May 1972.
Webb, Mrs. Walter Prescott, Austin, March 1972.
Webb, Walter Prescott, with Professor William A. Owens, taped inter-
    view in the possession of Professor Owens, Columbia University,
    dated August 18, 1953.
Wright, Mrs. Ima, Austin, February 1972.

Index

Abilene: Henry's early years in, 78

Adams, Andy, 77, 79; approach to literature of, 82; foundation of a Western literature by, 88; and idealization of the West, 109; and *Log of a Cowboy*, 94, 100–101, 150 n. 16; as Western writer, 82

Albany, 10

Alpine Normal School, 62

American Boy, The (magazine), 22

American Chemical Society, 28

American Commonwealth (Bryce), 58

American Historical Review, 103

Americanism, 79–81

Anderson, Sherwood: as a "Euro-American," 80

Appraisal of Walter Prescott Webb's "The Great Plains: A Study in Institutions and Environment," An (Shannon), 154 n. 24

Austin: Keasbey's home in, 40; new state university at, 28, 30, 53; Webb's early uncertainties in, 65; Webb's ranch near, 23; Webb's return to, 1923, 68–70

Bain, Read, 155 n. 7; and geographic determinism, 112

Barbed wire: and role in settlement of Great Plains, 94–95, 108, 150 n. 17

Barker, Eugene C.: academic standards of, 63; background of, 60; and Department of History, 59–62; and expectations of Webb, 69; influence of, 38; investments of, 114; and support of Webb, 65; and Webb's Ranger study, 91

Barrows, Harlan: geographic theory of, 111

Beeville: folklore of, 57, 72; Webb teaching at, 53–55; windmills of, 94

Benedict, Harry Yandell: as product of West Texas, 133 n. 1

Berle, Adolph A., Jr., and G. C. Means: and *The Modern Corporation and Private Property*, 115

Big Bend: Webb's impressions of, 70

Blumer, Herbert, 125

Boas, Franz: and *Primitive Art*, 115

Bolton, Herbert, 61

Boston: Webb's visit to, 1931, 112

Boucher, C. S., 62

Brigham, Albert Perry: and geographic determinism, 24, 136 n. 37

Bryce, James: and *American Commonwealth*, 58

Bryn Mawr, 47; Department of Political Science of, 44–45; Keasbey at, 40–41, 43

Buck, Solon J.: as local historian, 73–74

Burgess, John, 40

Burleson, Albert S., 34

Bye, Raymond T., 125

Caldwell, Robert G.: favorable reactions of, to *The Great Plains*, 103

Callaway, Morgan, Jr., 38, 138
n. 36
Cattleman's Frontier, The
(Pelzer), 152 n. 46
Central Texas: railroads in, 10
Chicago, 55; Webb's disappoint-
ment in, 66–69, 145 n. 19;
and Webb's study plans, 57
Cisco, 10, 12, 30
Civil War: era following, 72;
impact of, xii
Clark, Walter Van Tilburg, 89
Clayton-Bulwer Treaty: Keasbey's
study of, 41
Coker, Frederick: and appraisal of
Great Plains, 155 n. 7
Colt revolver: role of, in settle-
ment of Great Plains, 12–13,
93, 95, 98, 108, 117
Columbia, 55; and Webb's study
plans, 57
Columbia University: Keasbey at,
40
Comte, Auguste, 46
Coolidge, Calvin, 70
Coulanges, Fustel: and role of
hypothesis, 121, 156 n. 20
Craven, Avery, 67
Cross Timbers, 32, 37, 123;
imaginative existence of, 129;
Webb's boyhood in, 109;
Western parts of, 7
Cross Timbers, The (Dale), 156
n. 26
Cuero: folklore of, 72; Webb's
move from, 58; Webb teaching
at, 56–57

Dale, Edward Everett, 123; and
The Cross Timbers, 156 n. 26;
and the Plains history, 75
Dallas Morning News, 150 n. 17
Davenport, Harbert: as state
historian, 152 n. 43
Davis, E. E., 126
Davis, William Morris: approach
to geography of, 24; and
Physical Geography, 23, 135
n. 33
Deep South, 3, 6
De Patriarcha (Filmer), 141 n. 36

De Voto, Bernard Augustine, 71;
defense of Western literature
by, 87; and literature of twenties, 86; and regional outlook,
89
Divided We Stand (Webb), 114
Dobie, J. Frank: background of,
72, 146 n. 33; and creative
writing, 83; and regional outlook, 89
Dodd, William E., 67, 98; as
advisor to Webb, 65; and expectations of Webb, 69; as joint
author with Webb, 91
Duncalf, Frederic: as colleague
of Webb, 60; and Department
of History, 59; teaching of,
with Webb, 69
Dunning, William A.: and *History
of Political Theories*, 142 n. 36

East, the: cultural climate of, 89;
as distinct from the West, 92,
94, 108; as distinct region, 81
Eastland County: farming in, 9;
prior to Civil War, 9; the Webbs
in, 8; Webb teaching in, 20,
134 n. 18
East Texas: likeness to Old South
of, 6; movement of Webbs
away from, 7; settlement of, 3
*Economic Foundations of Society,
The* (Loria): Keasbey's translation of, 41–42, 51
Eliasville, 14
"European Americans," 79
European history: Webb's fading
interest in, 49

Fabre, Jean Henri: Webb's read-
ing of, 21
Ferguson, James, 60
Ferguson, Miriam, 70
Filmer, Sir Robert: and *De
Patriarcha*, 141 n. 36
Fincher, Amos: legendary figure
of, 12
Fitzgerald, F. Scott: as "Euro-
American," 80
Fleming, Richard: study under
Webb of, 142 n. 41

own education by, 20–21;
defense of Plains thesis by,
120–123, 124; degree plans
of, 53–54; and Department of
History, 127; and *Divided We
Stand*, 114; and early contact
with Keasbey, 40–41; early
education of, 16–19, 134
n. 10; early movements of, 8;
and geographic determinism,
xvii, 50, 93–97, 104–110;
graduate study plans of, 57;
and *The Great Frontier*,
50, 128; imagination of, 7, 18,
133 n. 8; informal education
of, 9; and institutional history,
47–49, 141 n. 32; intellectual
development of, xv–xvi; and
interest in physical geography,
22–24; investments of, 114,
154 n. 34; as joint editor of
Handbook of Texas, 75; and
journey to Chicago, 1922,
65–68; and journey north, 1931,
112; Keasbey's influence on,
xvi, 51, 61, 63, 128; literary
background of, 22, 134 n. 25;
and literature of the West,
81–90; and local history, 75;
and love of the West, 70, 79;
marriage plans of, 56; and need
for higher degree, 60; oil
speculations of, 71, 144 n. 41;
at Oxford, 127; Plains theory
of, 96–97; return to Austin of,
1923, 68–69, 70; and rural

America, 72, 145 n. 30; secondary education of, 19, 134
n. 15; at University of Texas,
1909, 33–39, 41; and visit to
Mexican border, 70; and William Hinds, 18–19; as a writer
of the West, 101–102. *See also
The Great Plains*
West, the: cultural climate of, 88;
development of, 31; as distinct
region, 81, 108, 123; factors in
settlement of, 92; honor of, 77;
imaginative concept of, 12,
109; intellectual pioneering of,
64; railroads in, 10–11, 31, 137
n. 10; realities of, 9; romantic
view of, under attack, 76;
settlement of, xii-xiii; as source
of history, 82–83; special problems of, 51; unique values of,
77, 79, 83; Webb's interest in,
61
Windmills: and role in settlement
of Great Plains, 94–95, 108,
150 n. 17
Wirth, Louis, 124; and appraisal
of *Great Plains*, 155 n. 7
Wissler, Clark, 98
Wolfe, Thomas: and *Look Homeward, Angel*, 25, 136 n. 39
World War I: impact on local
history of, 73; nationalism
generated by, 80

Young, Stark, 38